Flying Witch

Chihiro Ishizuka

10667754

Contents

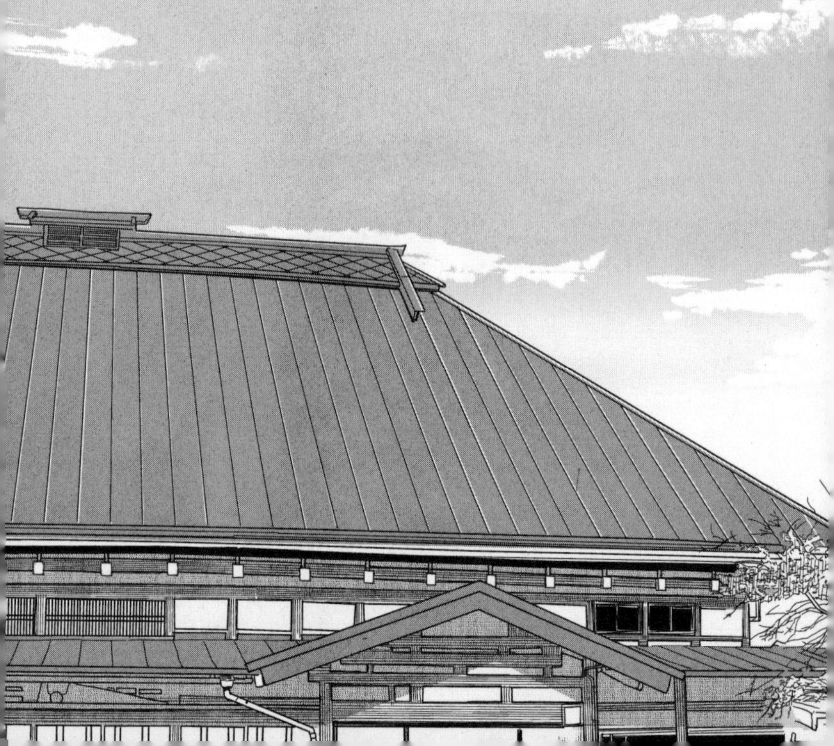

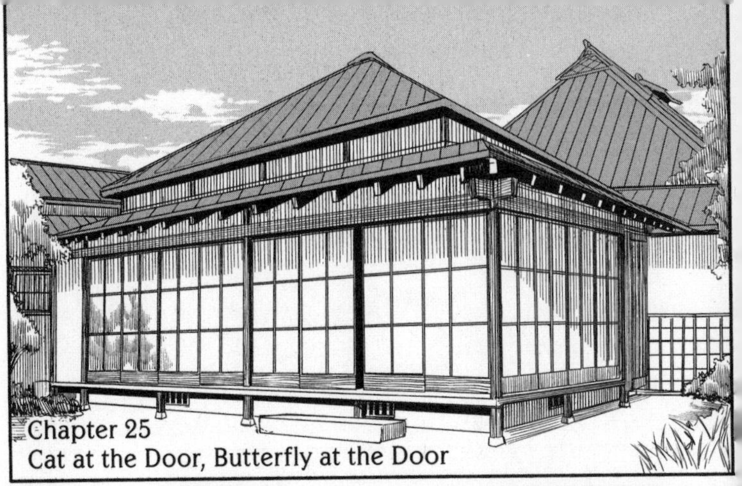

Chapter 25
Cat at the Door, Butterfly at the Door

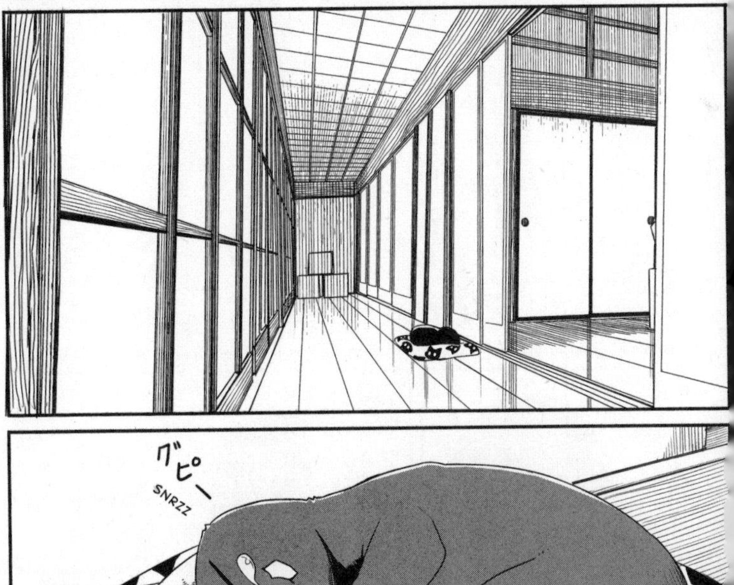

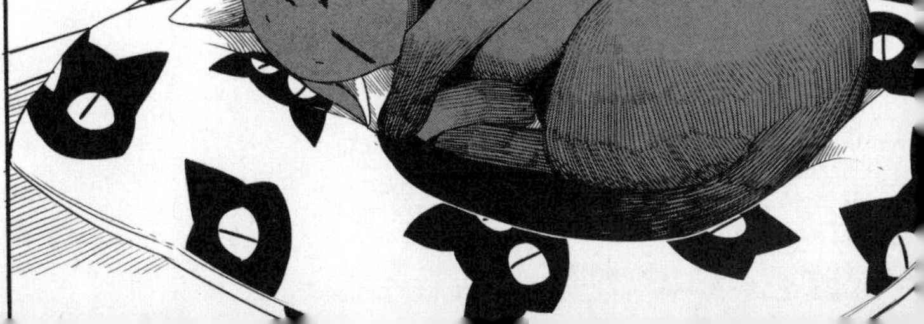
グピー
SNRZZ

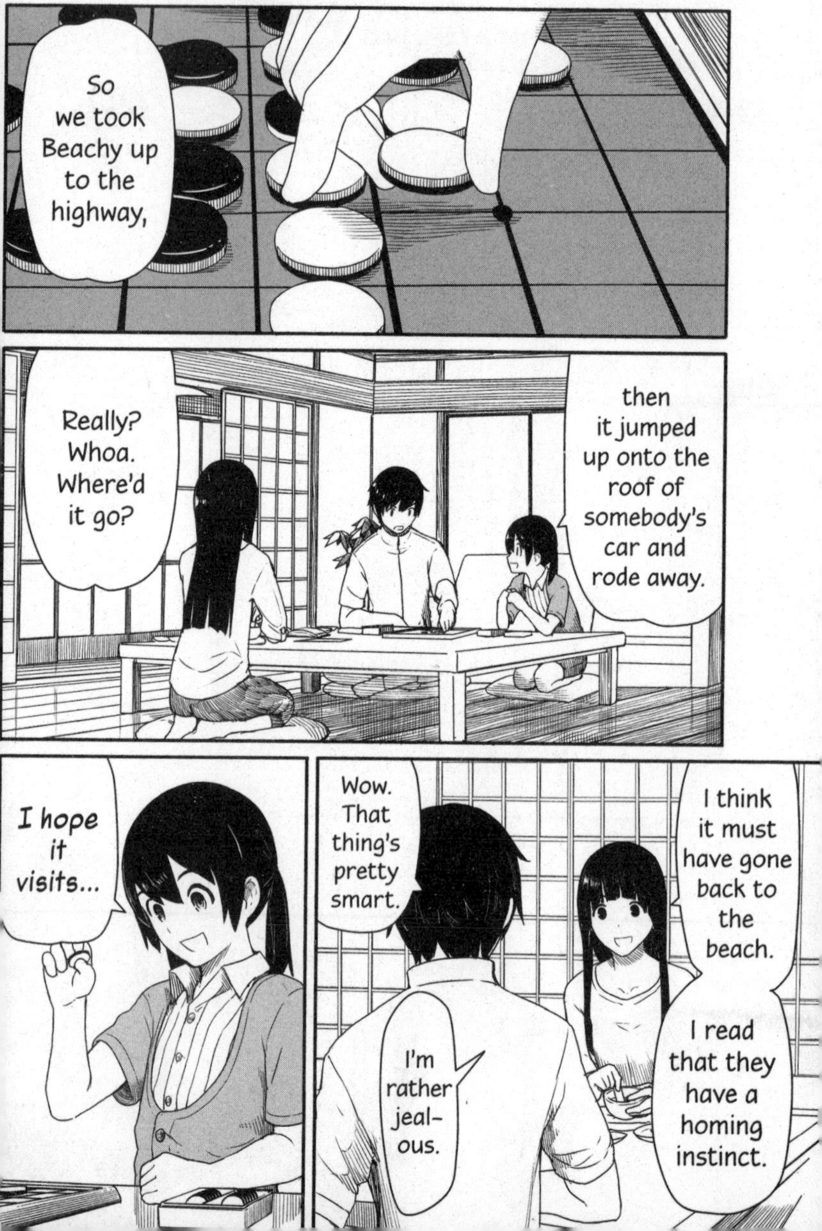
So we took Beachy up to the highway,
then it jumped up onto the roof of somebody's car and rode away.
Really? Whoa. Where'd it go?
I think it must have gone back to the beach.
Wow. That thing's pretty smart.
I read that they have a homing instinct.
I'm rather jeal- ous.
I hope it visits...

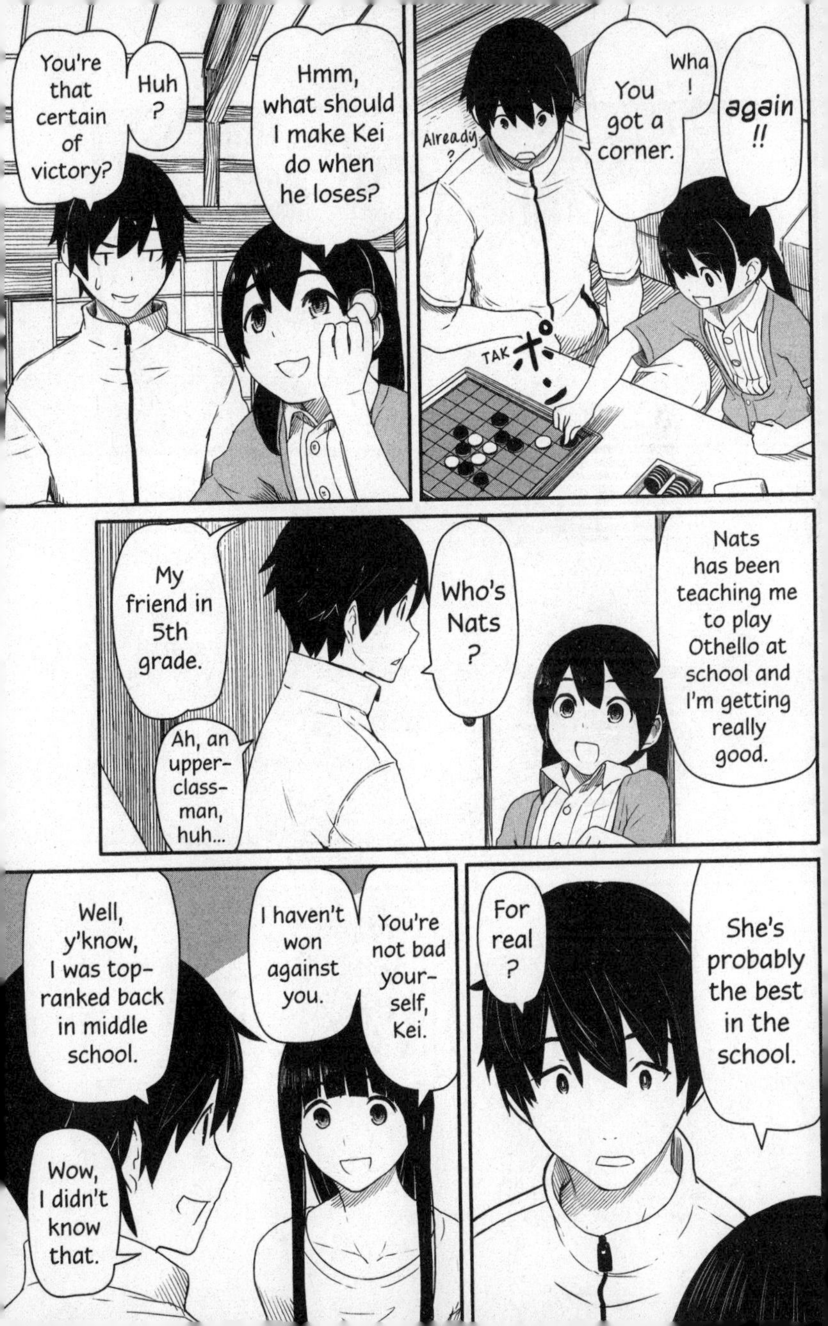
again !!
Wha !
You got a corner.
Already ?
TAK
Hmm, what should I make Kei do when he loses?
Huh ?
You're that certain of victory?
Nats has been teaching me to play Othello at school and I'm getting really good.
Who's Nats ?
My friend in 5th grade.
Ah, an upper-class-man, huh...
She's probably the best in the school.
For real ?
You're not bad your-self, Kei.
I haven't won against you.
Well, y'know, I was top-ranked back in middle school.
Wow, I didn't know that.

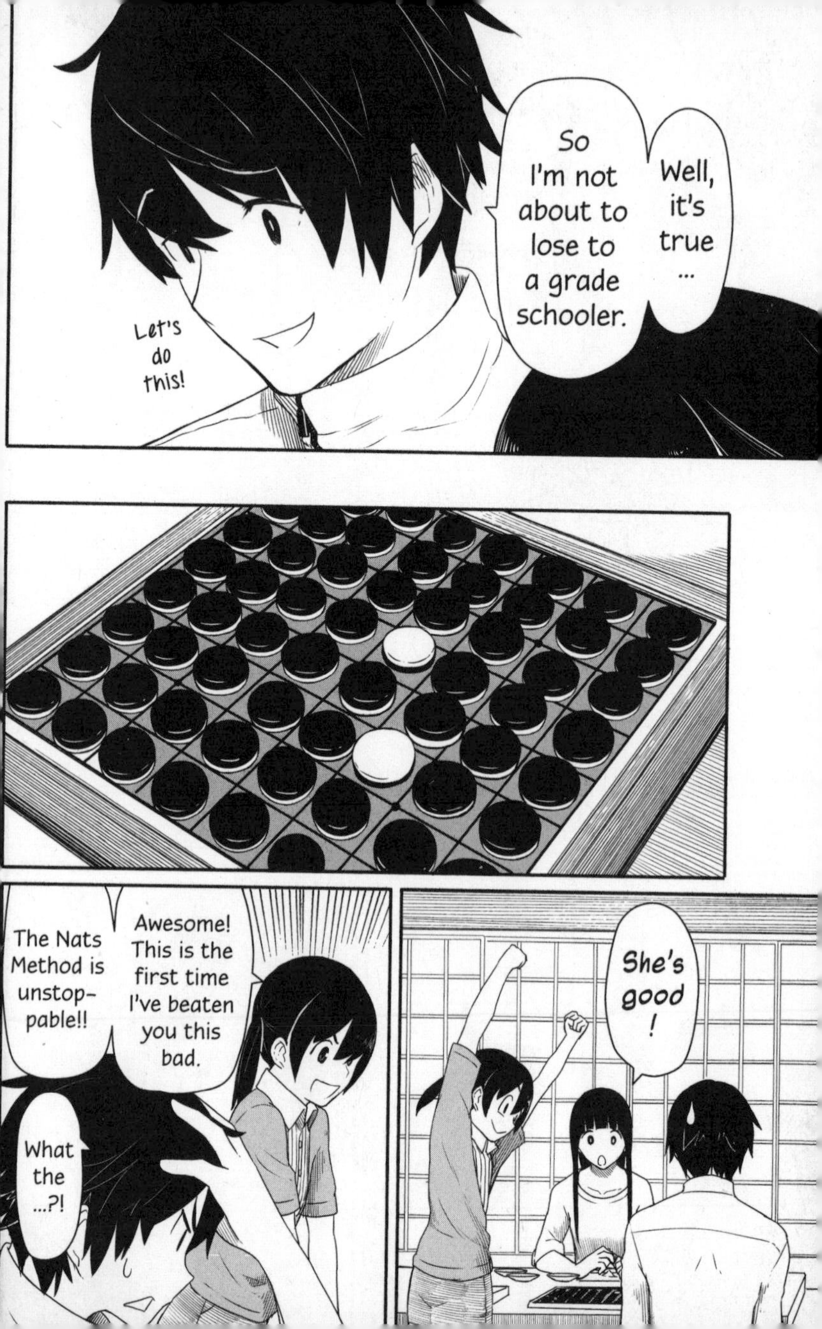
Well, it's true ...
So I'm not about to lose to a grade schooler.
Let's do this!
She's good!
Awesome! This is the first time I've beaten you this bad.
The Nats Method is unstop-pable!!
What the ...?!

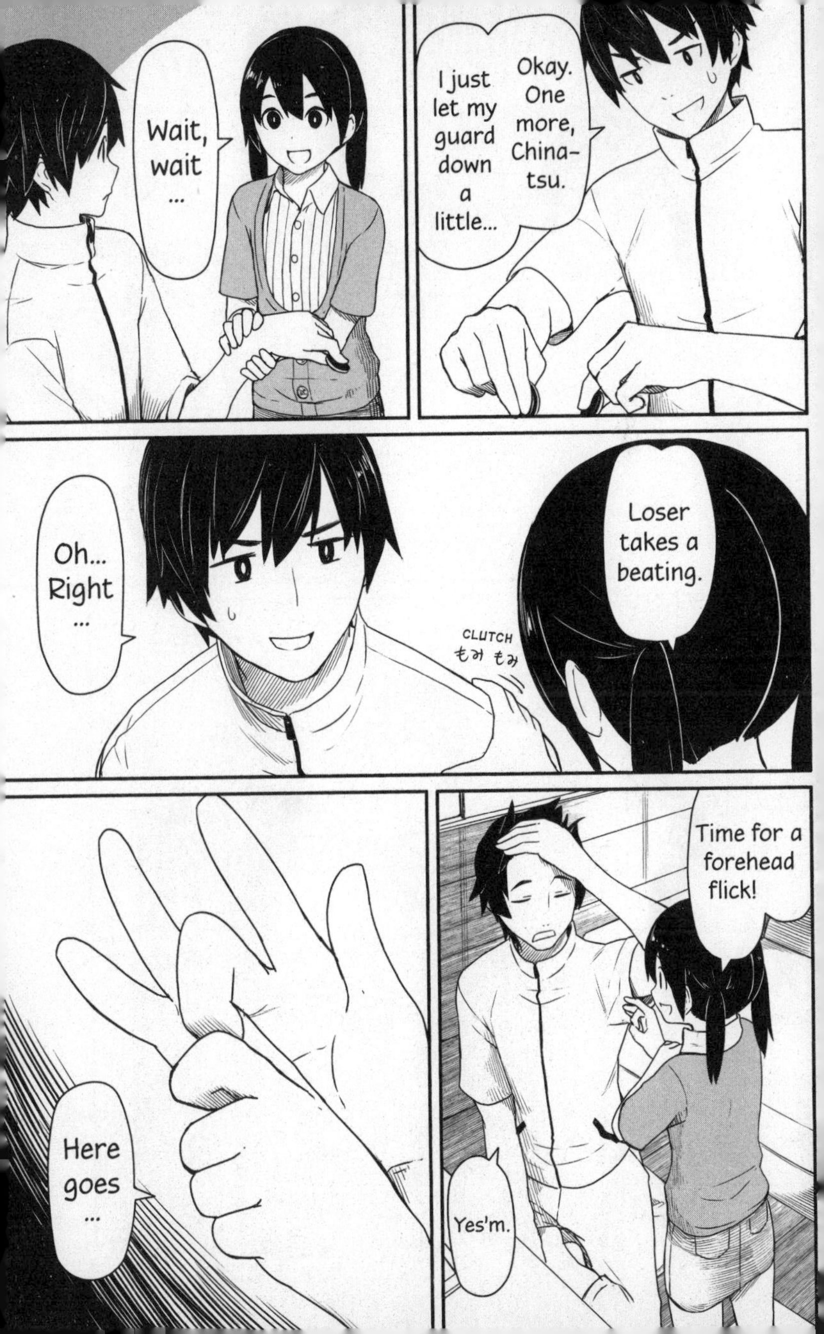
Okay. One more, China-tsu.
I just let my guard down a little...
Wait, wait ...
Loser takes a beating.
CLUTCH
もみ もみ
Oh... Right ...
Time for a forehead flick!
Yes'm.
Here goes ...

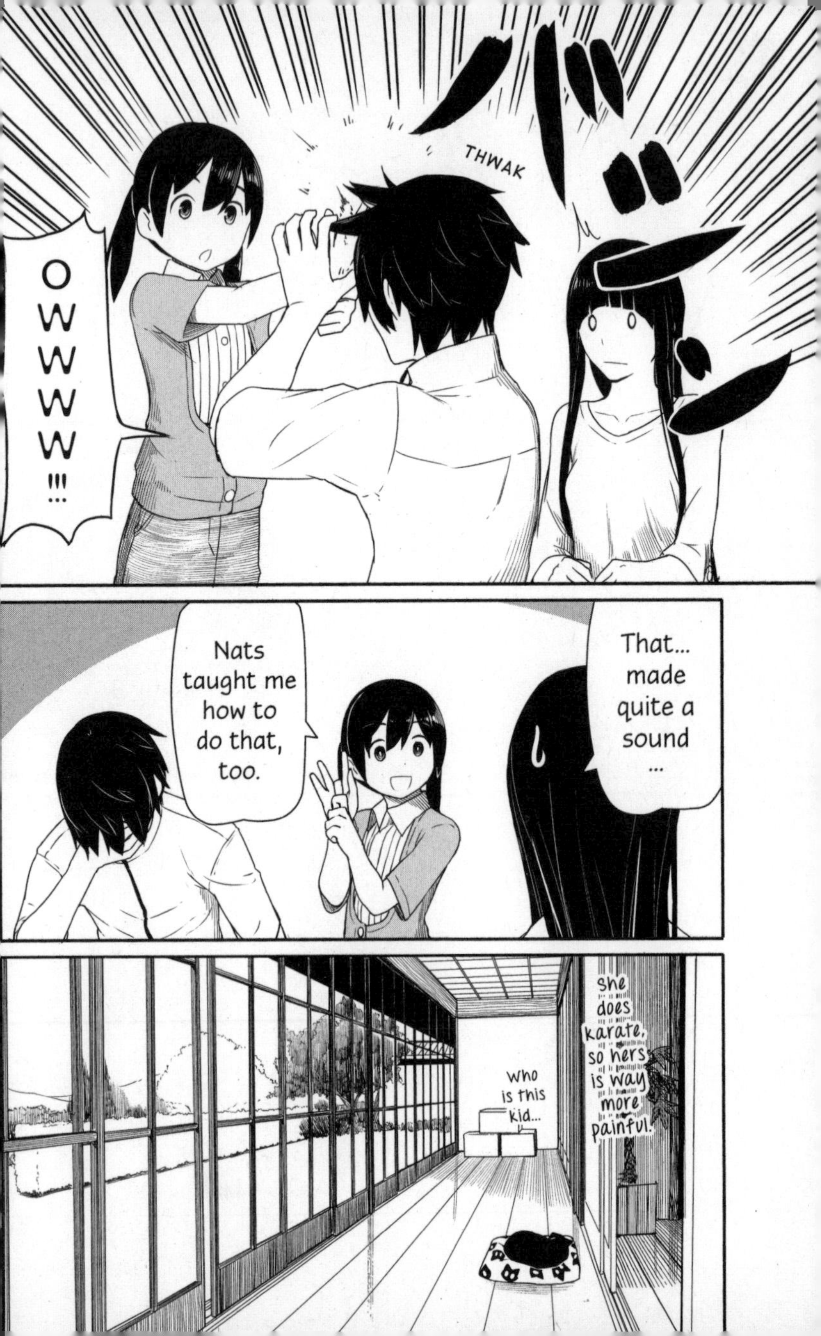
THWAK
OWWWWW!!!
That... made quite a sound ...
Nats taught me how to do that, too.
She does karate, so hers is way more painful.
Who is this kid...

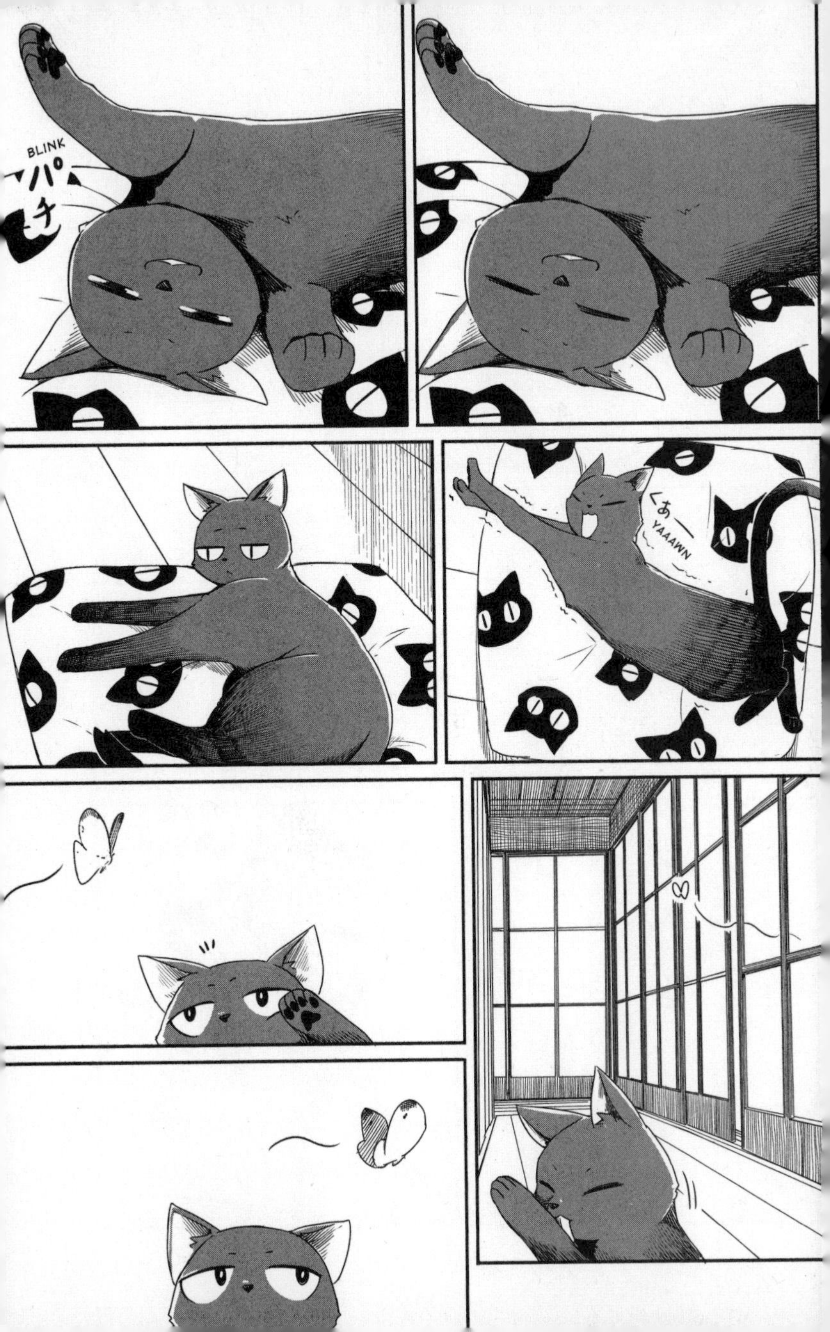
パチ
BLINK
くあ—
YAAAWN

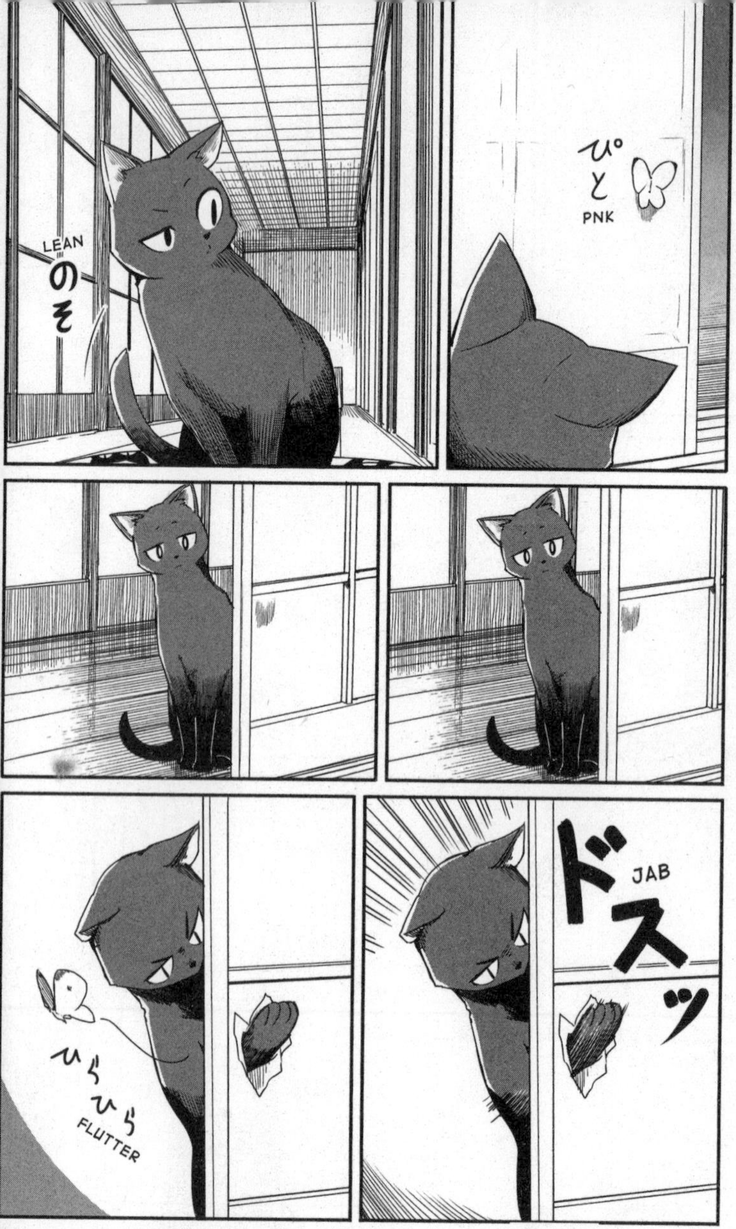
ぴと
PNK
のそ
LEAN
ドスッ
JAB
ひらひら
FLUTTER

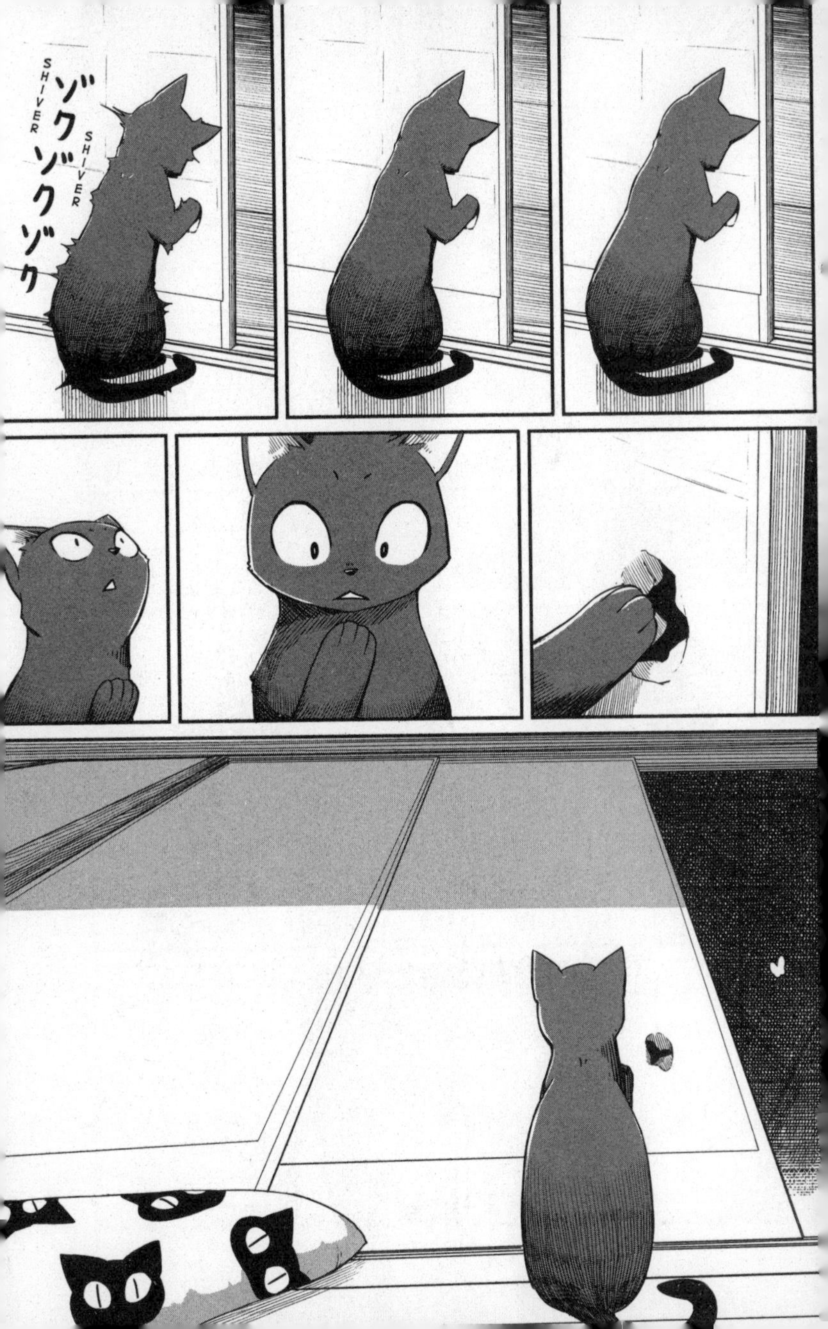
ゾクゾクゾクゾク
SHIVER SHIVER

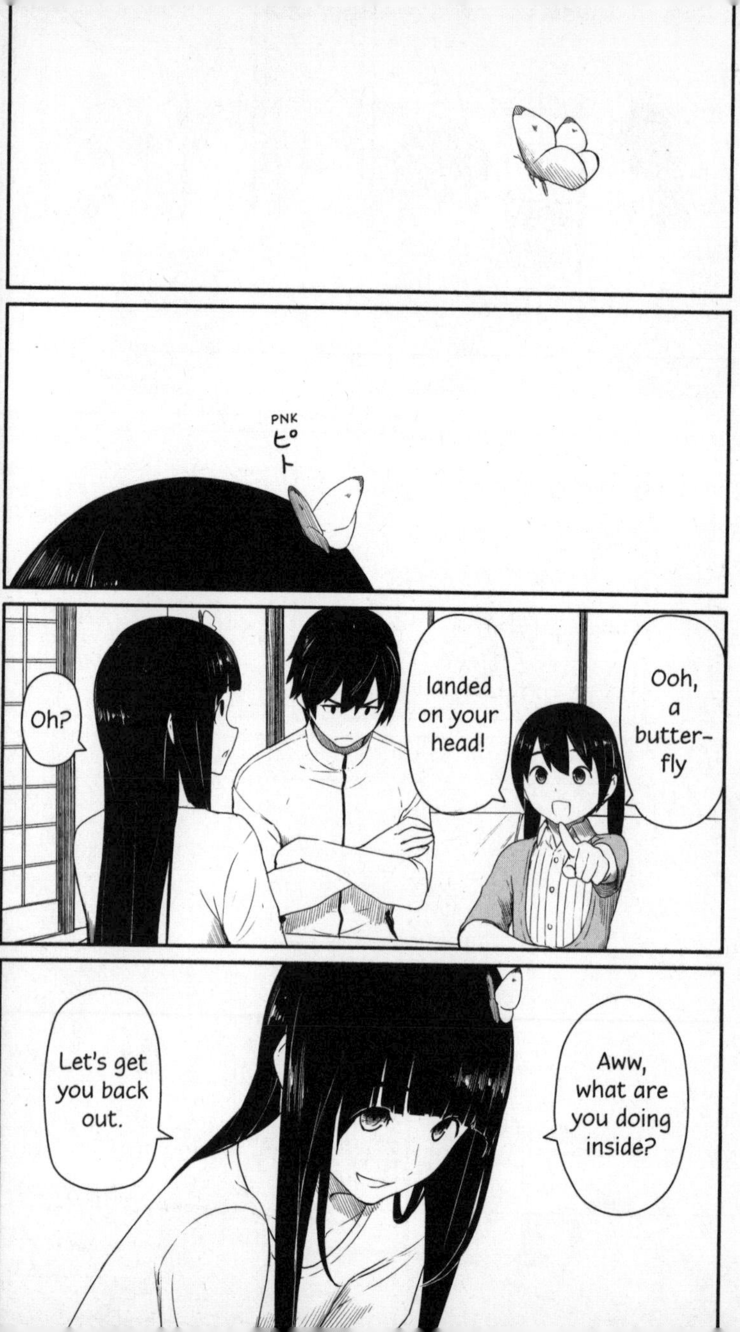
PNK
ピト
Ooh, a butter-fly
landed on your head!
Oh?
Aww, what are you doing inside?
Let's get you back out.

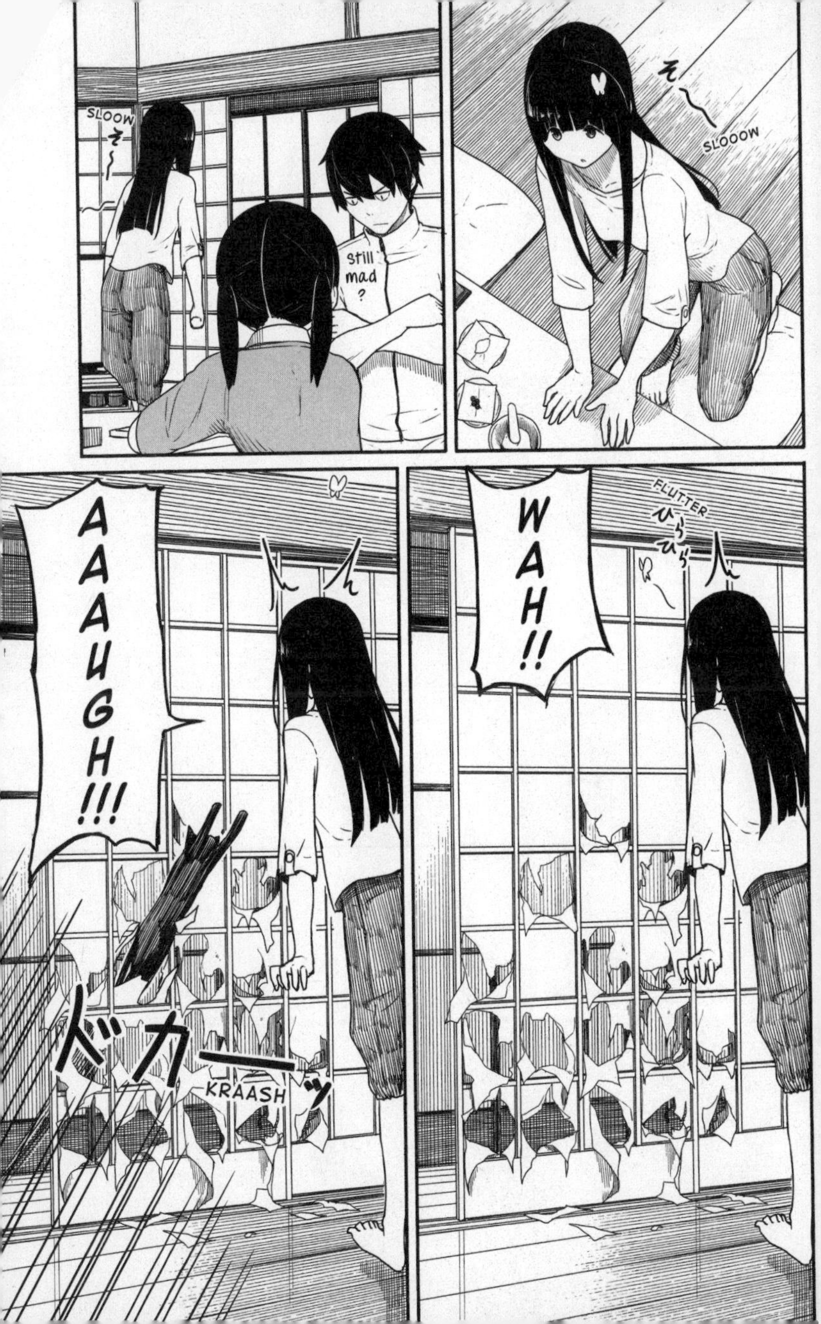
そ～
SLOOOW
Still mad?
SLOOW
そ～
FLUTTER
ひらひら
WAH!!
AAAAUGH!!!
ドカーッ
KRAASH

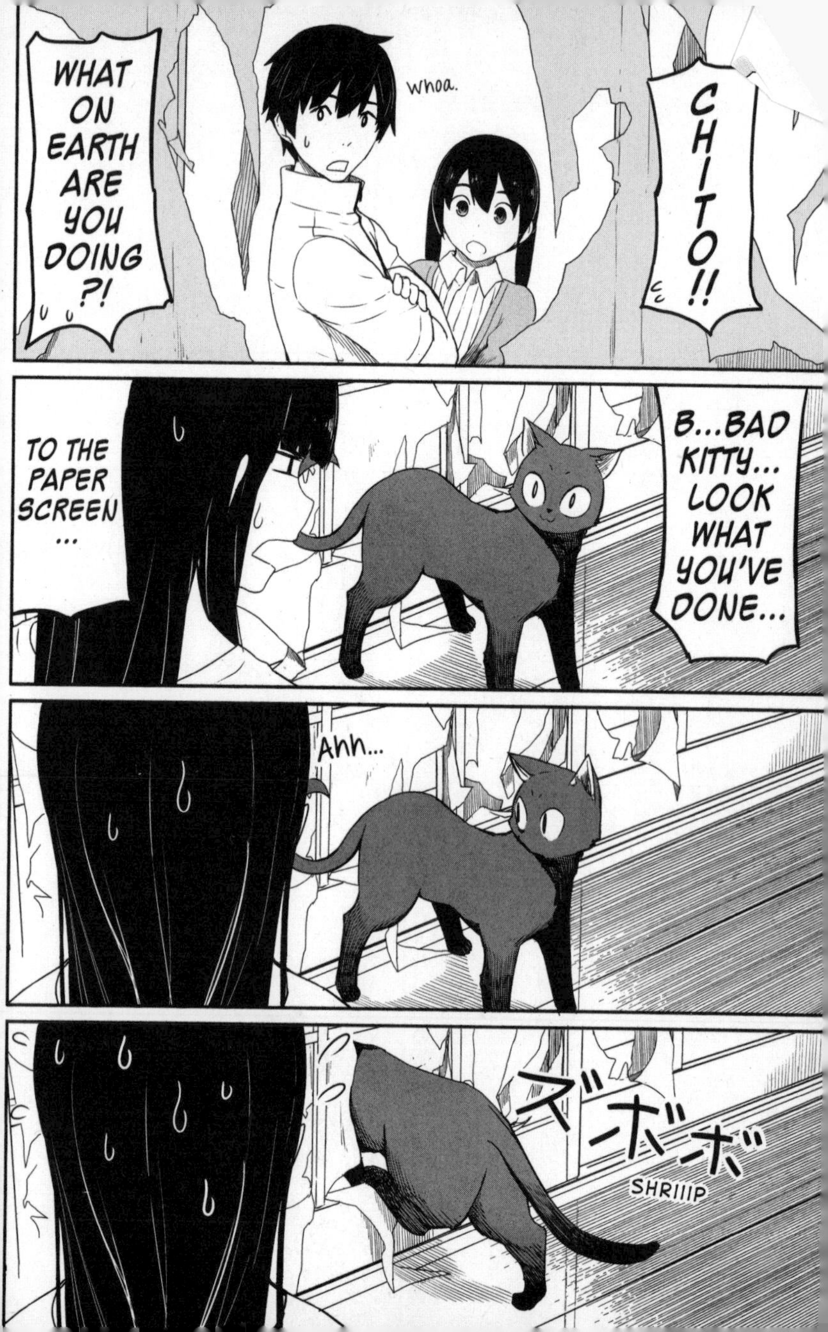
CHITO!!
Whoa.
WHAT ON EARTH ARE YOU DOING?!
B...BAD KITTY... LOOK WHAT YOU'VE DONE...
TO THE PAPER SCREEN...
Ahn...
ズーボボ
SHRIIIP

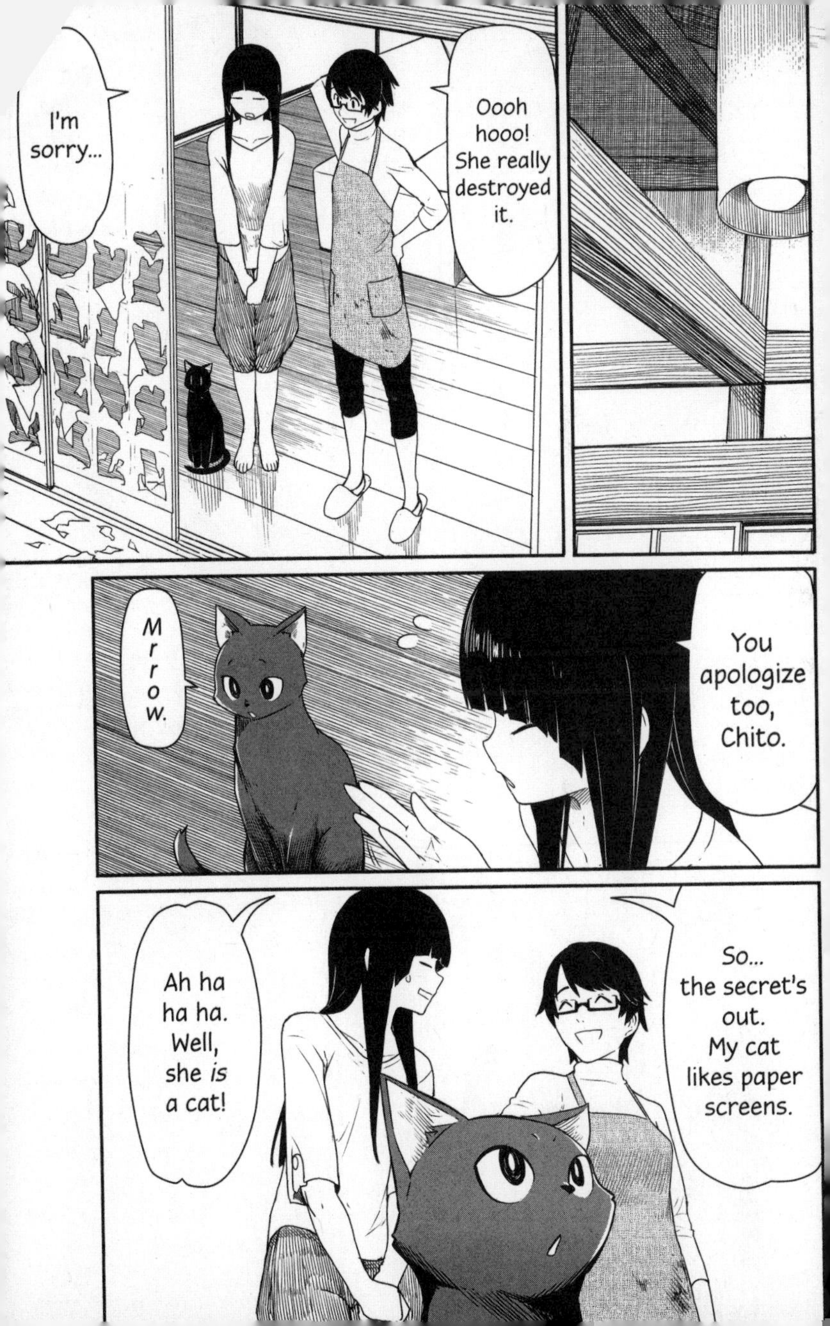
Oooh hooo! She really destroyed it.
I'm sorry...
You apologize too, Chito.
Mrrow.
So... the secret's out. My cat likes paper screens.
Ah ha ha ha. Well, she *is* a cat!

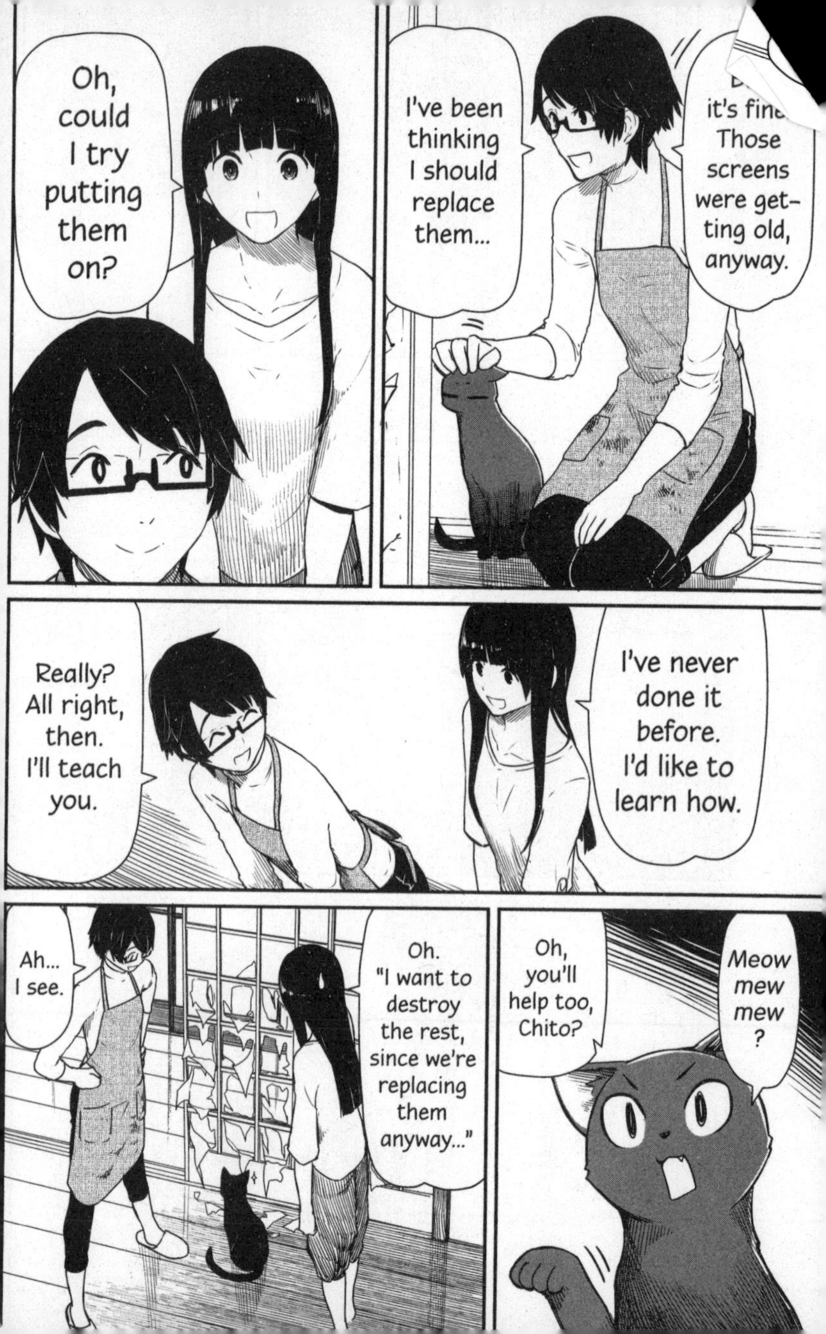
it's fin Those screens were get-ting old, anyway.
I've been thinking I should replace them...
Oh, could I try putting them on?
I've never done it before. I'd like to learn how.
Really? All right, then. I'll teach you.
Meow mew mew ?
Oh, you'll help too, Chito?
Oh. "I want to destroy the rest, since we're replacing them anyway..."
Ah... I see.

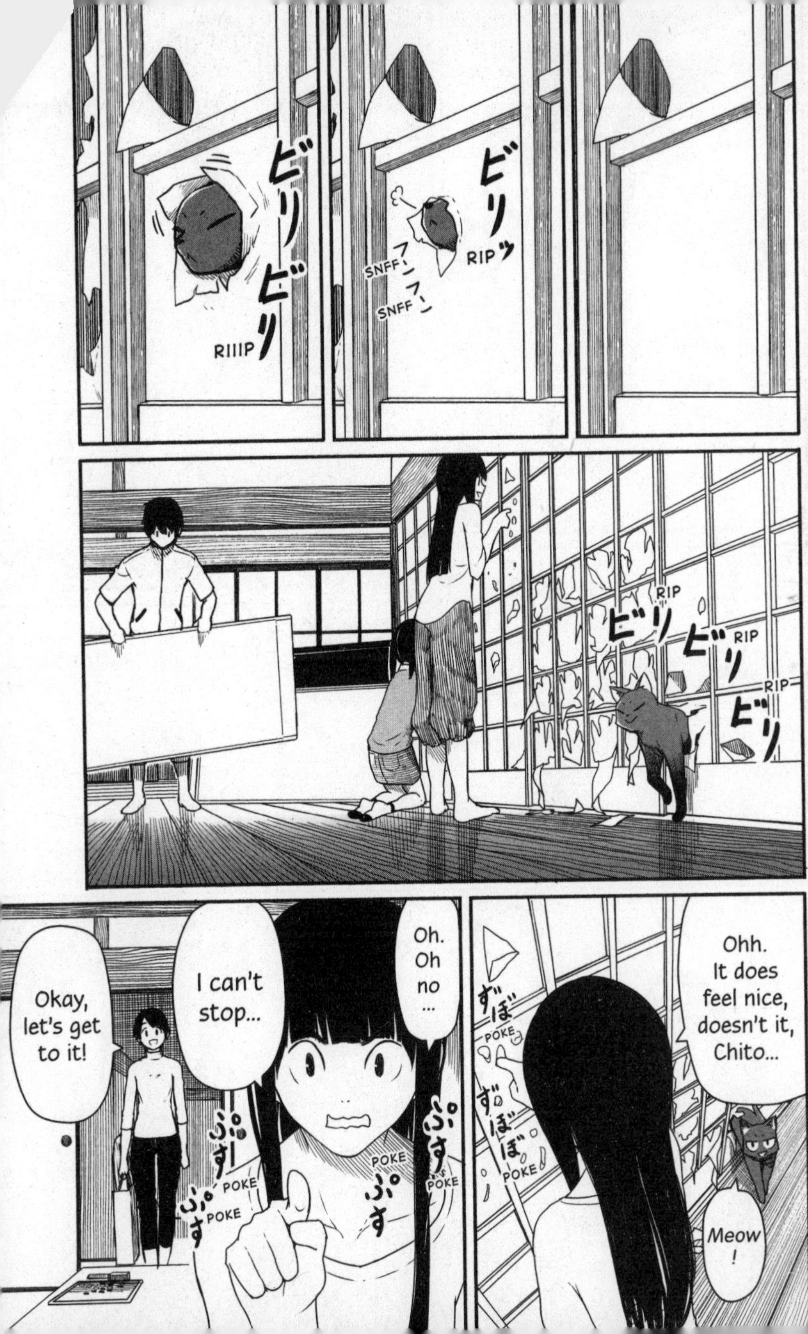

ビリッ
RIP
フンフン
SNFF
SNFF
ビリビリ
RIIIP
RIP
ビリ
RIP
ビリ
RIP
ビリ
Ohh. It does feel nice, doesn't it, Chito...
ずぼ
POKE
ずぼぼ
POKE
Meow!
Oh. Oh no ...
ぷす
POKE
ぷす
POKE
I can't stop...
ぷす
POKE
ぷす
POKE
Okay, let's get to it!

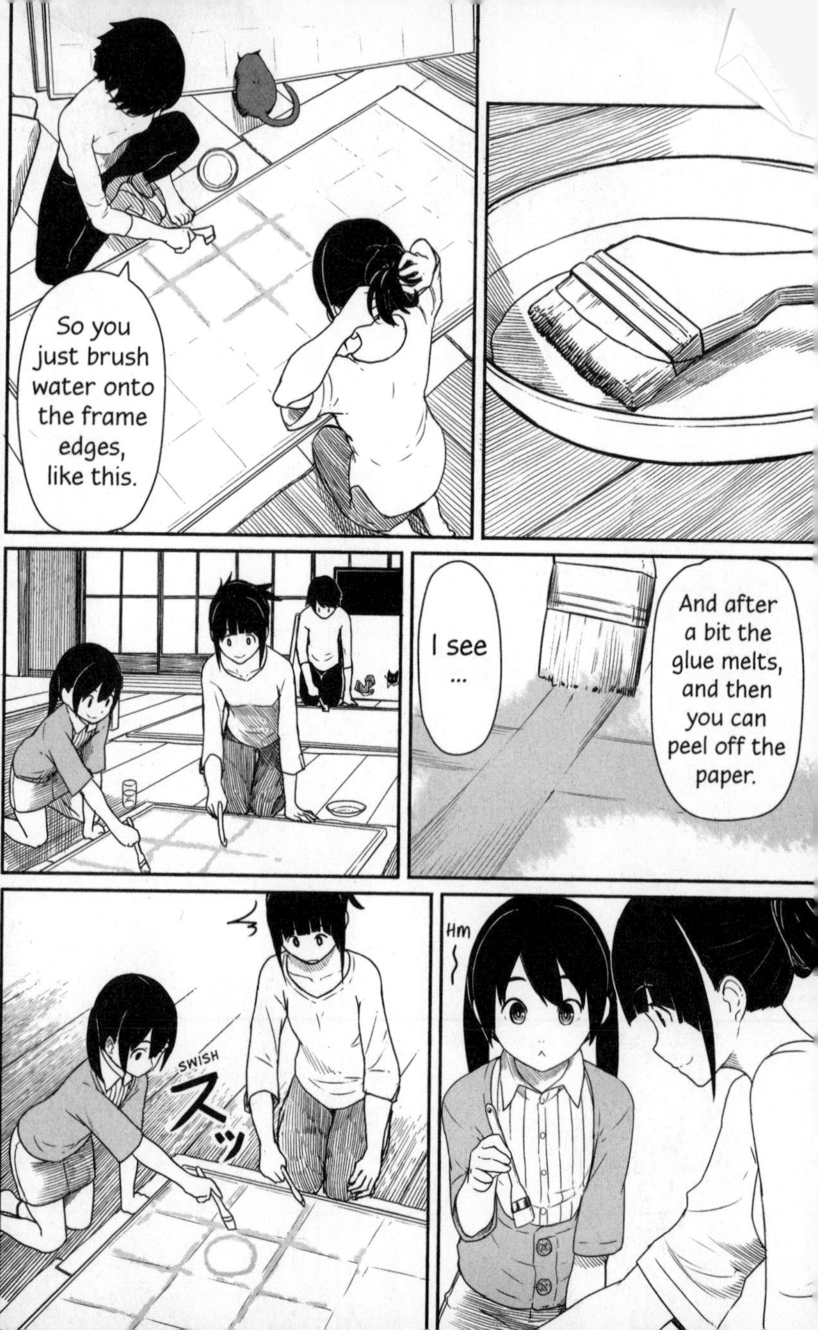
So you just brush water onto the frame edges, like this.
And after a bit the glue melts, and then you can peel off the paper.
I see ...
HM
SWISH

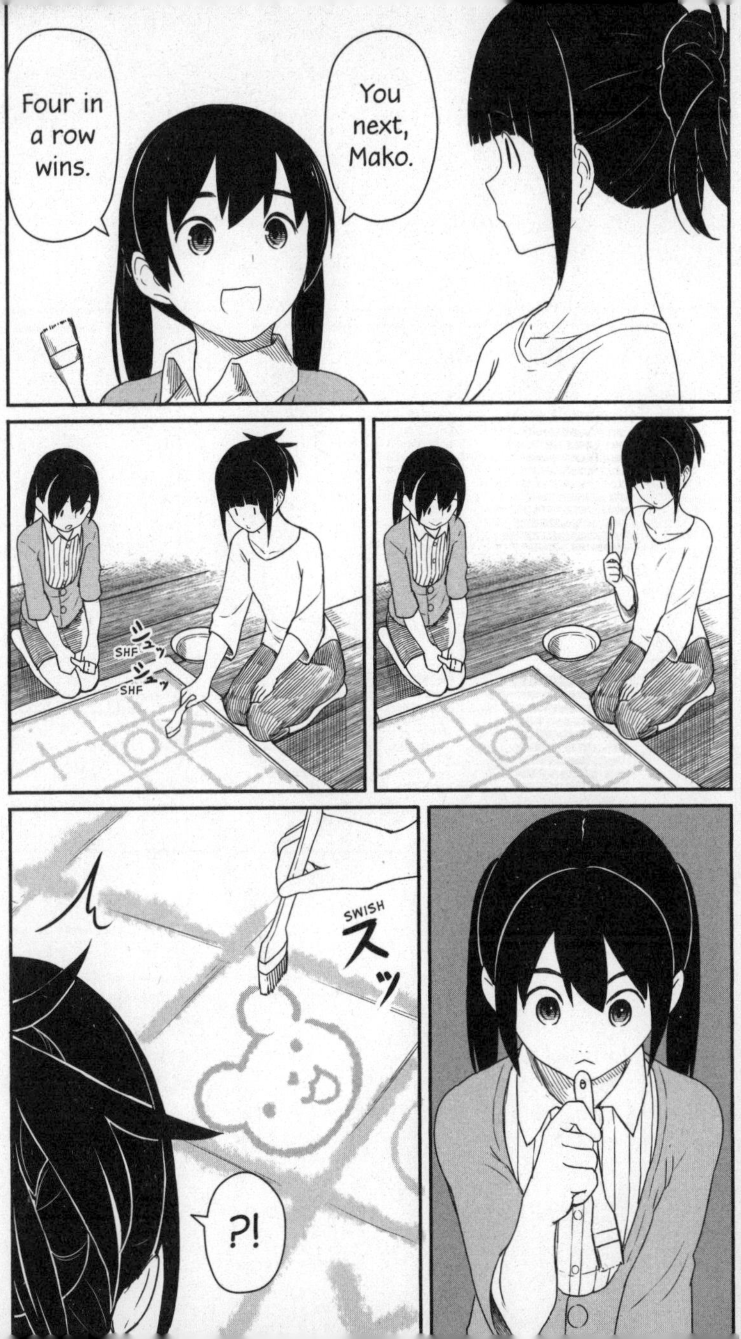
You next, Mako.
Four in a row wins.
シュッ
SHF
シュッ
SHF
SWISH
スッ
?!

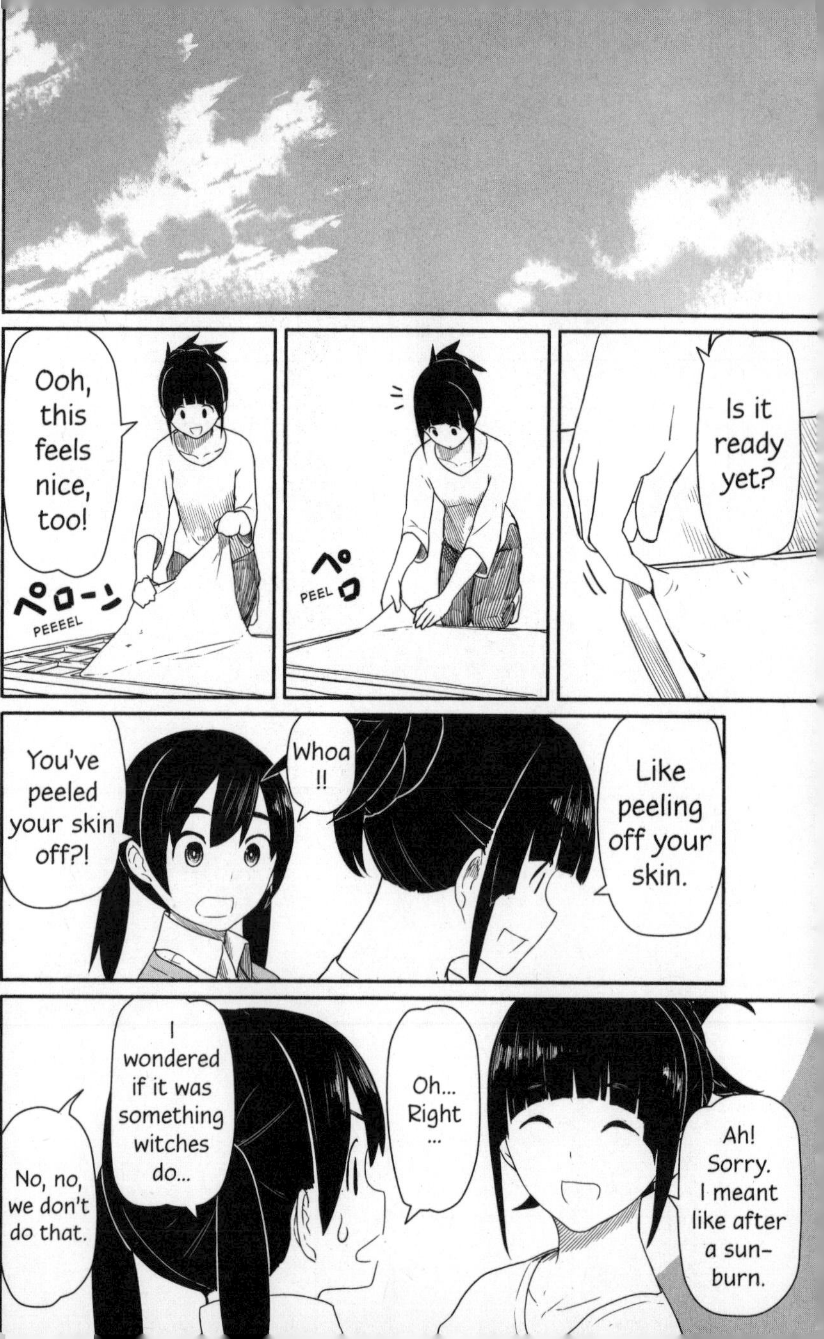
Is it ready yet?
ペロ
PEEL
Ooh, this feels nice, too!
ペローン
PEEEEL
Like peeling off your skin.
Whoa !!
You've peeled your skin off?!
Ah! Sorry. I meant like after a sun-burn.
Oh... Right ...
I wondered if it was something witches do...
No, no, we don't do that.

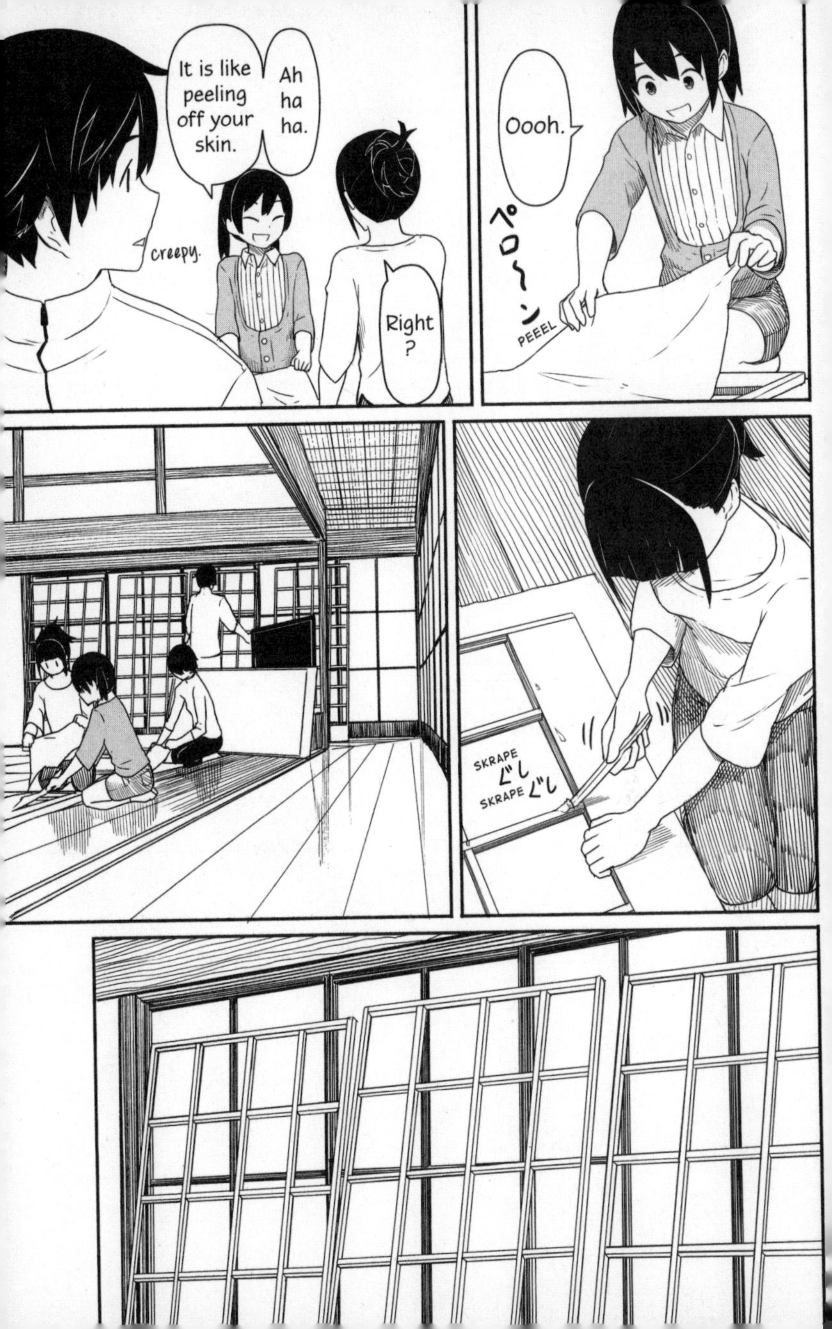
Oooh.
ペロ～ン
PEEEL
Right?
Ah ha ha.
It is like peeling off your skin.
creepy.
SKRAPE ぐし
SKRAPE ぐし

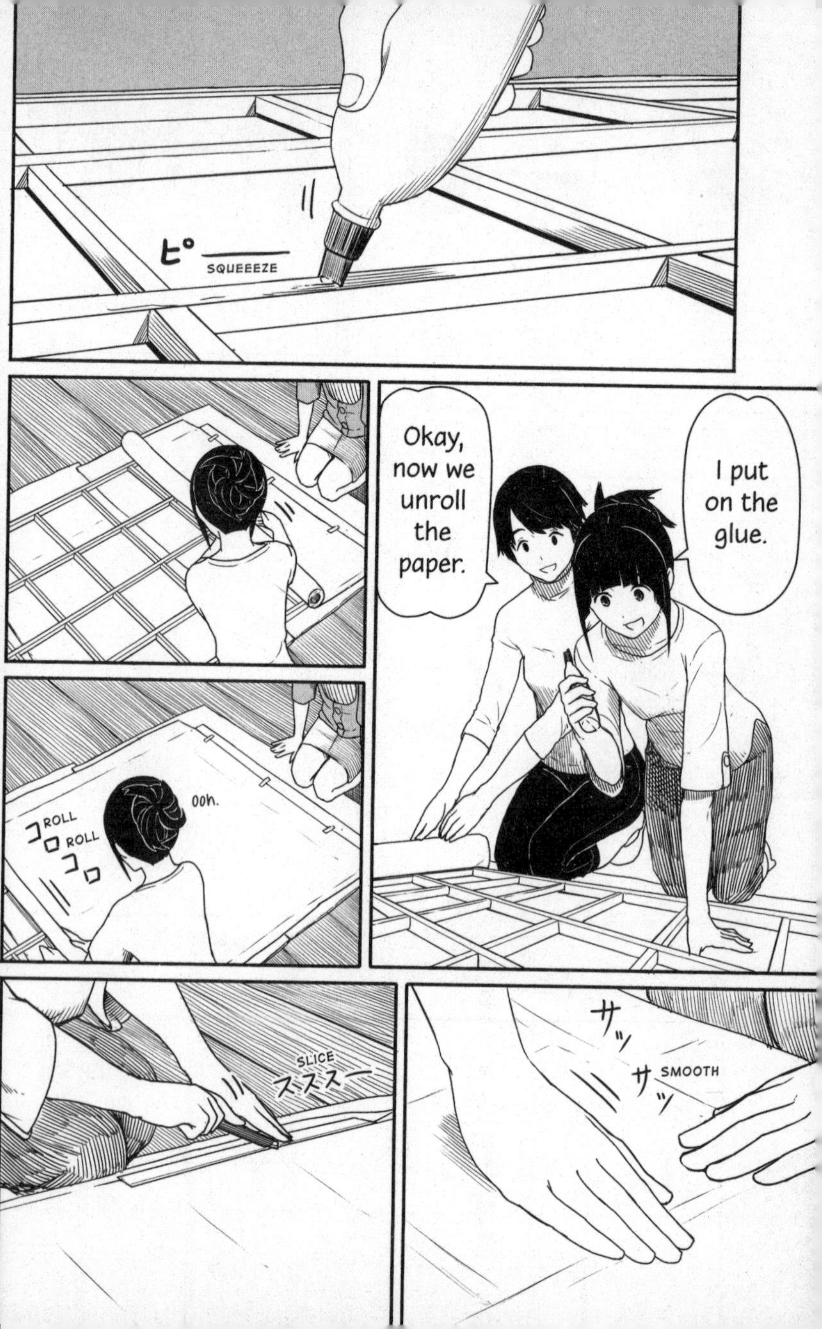
ピー
SQUEEEZE
I put on the glue.
Okay, now we unroll the paper.
Ooh.
コロコロ
ROLL ROLL
サッサッ
SMOOTH
スススー
SLICE

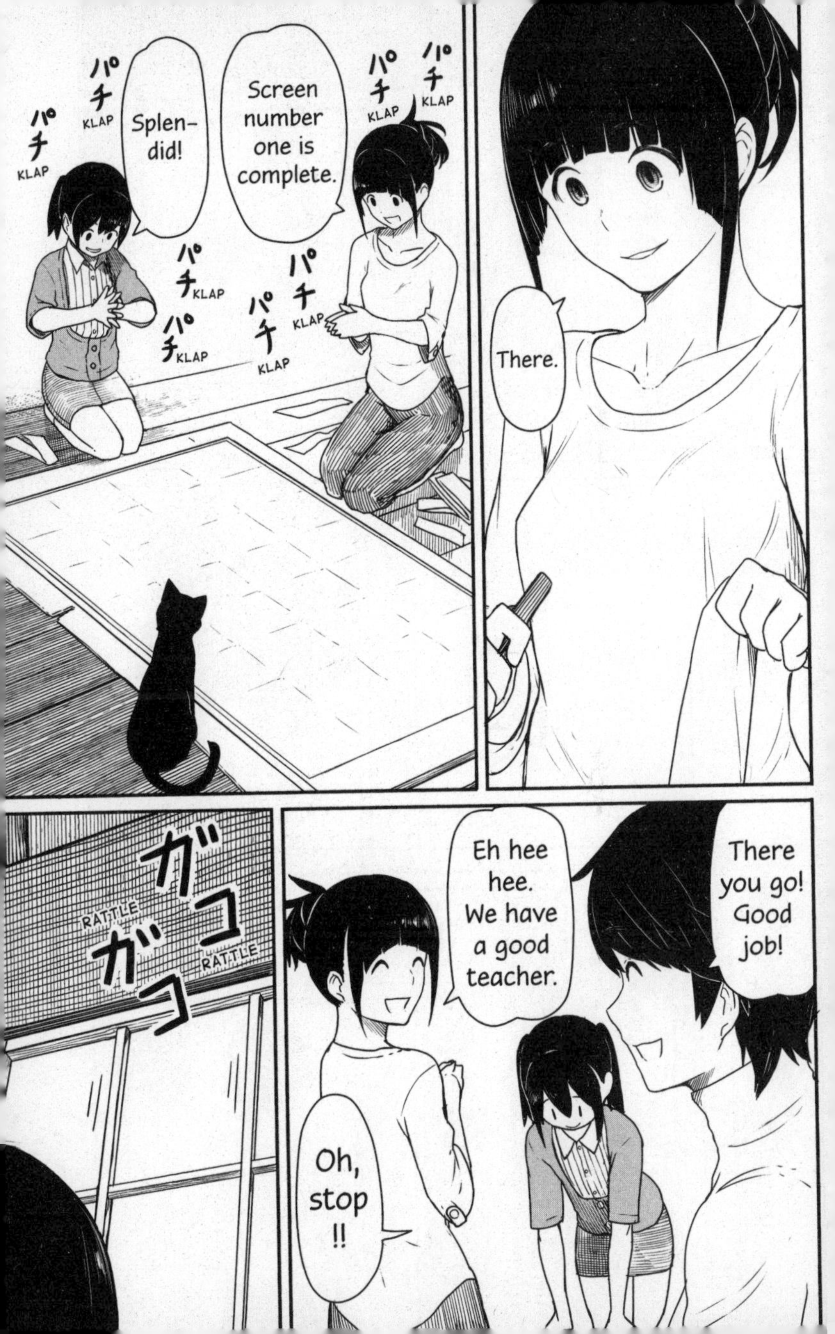
There.
パチ KLAP
パチ KLAP
Screen number one is complete.
Splendid!
パチ KLAP
パチ KLAP
パチ KLAP
パチ KLAP
パチ KLAP
パチ KLAP
There you go! Good job!
Eh hee hee. We have a good teacher.
Oh, stop!!
ガコ RATTLE
ガコ RATTLE

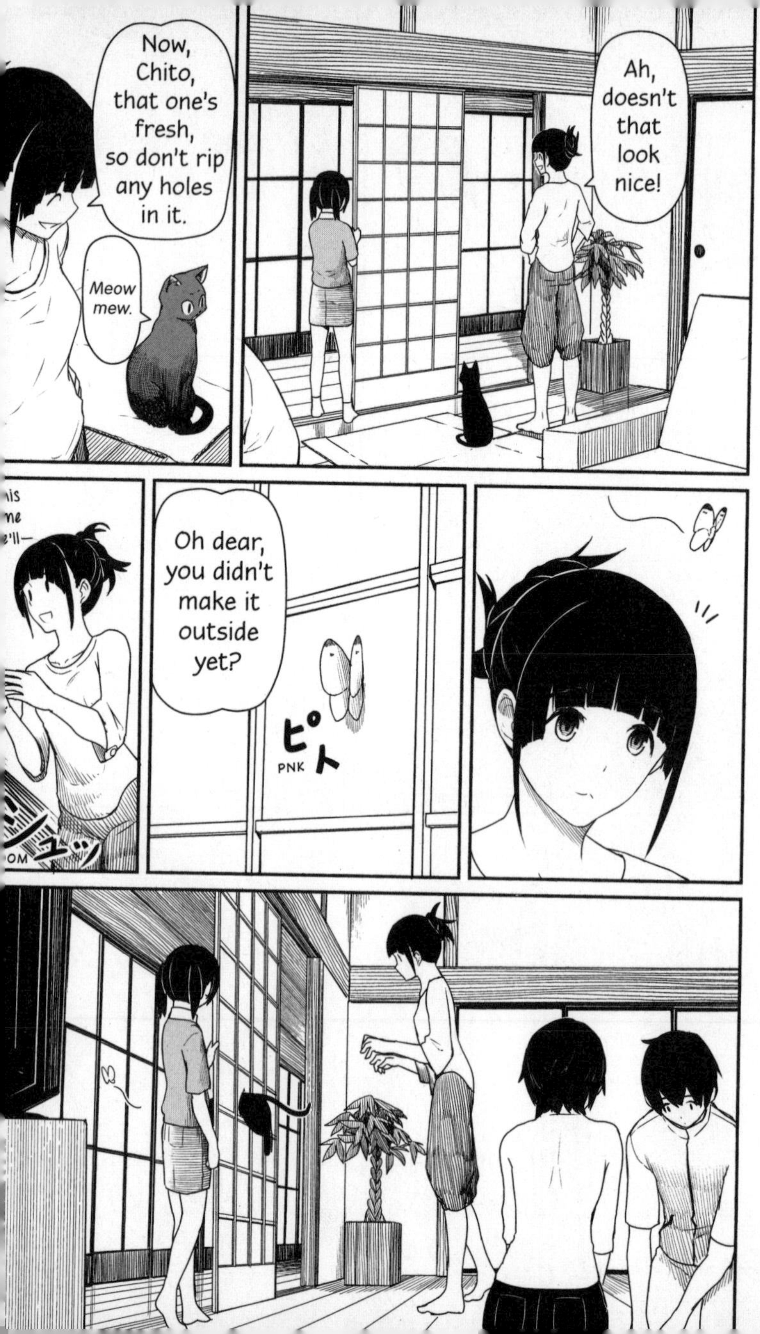
Ah, doesn't that look nice!
Now, Chito, that one's fresh, so don't rip any holes in it.
Meow mew.
Oh dear, you didn't make it outside yet?
PNK

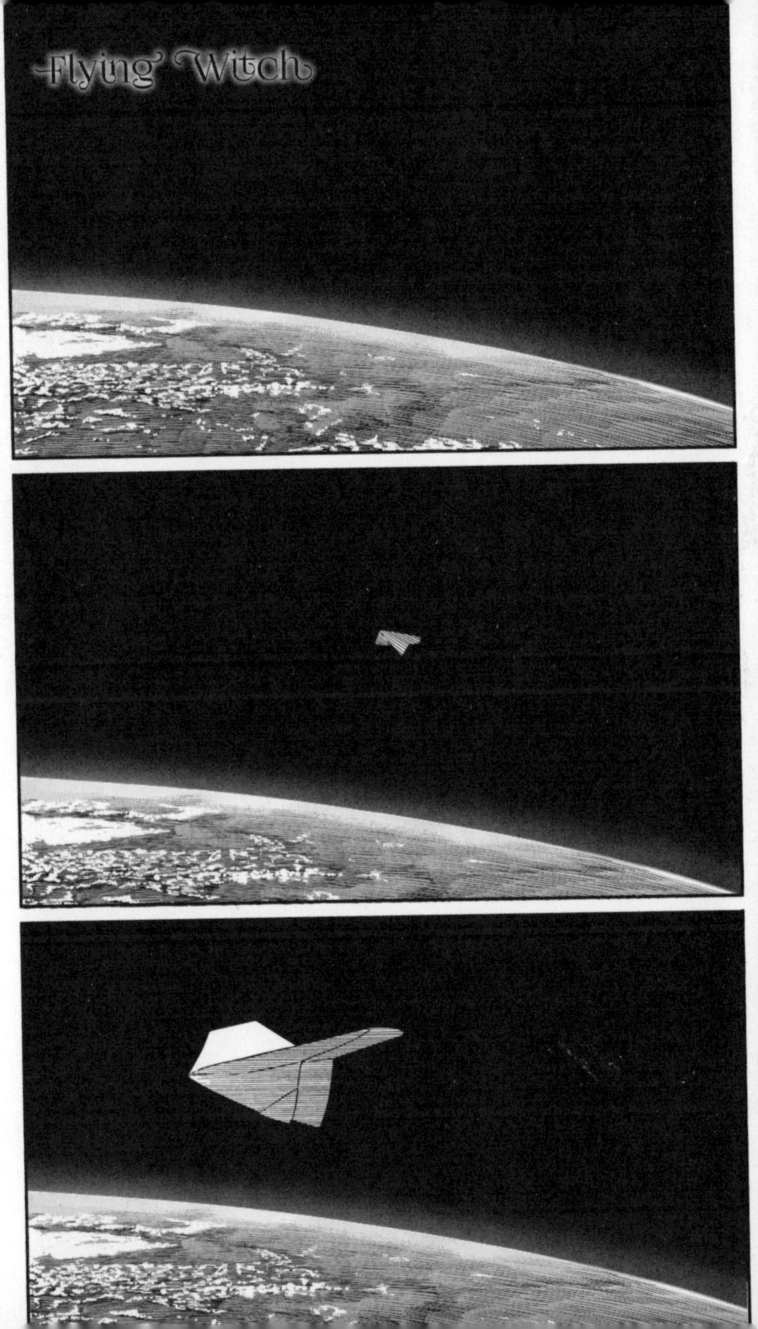
Flying Witch

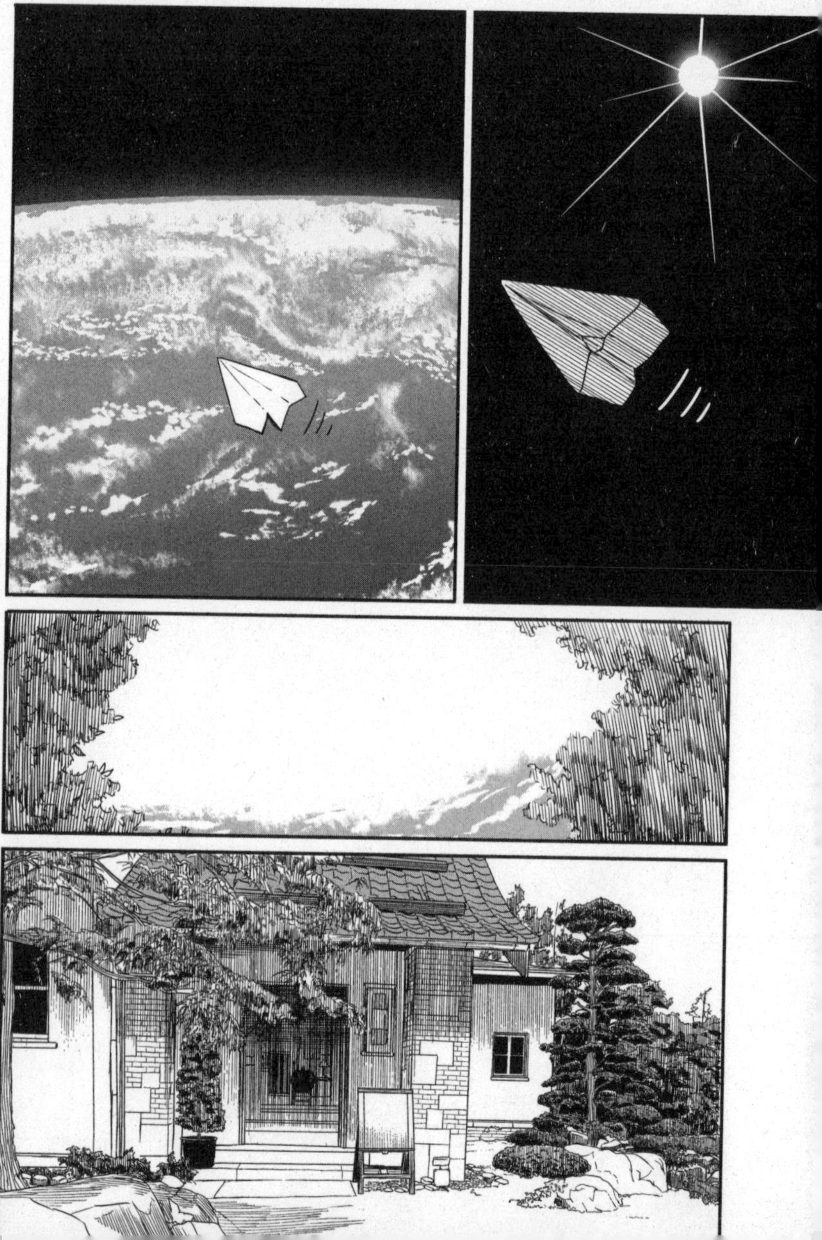

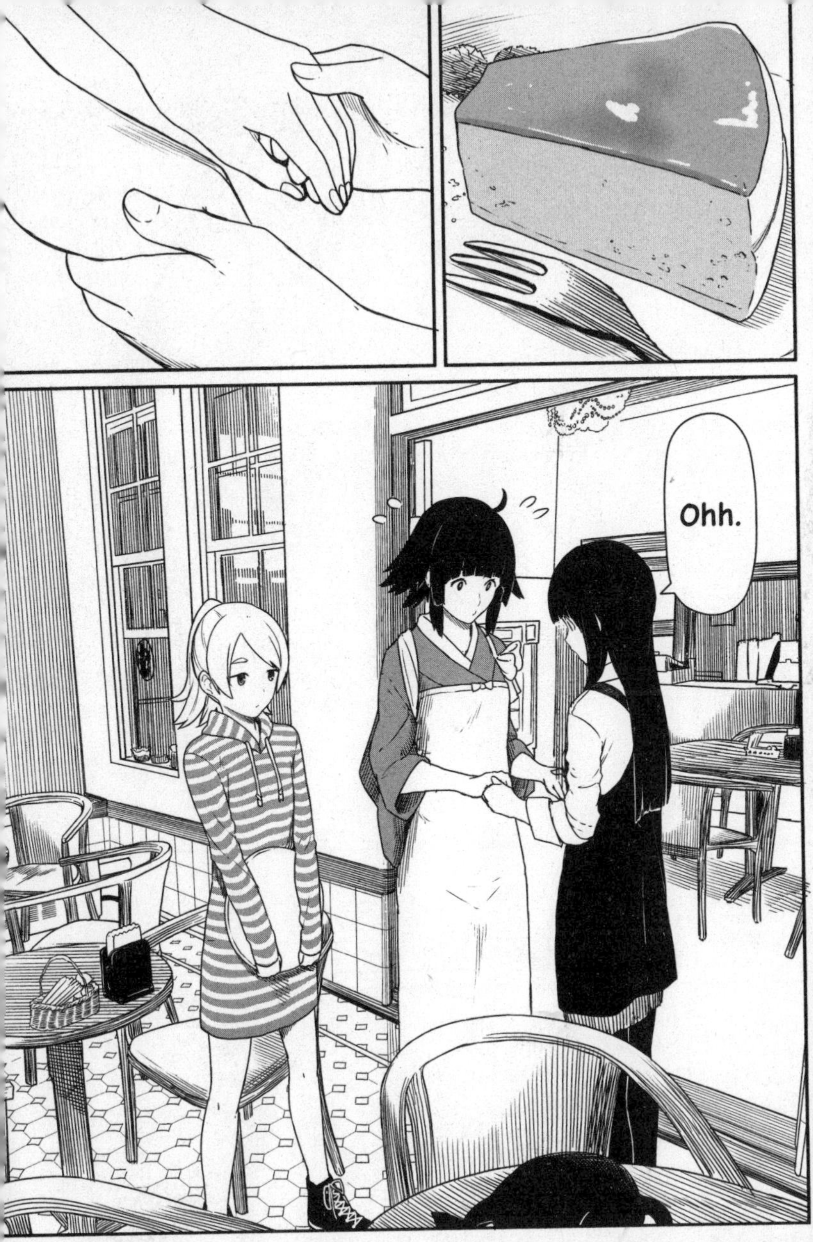
Ohh.

Chapter 26
Nasty Weather, Nasty Mood

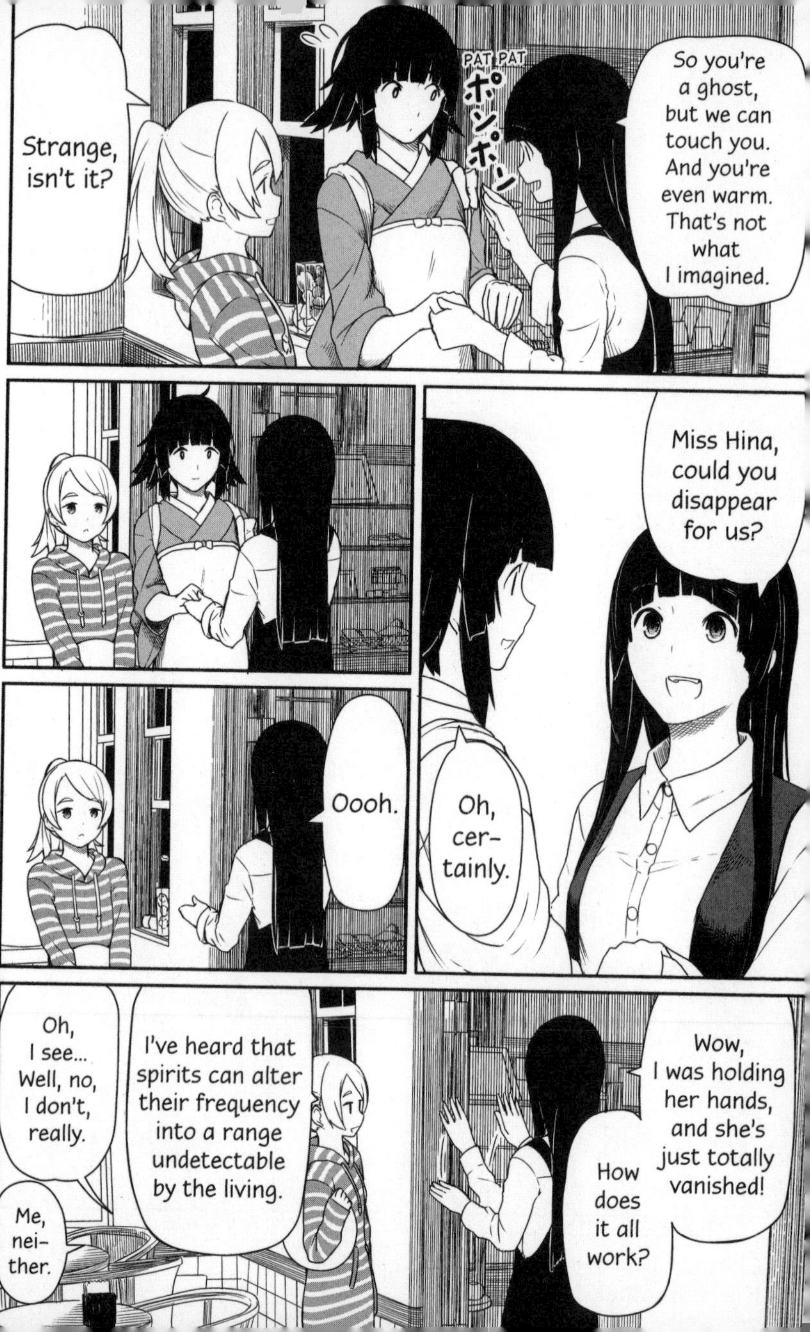
So you're a ghost, but we can touch you. And you're even warm. That's not what I imagined.
PAT PAT
ポンポン
Strange, isn't it?
Miss Hina, could you disappear for us?
Oh, certainly.
Oooh.
Wow, I was holding her hands, and she's just totally vanished!
How does it all work?
I've heard that spirits can alter their frequency into a range undetectable by the living.
Oh, I see... Well, no, I don't, really.
Me, neither.

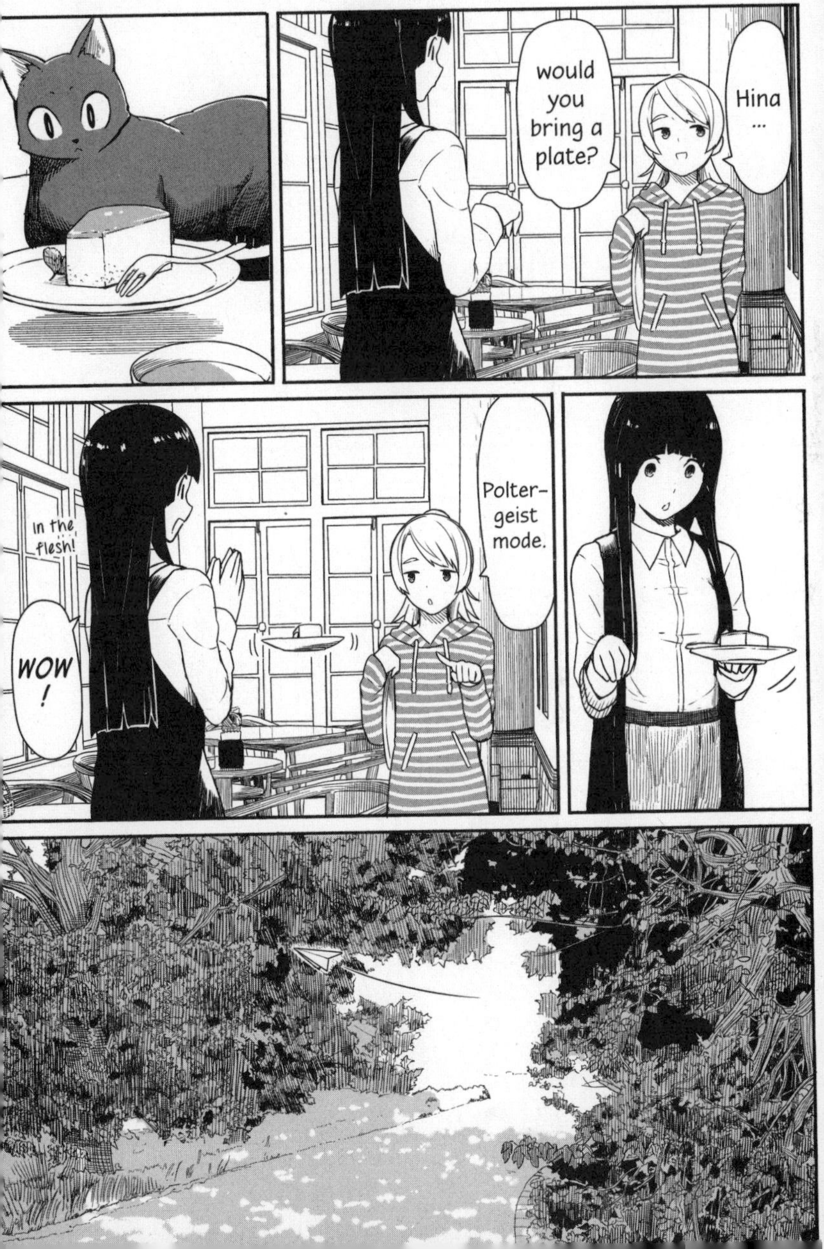

Hina...
would you bring a plate?
Polter-geist mode.
In the flesh!
WOW!

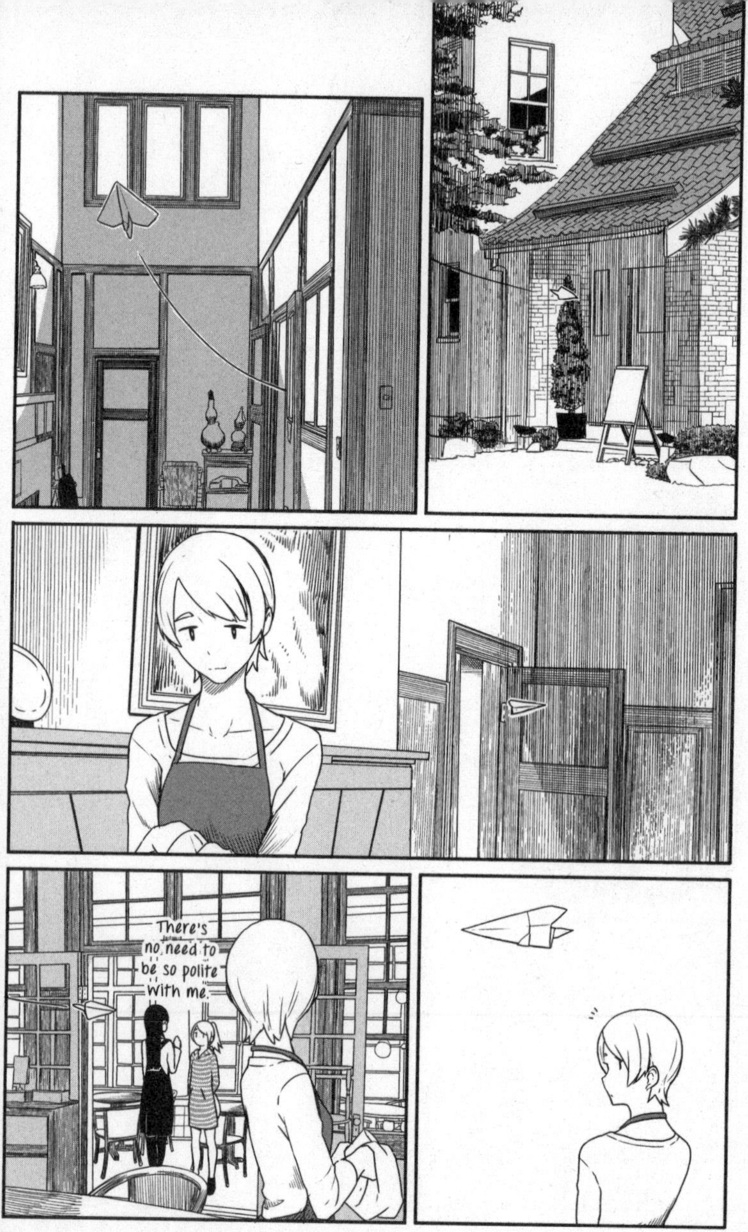
There's no need to be so polite with me.

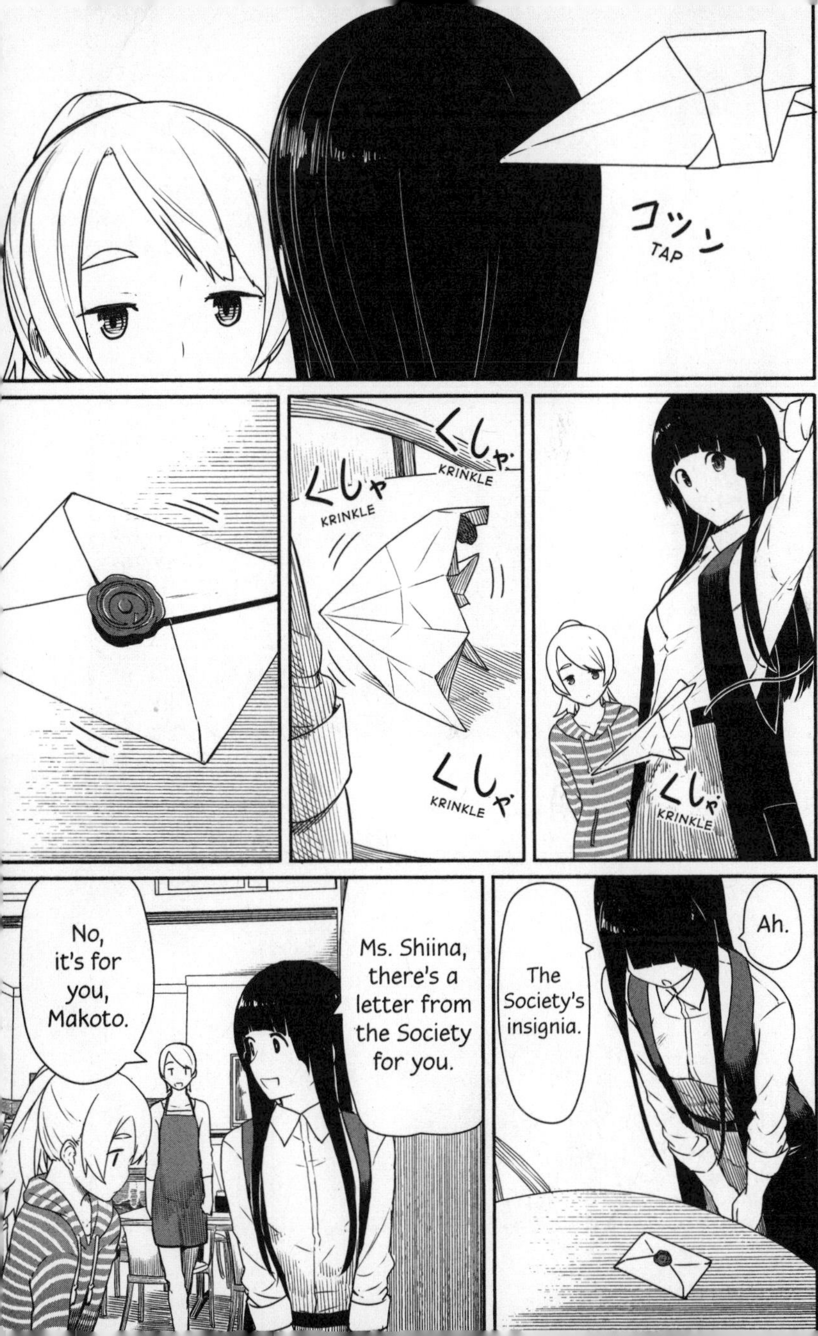
コッン
TAP
くしゃ
KRINKLE
くしゃ
KRINKLE
くしゃ
KRINKLE
くしゃ
KRINKLE
Ah.
The Society's insignia.
Ms. Shiina, there's a letter from the Society for you.
No, it's for you, Makoto.

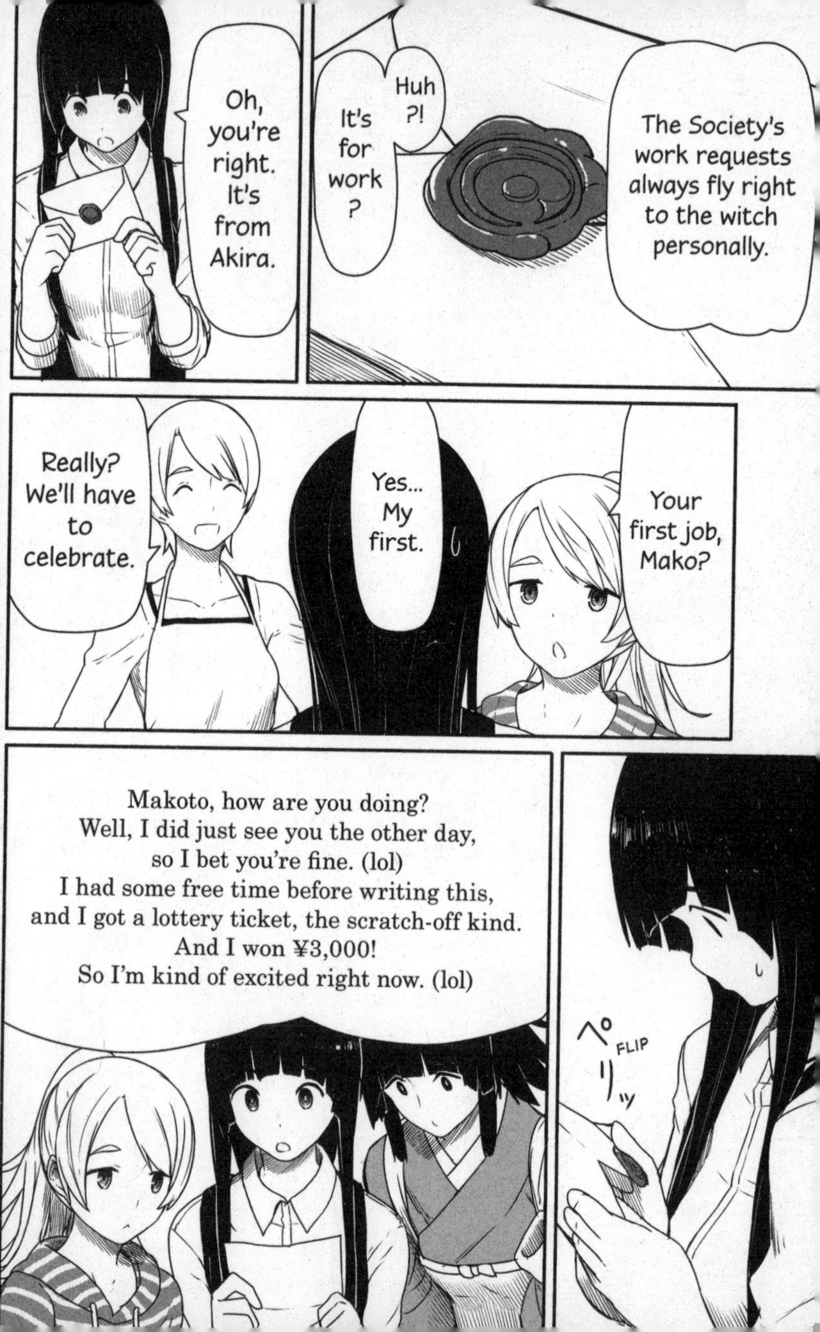
The Society's work requests always fly right to the witch personally.
Huh ?!
It's for work ?
Oh, you're right. It's from Akira.
Your first job, Mako?
Yes... My first.
Really? We'll have to celebrate.
ペ リッ FLIP
Makoto, how are you doing? Well, I did just see you the other day, so I bet you're fine. (lol) I had some free time before writing this, and I got a lottery ticket, the scratch-off kind. And I won ¥3,000! So I'm kind of excited right now. (lol)

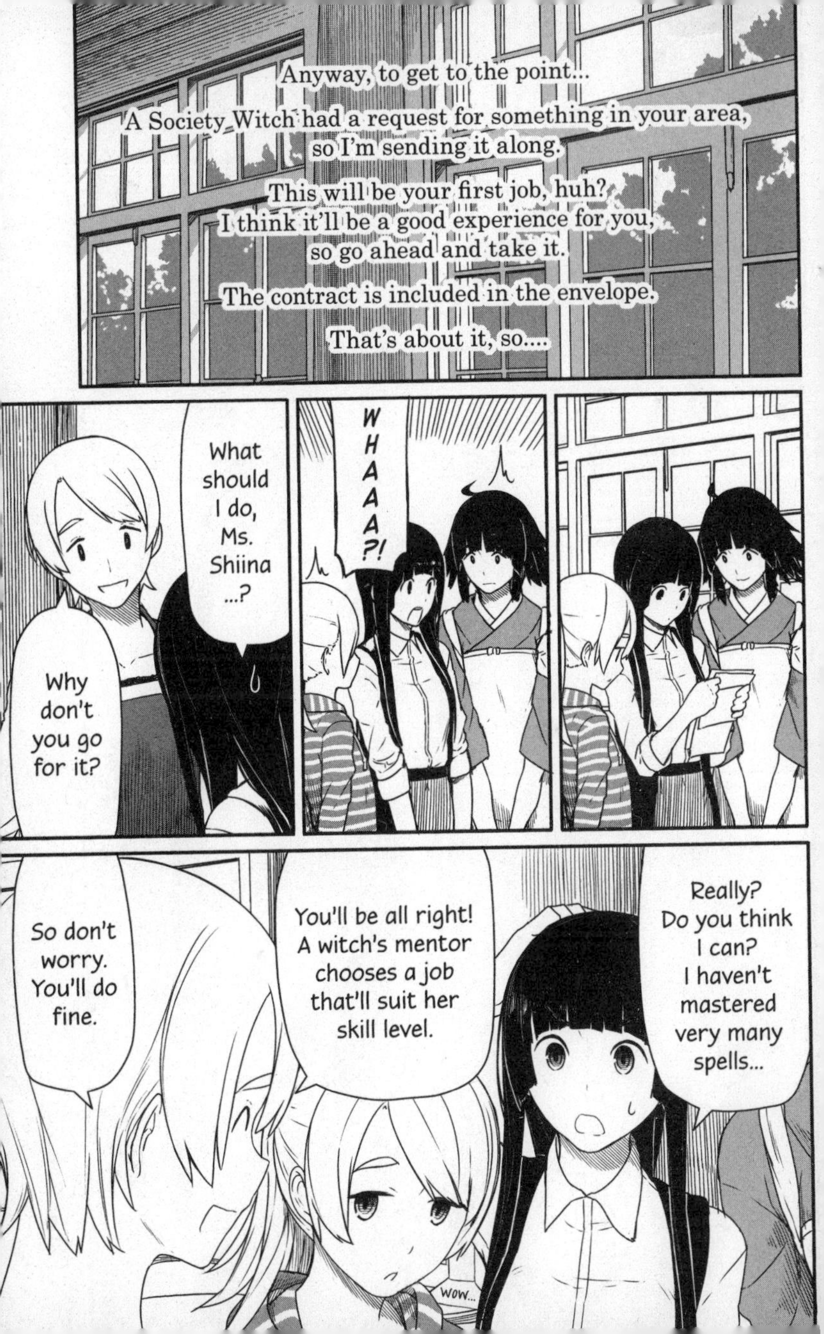
Anyway, to get to the point...
A Society Witch had a request for something in your area, so I'm sending it along.
This will be your first job, huh? I think it'll be a good experience for you, so go ahead and take it.
The contract is included in the envelope.
That's about it, so....
WHAAAA?!
What should I do, Ms. Shiina ...?
Why don't you go for it?
Really? Do you think I can? I haven't mastered very many spells...
You'll be all right! A witch's mentor chooses a job that'll suit her skill level.
So don't worry. You'll do fine.
wow...

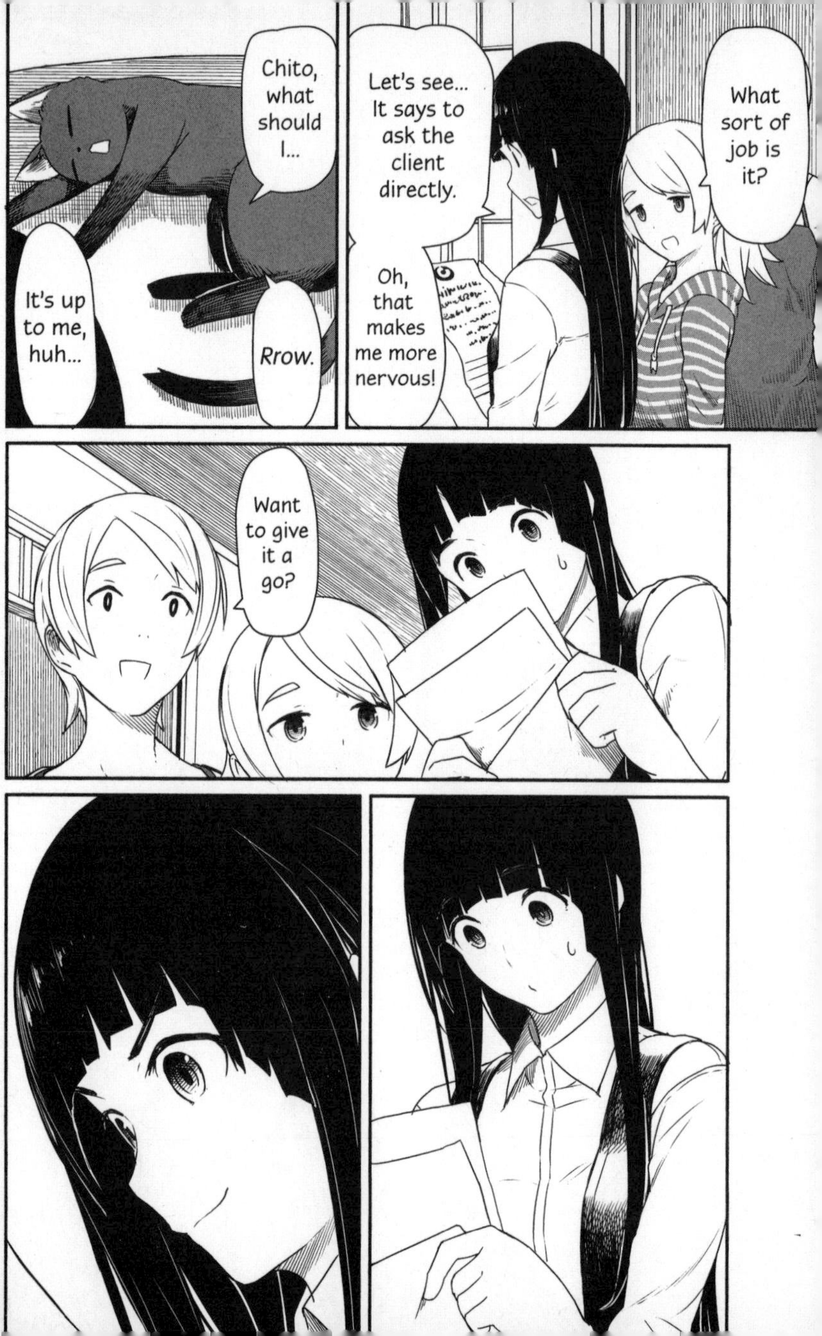
What sort of job is it?
Let's see... It says to ask the client directly.
Oh, that makes me more nervous!
Chito, what should I...
Rrow.
It's up to me, huh...
Want to give it a go?

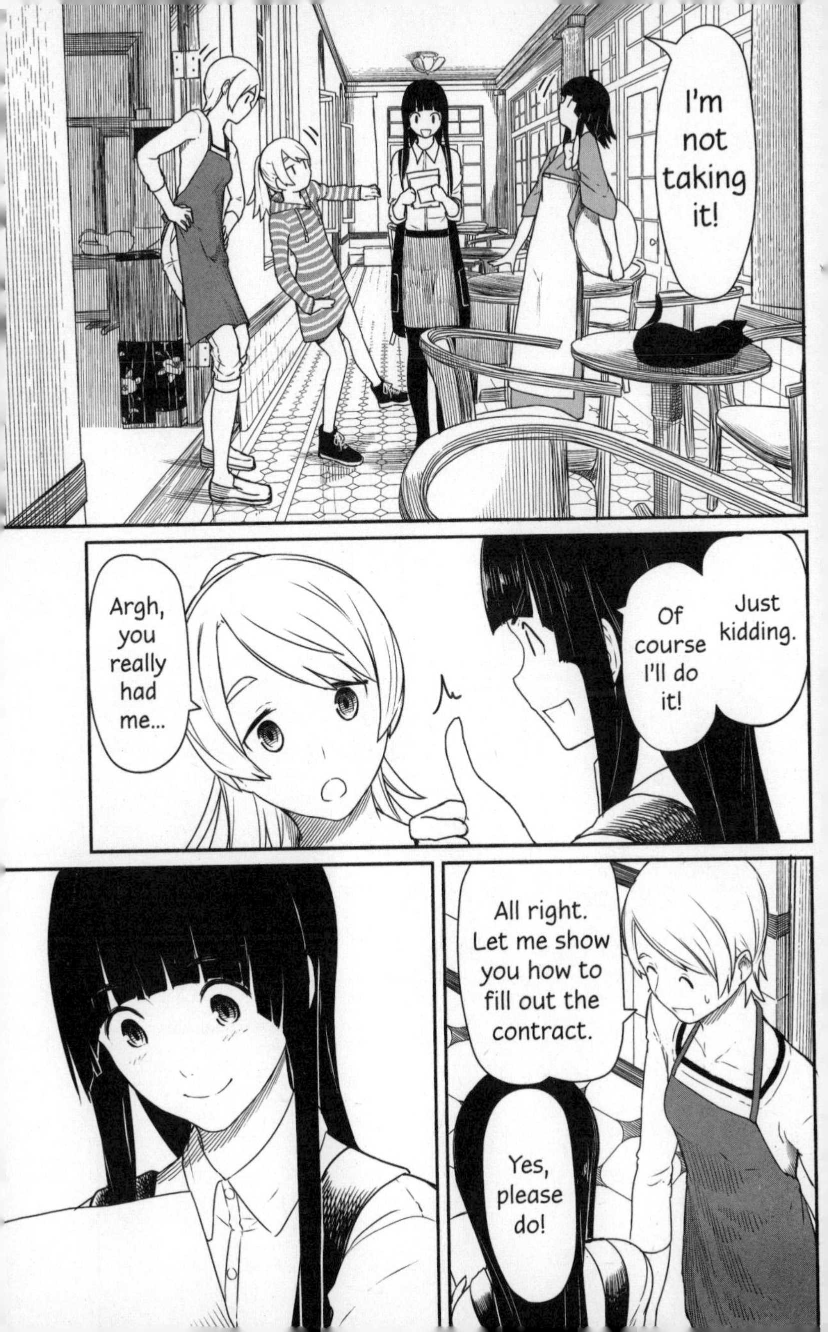
I'm not taking it!
Just kidding.
Of course I'll do it!
Argh, you really had me...
All right. Let me show you how to fill out the contract.
Yes, please do!

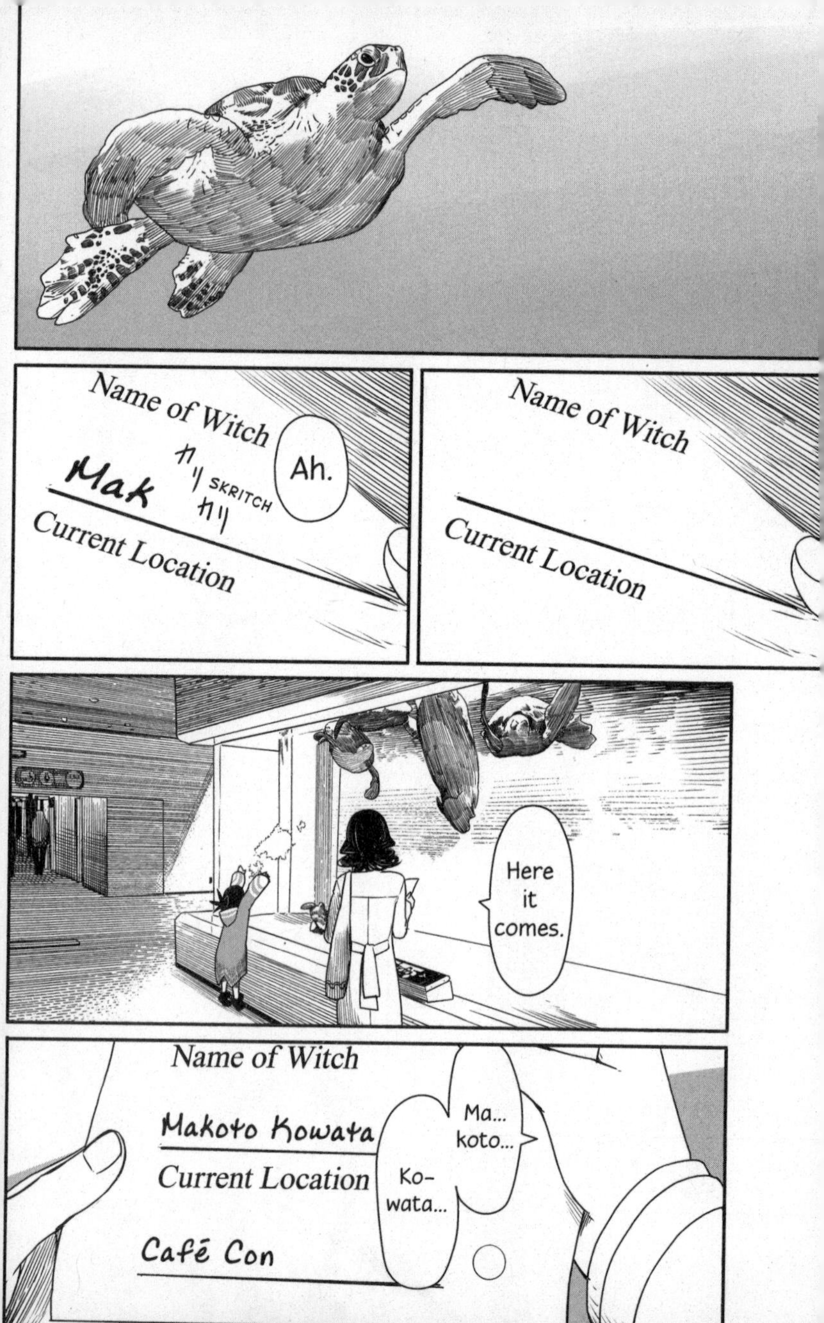
Name of Witch
Current Location
Name of Witch
Ah.
Mak
カリ
SKRITCH
カリ
Current Location
Here it comes.
Name of Witch
Makoto Kowata
Current Location
Café Con
Ma... koto...
Ko-wata...

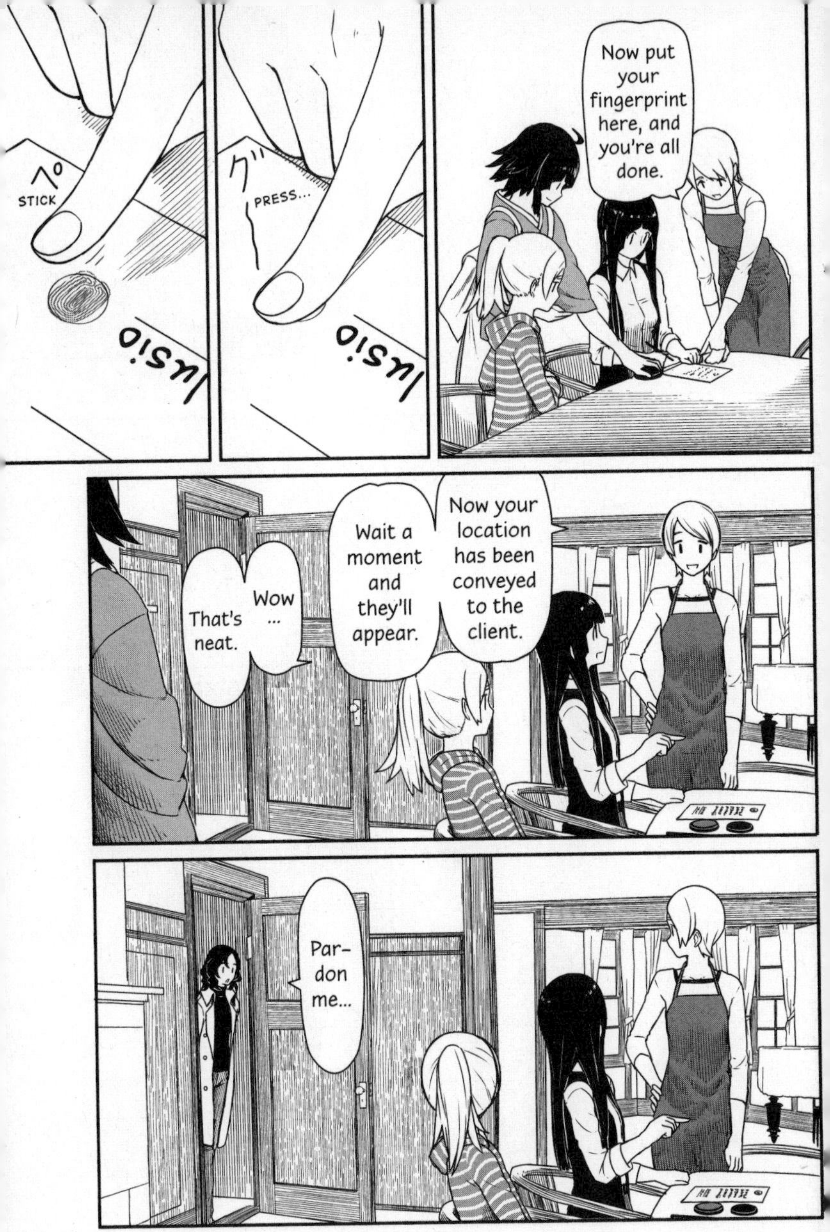
Now put your fingerprint here, and you're all done.
グ
PRESS...
ペ
STICK
Now your location has been conveyed to the client.
Wait a moment and they'll appear.
Wow ...
That's neat.
Par-don me...

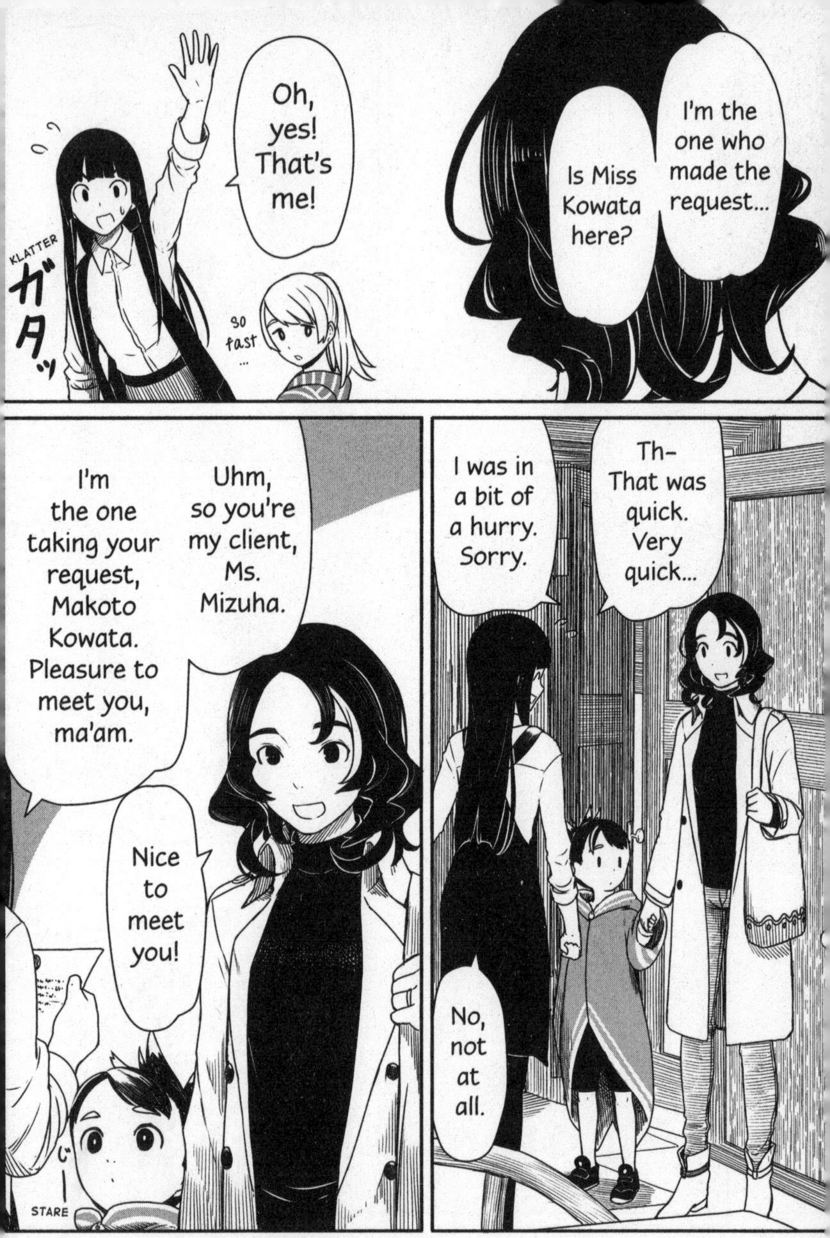
I'm the one who made the request...
Is Miss Kowata here?
Oh, yes! That's me!
KLATTER
ガタッ
so fast ...
Th- That was quick. Very quick...
I was in a bit of a hurry. Sorry.
No, not at all.
Uhm, so you're my client, Ms. Mizuha.
I'm the one taking your request, Makoto Kowata. Pleasure to meet you, ma'am.
Nice to meet you!
じー
STARE

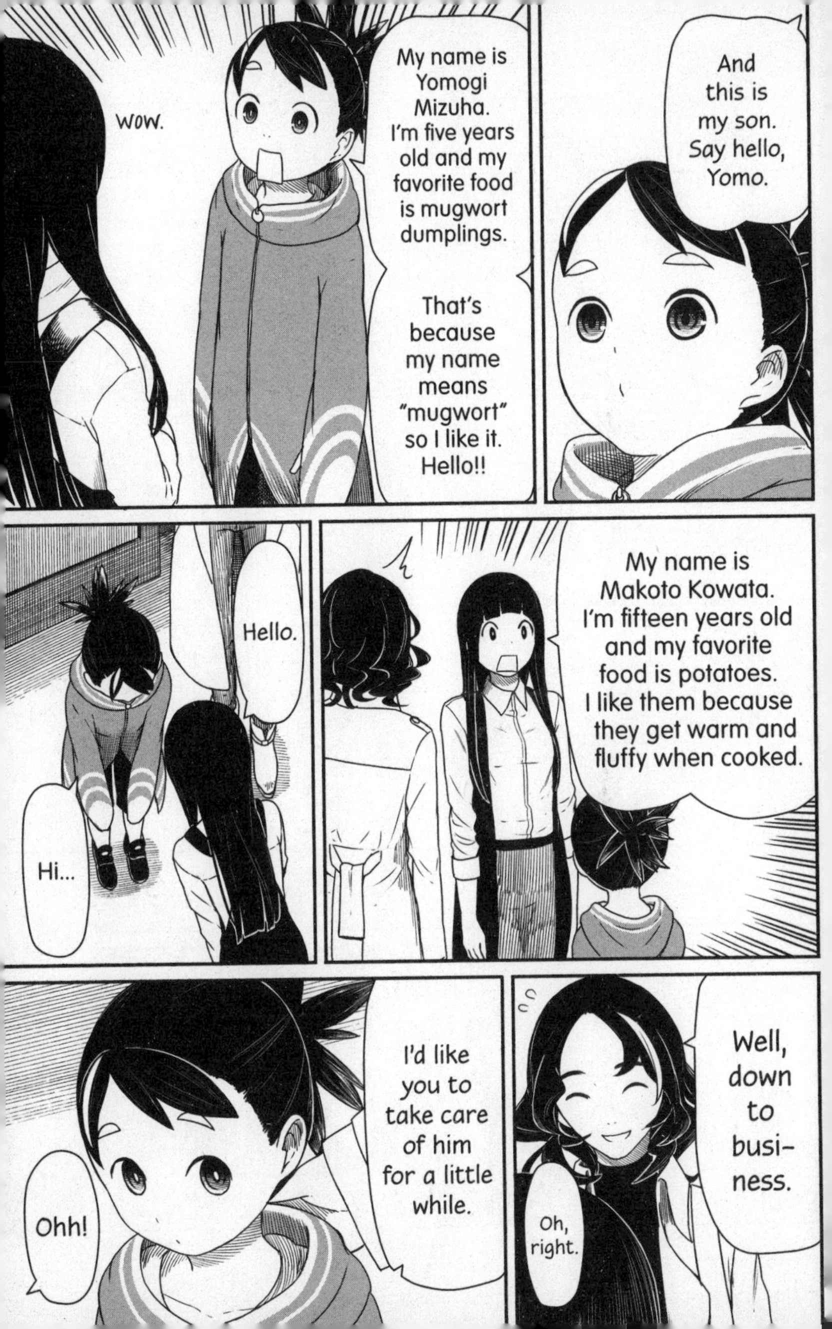
And this is my son. Say hello, Yomo.
My name is Yomogi Mizuha. I'm five years old and my favorite food is mugwort dumplings.
That's because my name means "mugwort" so I like it. Hello!!
wow.
My name is Makoto Kowata. I'm fifteen years old and my favorite food is potatoes. I like them because they get warm and fluffy when cooked.
Hello.
Hi...
Well, down to busi-ness.
Oh, right.
I'd like you to take care of him for a little while.
Ohh!

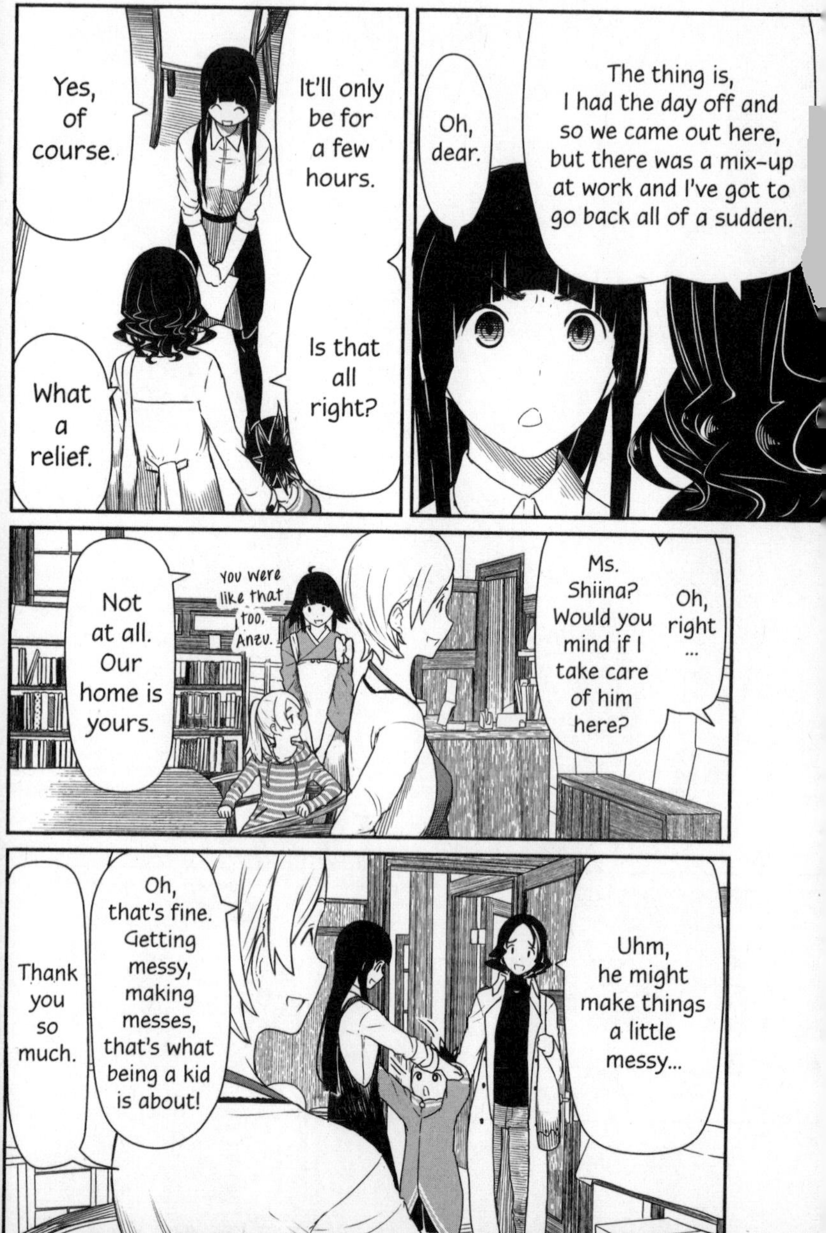
The thing is, I had the day off and so we came out here, but there was a mix-up at work and I've got to go back all of a sudden.
Oh, dear.
It'll only be for a few hours.
Is that all right?
Yes, of course.
What a relief.
Oh, right ...
Ms. Shiina? Would you mind if I take care of him here?
You were like that too, Anzu.
Not at all. Our home is yours.
Uhm, he might make things a little messy...
Oh, that's fine. Getting messy, making messes, that's what being a kid is about!
Thank you so much.

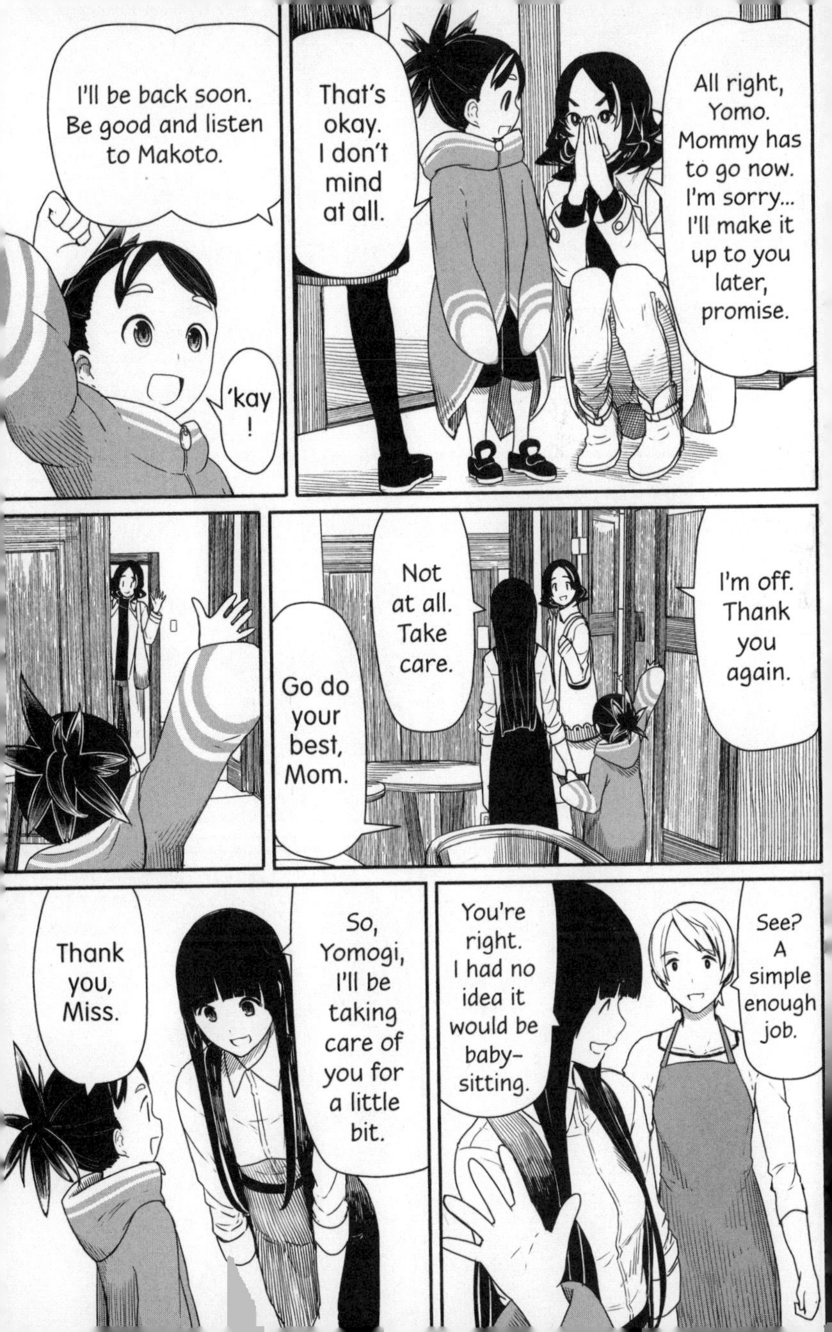
All right, Yomo. Mommy has to go now. I'm sorry... I'll make it up to you later, promise.
That's okay. I don't mind at all.
I'll be back soon. Be good and listen to Makoto.
'kay!
I'm off. Thank you again.
Not at all. Take care.
Go do your best, Mom.
See? A simple enough job.
You're right. I had no idea it would be baby-sitting.
So, Yomogi, I'll be taking care of you for a little bit.
Thank you, Miss.

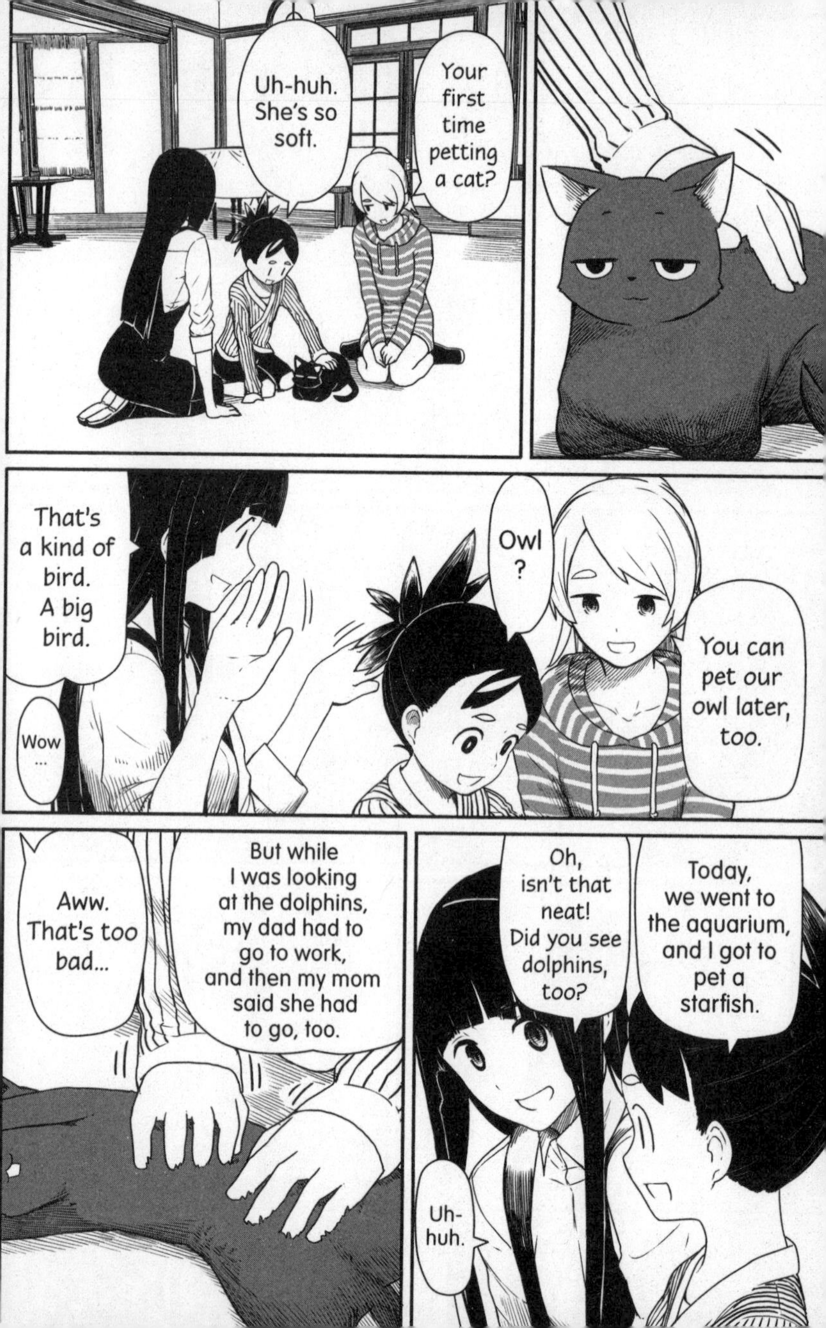
Your first time petting a cat?
Uh-huh. She's so soft.
You can pet our owl later, too.
Owl?
That's a kind of bird. A big bird.
Wow...
Today, we went to the aquarium, and I got to pet a starfish.
Oh, isn't that neat! Did you see dolphins, too?
Uh-huh.
But while I was looking at the dolphins, my dad had to go to work, and then my mom said she had to go, too.
Aww. That's too bad...

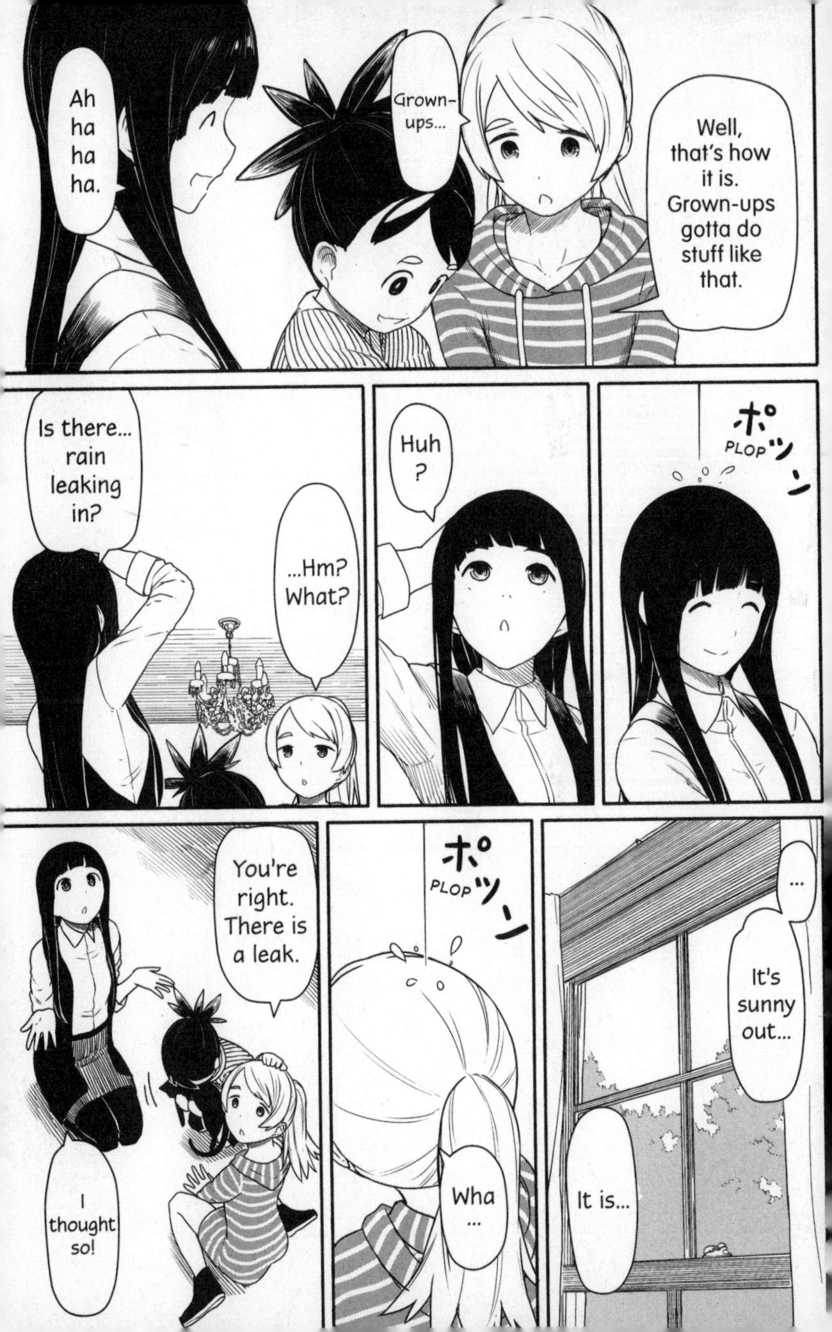
Well, that's how it is. Grown-ups gotta do stuff like that.
Grown-ups...
Ah ha ha ha.
ポツン PLOP
Huh?
Is there... rain leaking in?
...Hm? What?
...
It's sunny out...
It is...
ポツン PLOP
Wha...
You're right. There is a leak.
I thought so!

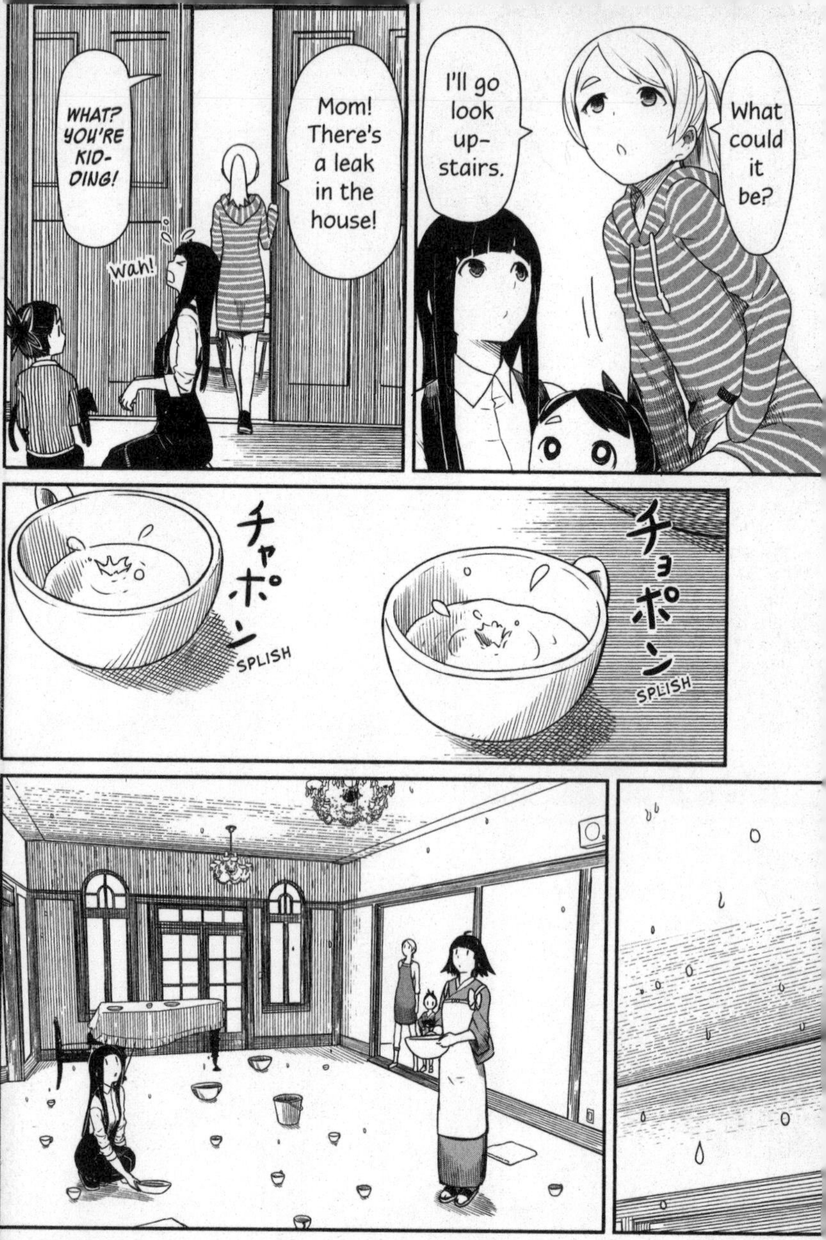
What could it be?
I'll go look up-stairs.
Mom! There's a leak in the house!
WHAT? YOU'RE KID-DING!
Wah!
チョポン
SPLISH
チャポン
SPLISH

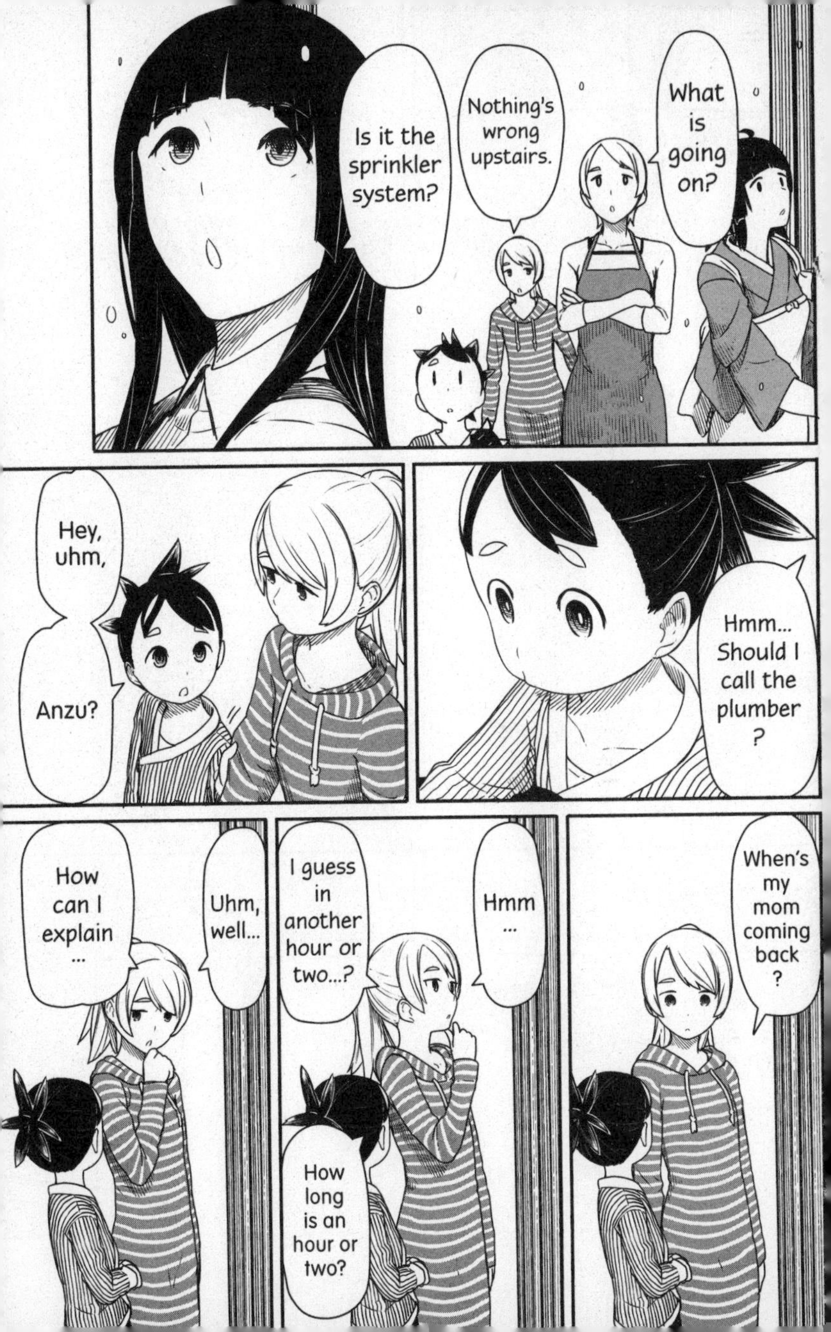
What is going on?
Nothing's wrong upstairs.
Is it the sprinkler system?
Hmm... Should I call the plumber?
Hey, uhm,
Anzu?
When's my mom coming back?
Hmm ...
I guess in another hour or two...?
How long is an hour or two?
Uhm, well...
How can I explain ...

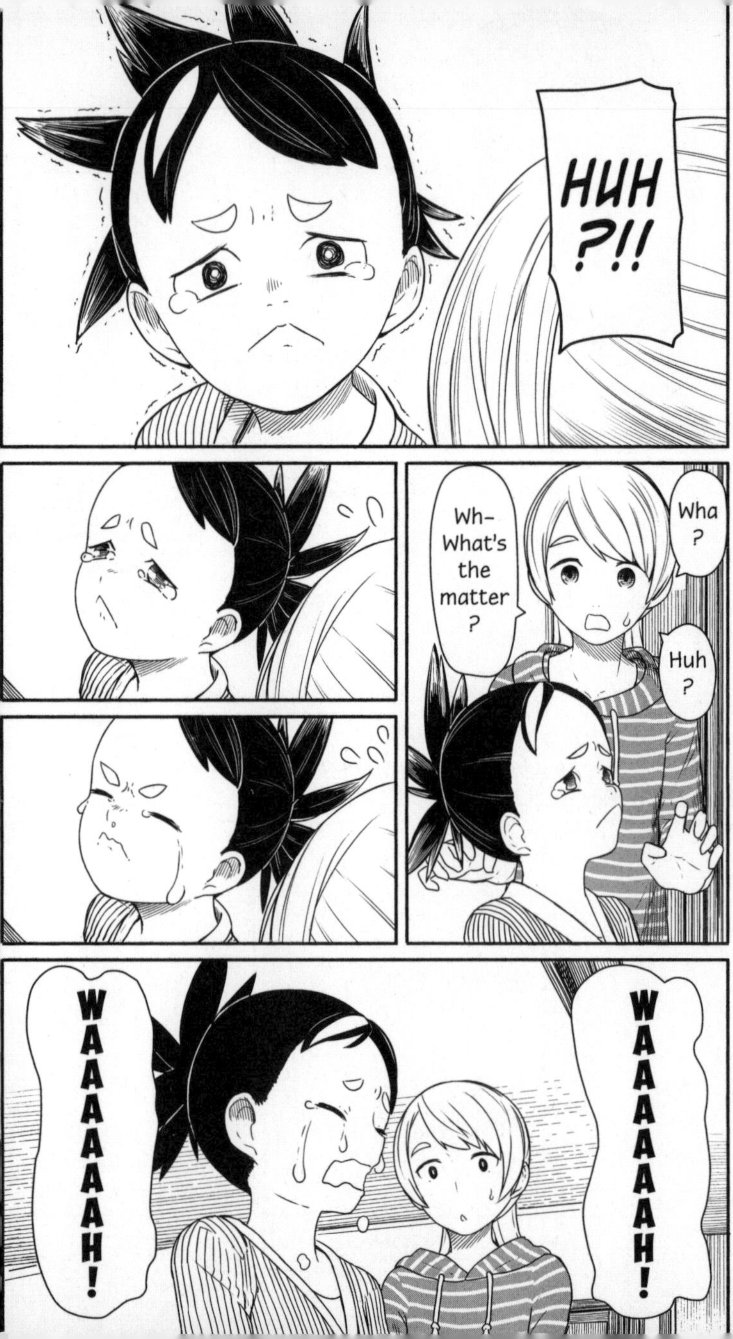
HUH ?!!
Wha ?
Wh- What's the matter ?
Huh ?
WAAAAAAAH!
WAAAAAAAH!

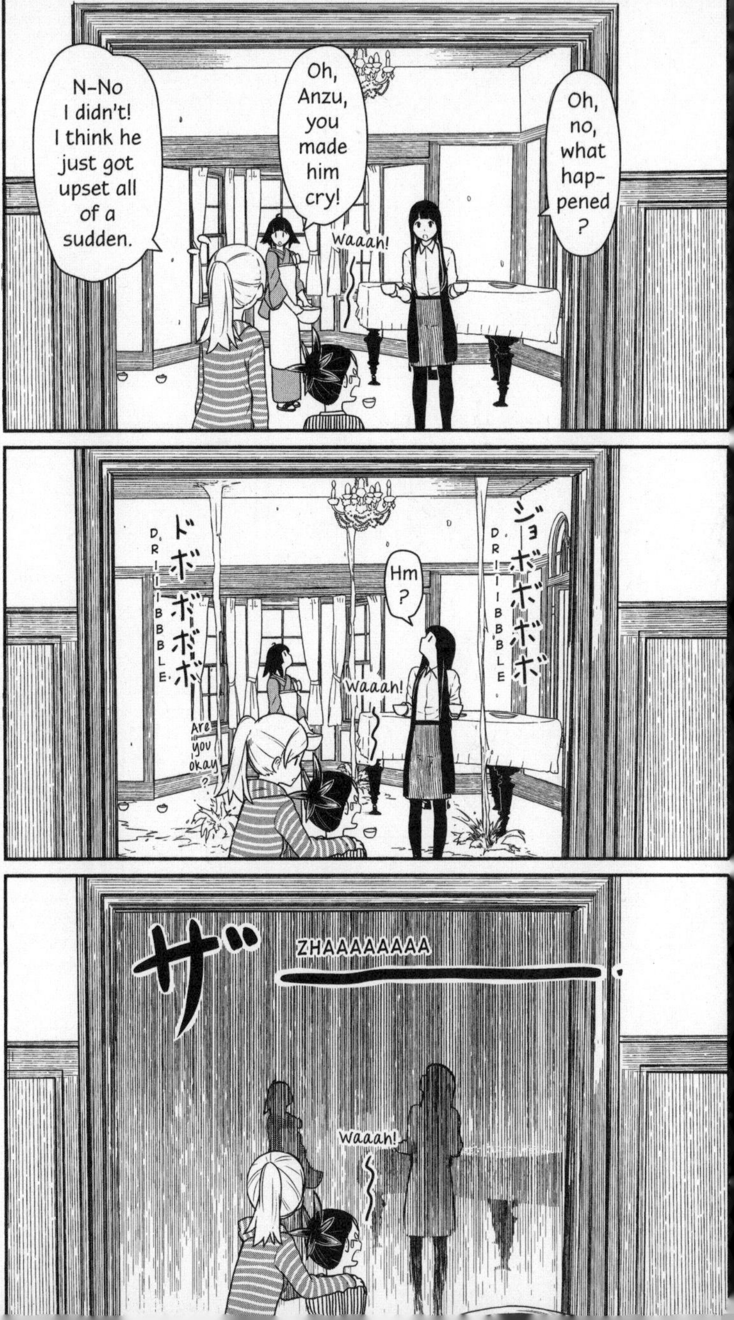
Oh, no, what hap-pened?
Oh, Anzu, you made him cry!
N-No I didn't! I think he just got upset all of a sudden.
Waaah!
ジョボボボボ
DRIIIBBBLE
Hm?
Waaah!
ドボボボボ
DRIIIBBBLE
Are you okay?
ザ
ZHAAAAAAAA
Waaah!

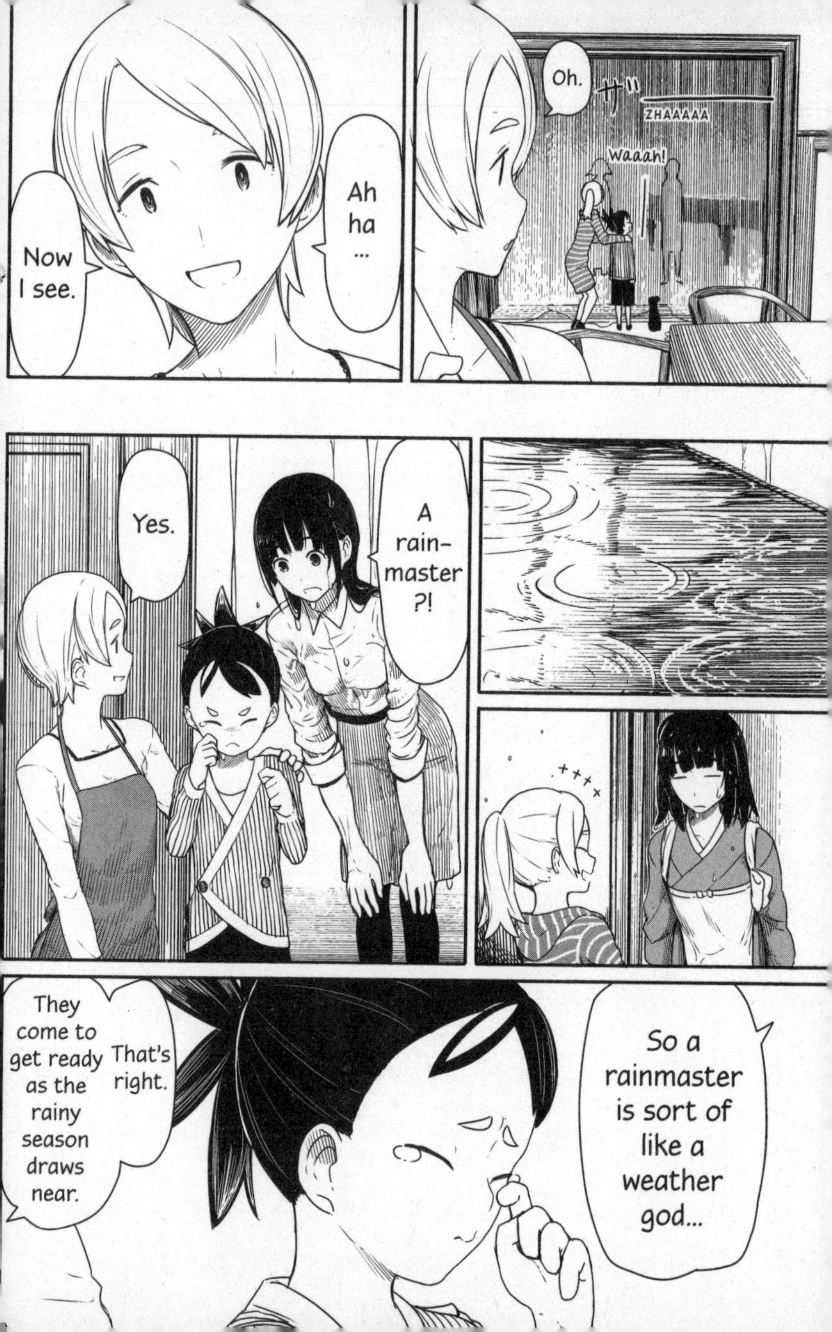
Oh.
ZHAAAAA
Waaah!
Ah ha ...
Now I see.
A rain-master ?!
Yes.
So a rainmaster is sort of like a weather god...
That's right.
They come to get ready as the rainy season draws near.

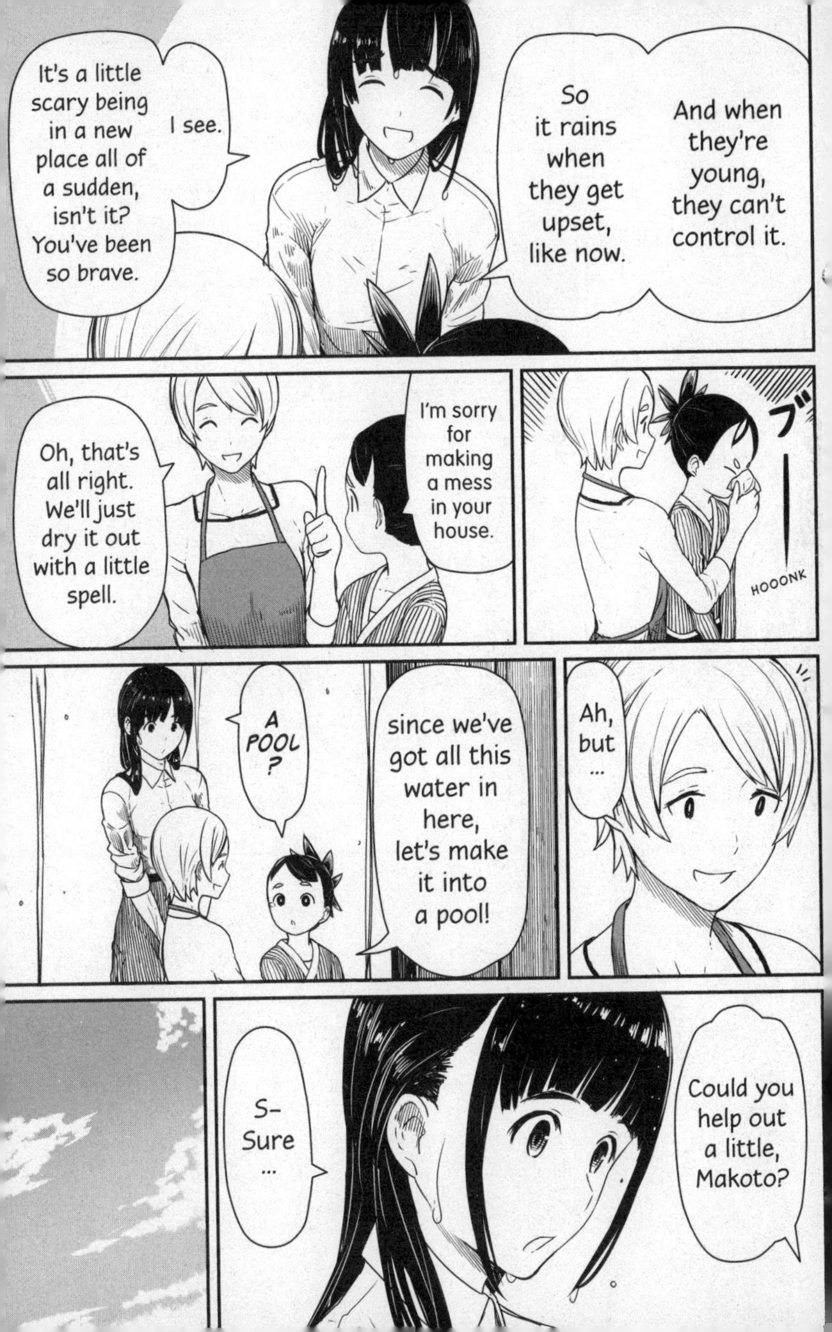
And when they're young, they can't control it.
So it rains when they get upset, like now.
I see.
It's a little scary being in a new place all of a sudden, isn't it? You've been so brave.
ブー
HOOONK
I'm sorry for making a mess in your house.
Oh, that's all right. We'll just dry it out with a little spell.
Ah, but ...
since we've got all this water in here, let's make it into a pool!
A POOL?
Could you help out a little, Makoto?
S-Sure ...

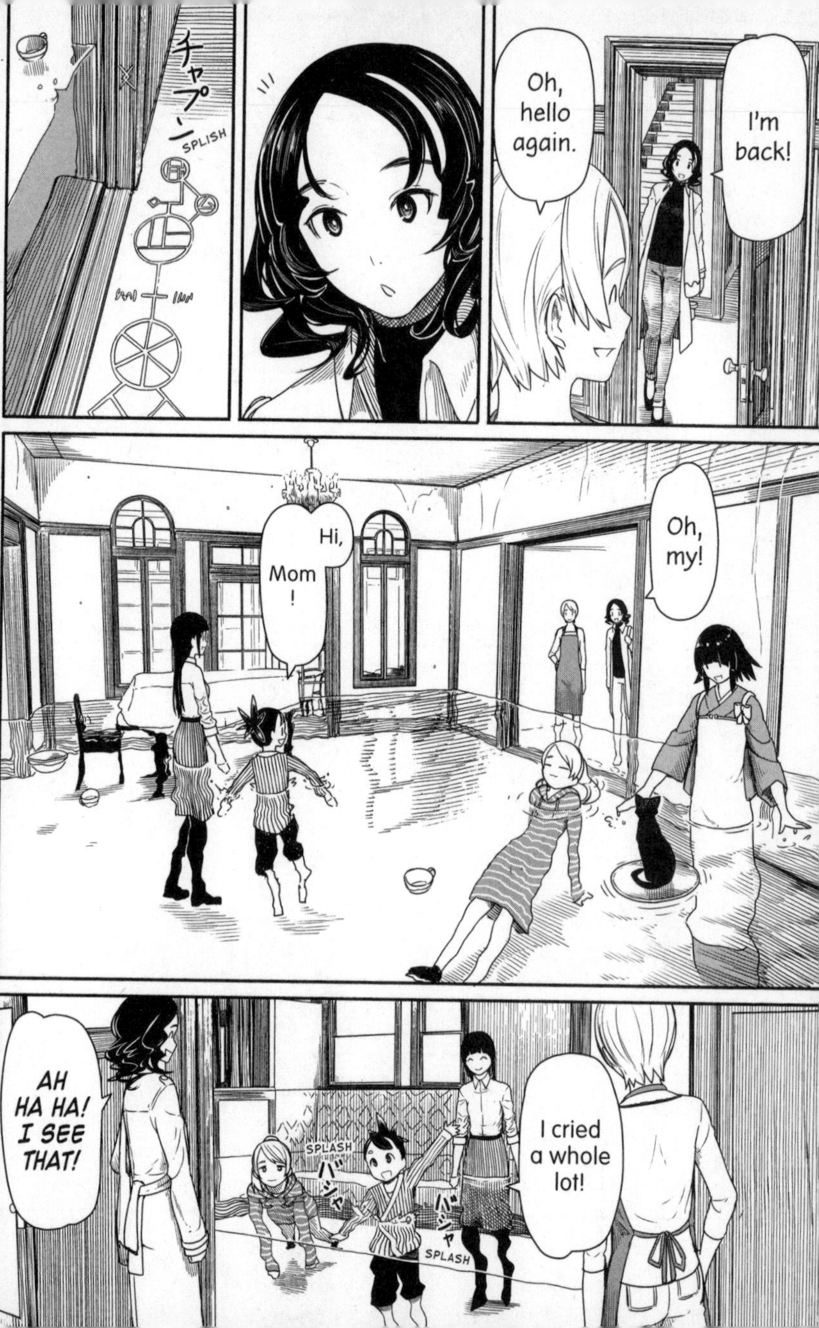
I'm back!
Oh, hello again.
チャプン
SPLISH
Oh, my!
Hi, Mom!
I cried a whole lot!
バシャ
SPLASH
バシャ
SPLASH
AH HA HA! I SEE THAT!

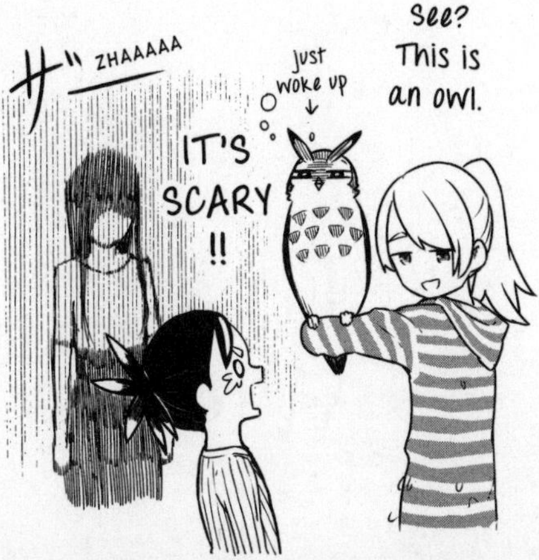
See? This is an owl.
just woke up
IT'S SCARY !!
ZHAAAAA

Flying
Witch

Chapter 27
Thai-Style Shrimp Fishing

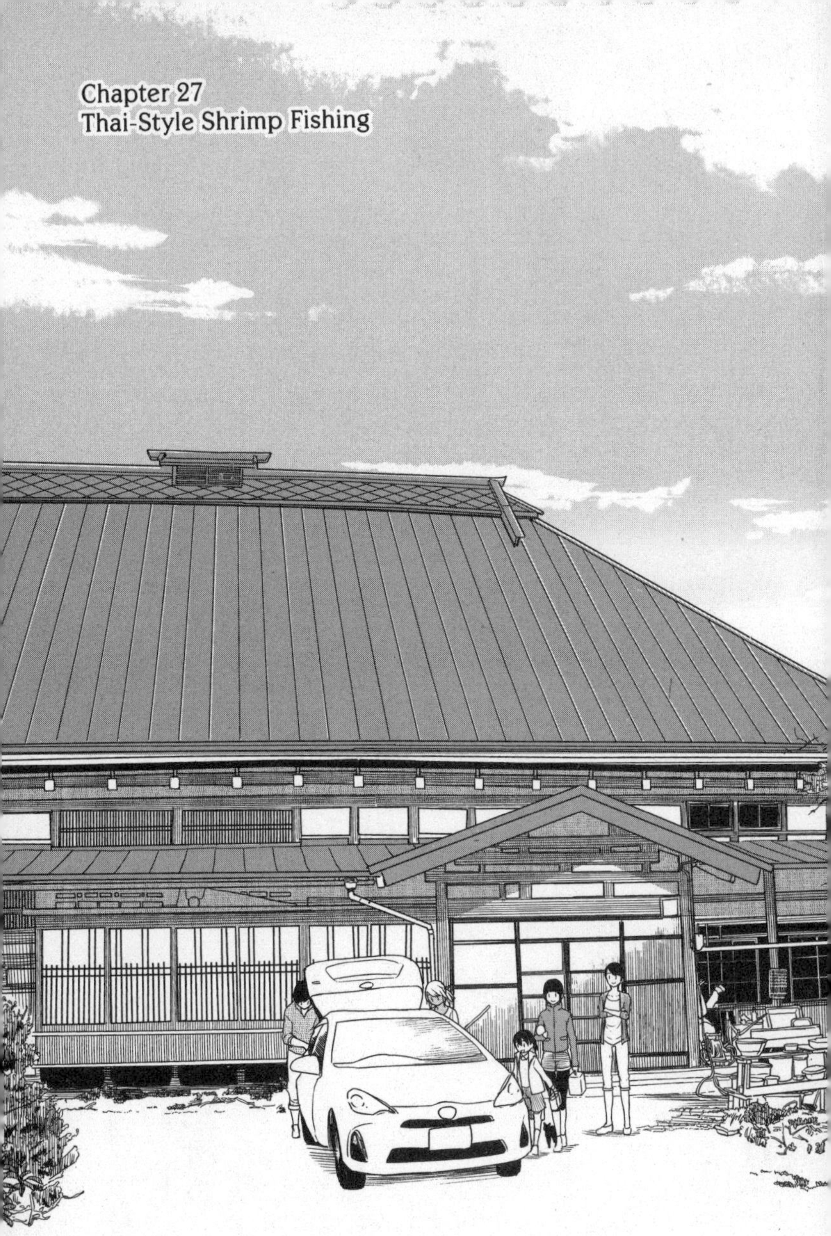

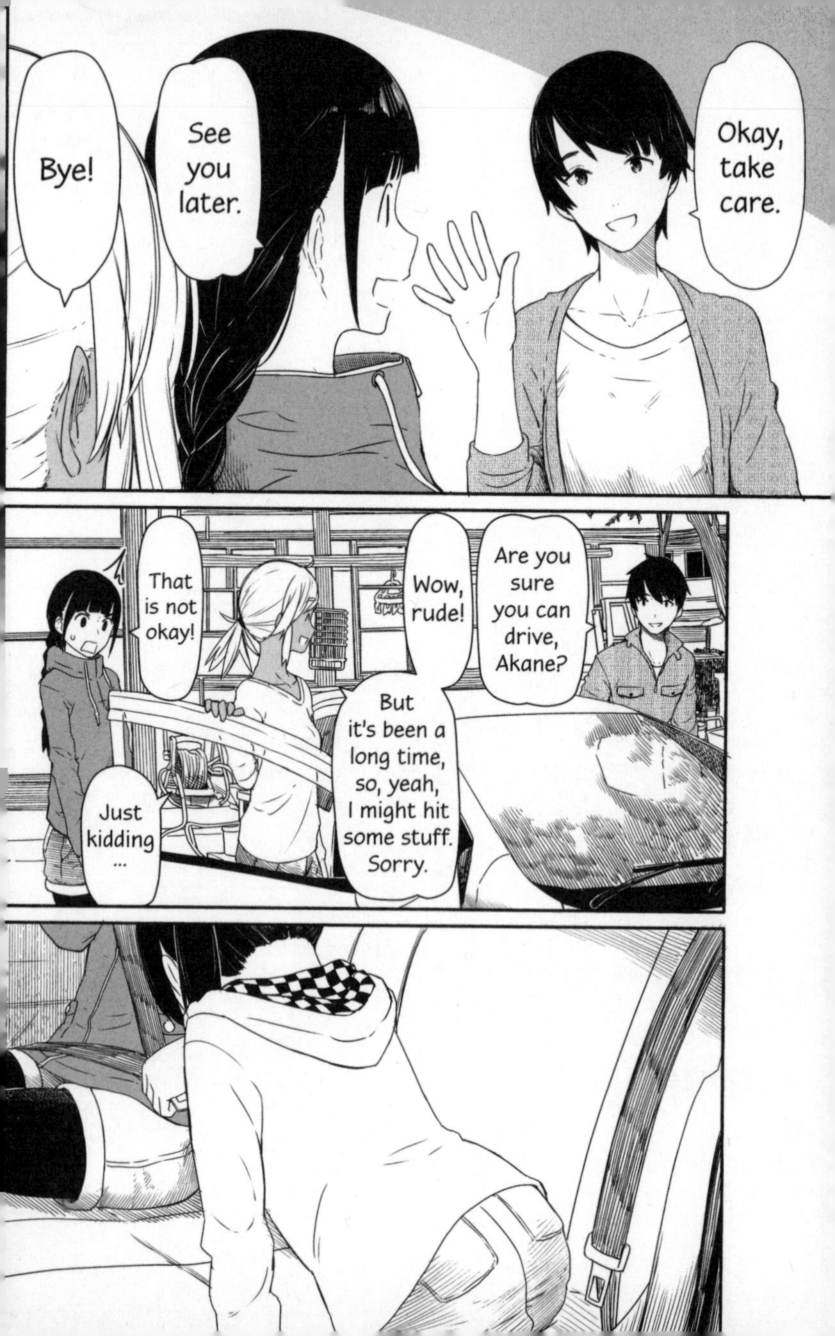
Okay, take care.
See you later.
Bye!
Are you sure you can drive, Akane?
Wow, rude!
But it's been a long time, so, yeah, I might hit some stuff. Sorry.
That is not okay!
Just kidding...

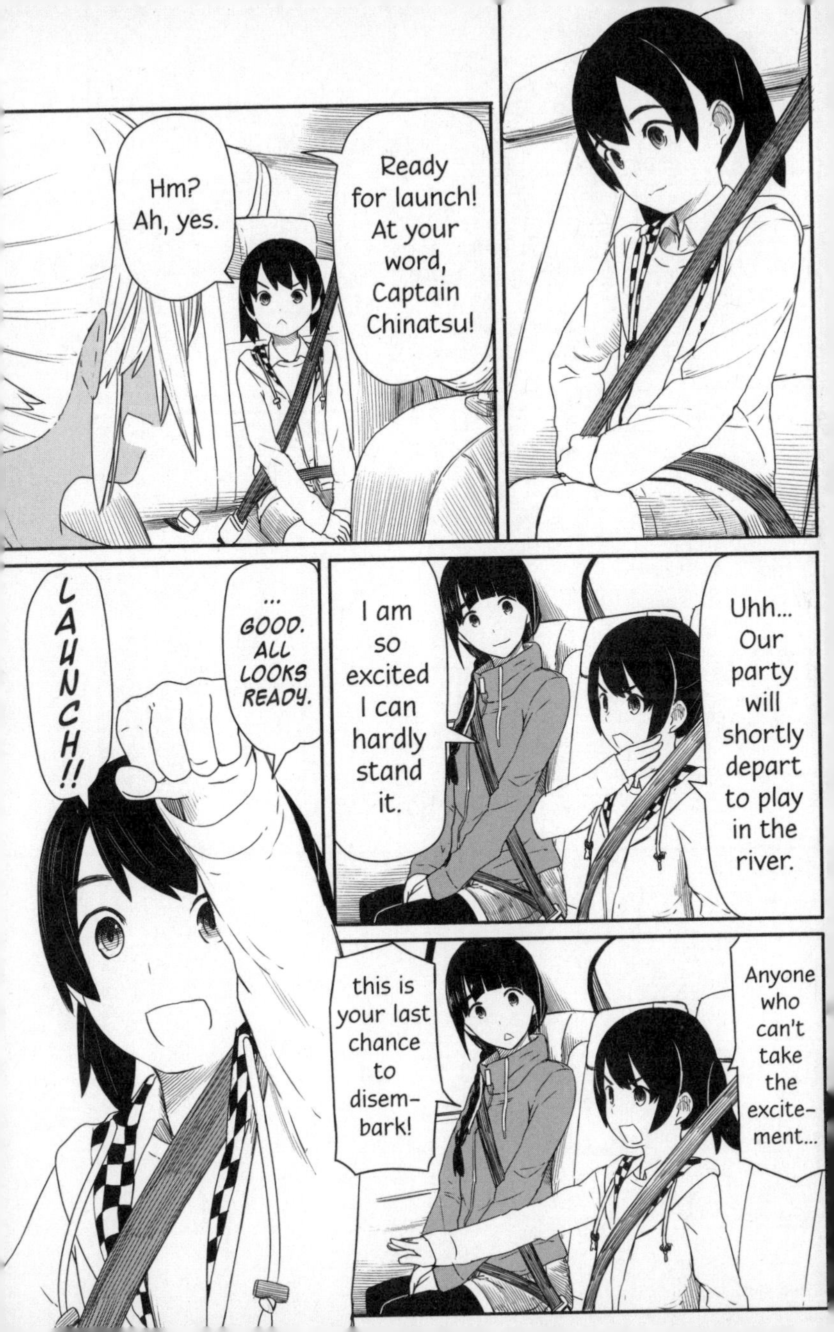
Ready for launch! At your word, Captain Chinatsu!
Hm? Ah, yes.
Uhh... Our party will shortly depart to play in the river.
I am so excited I can hardly stand it.
Anyone who can't take the excitement...
this is your last chance to disembark!
... GOOD. ALL LOOKS READY.
LAUNCH!!

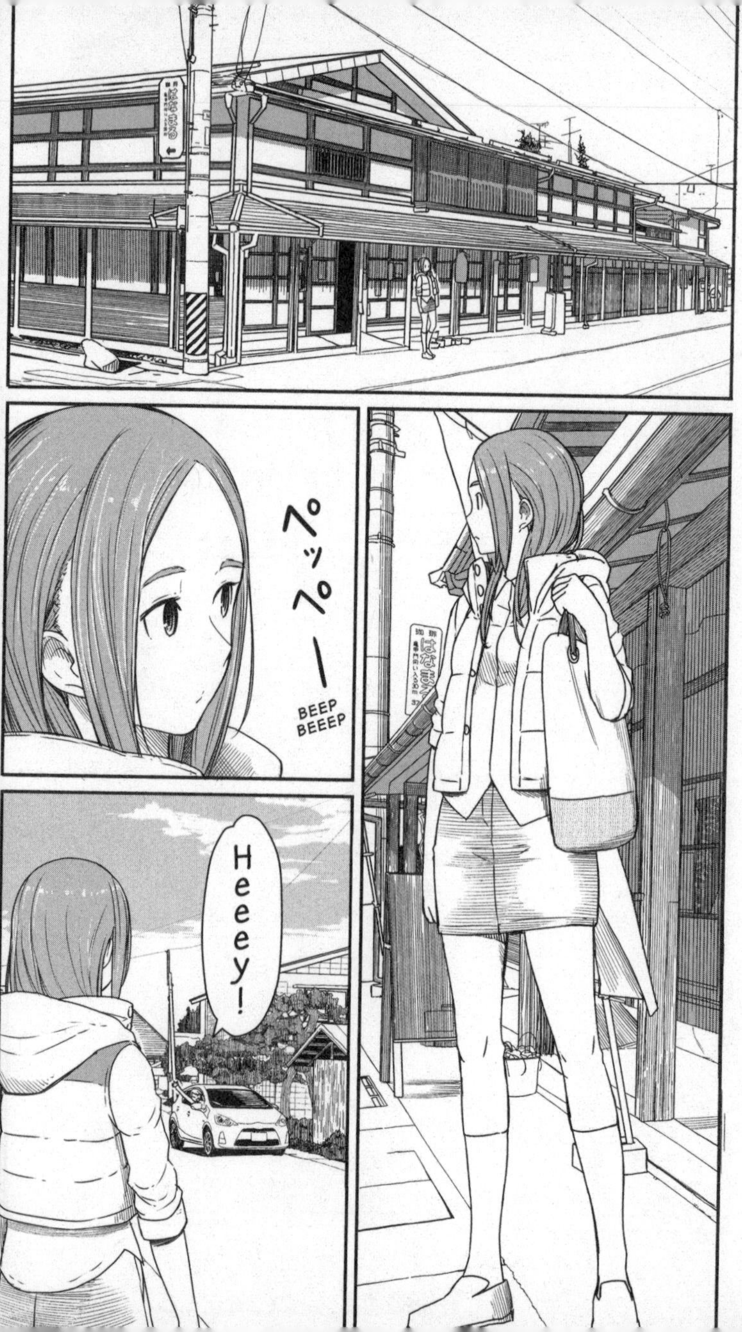
ペッペー
BEEP BEEEP
Heeey!

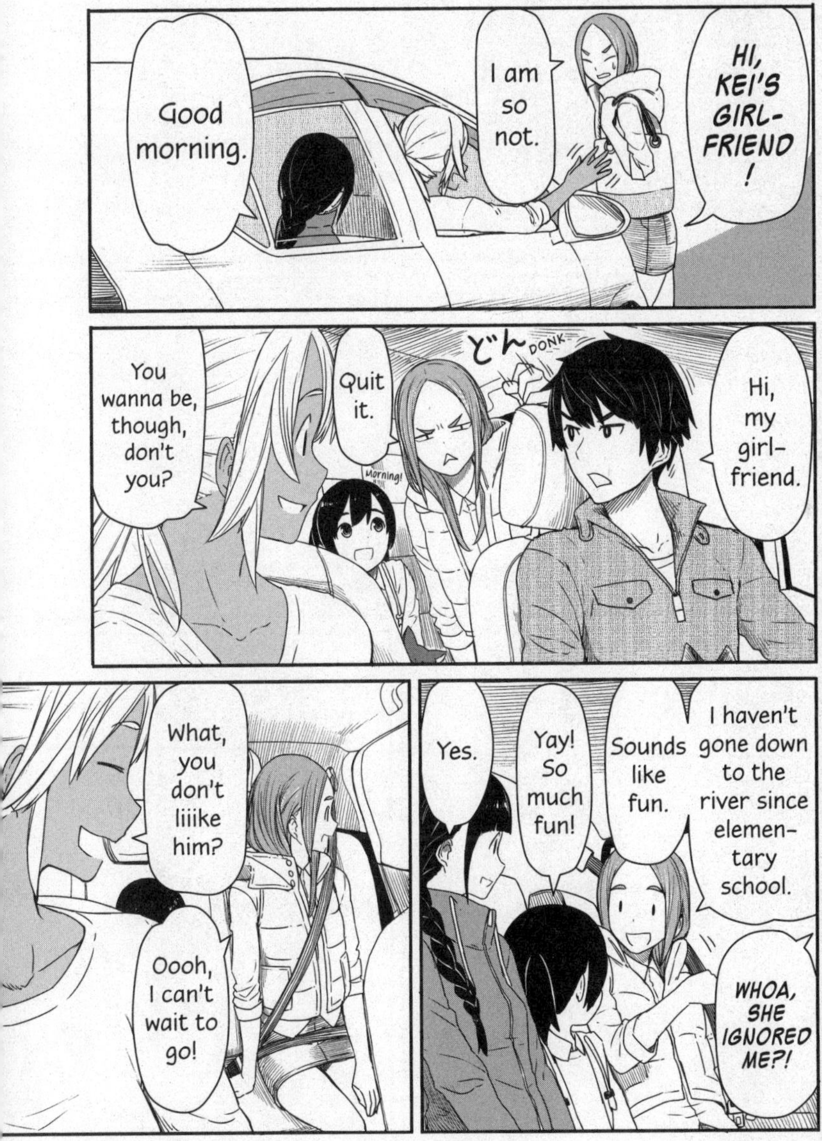
HI, KEI'S GIRL-FRIEND!
I am so not.
Good morning.
Hi, my girl-friend.
どん DONK
Quit it.
Morning!
You wanna be, though, don't you?
I haven't gone down to the river since elemen-tary school.
Sounds like fun.
Yay! So much fun!
Yes.
WHOA, SHE IGNORED ME?!
What, you don't liiike him?
Oooh, I can't wait to go!

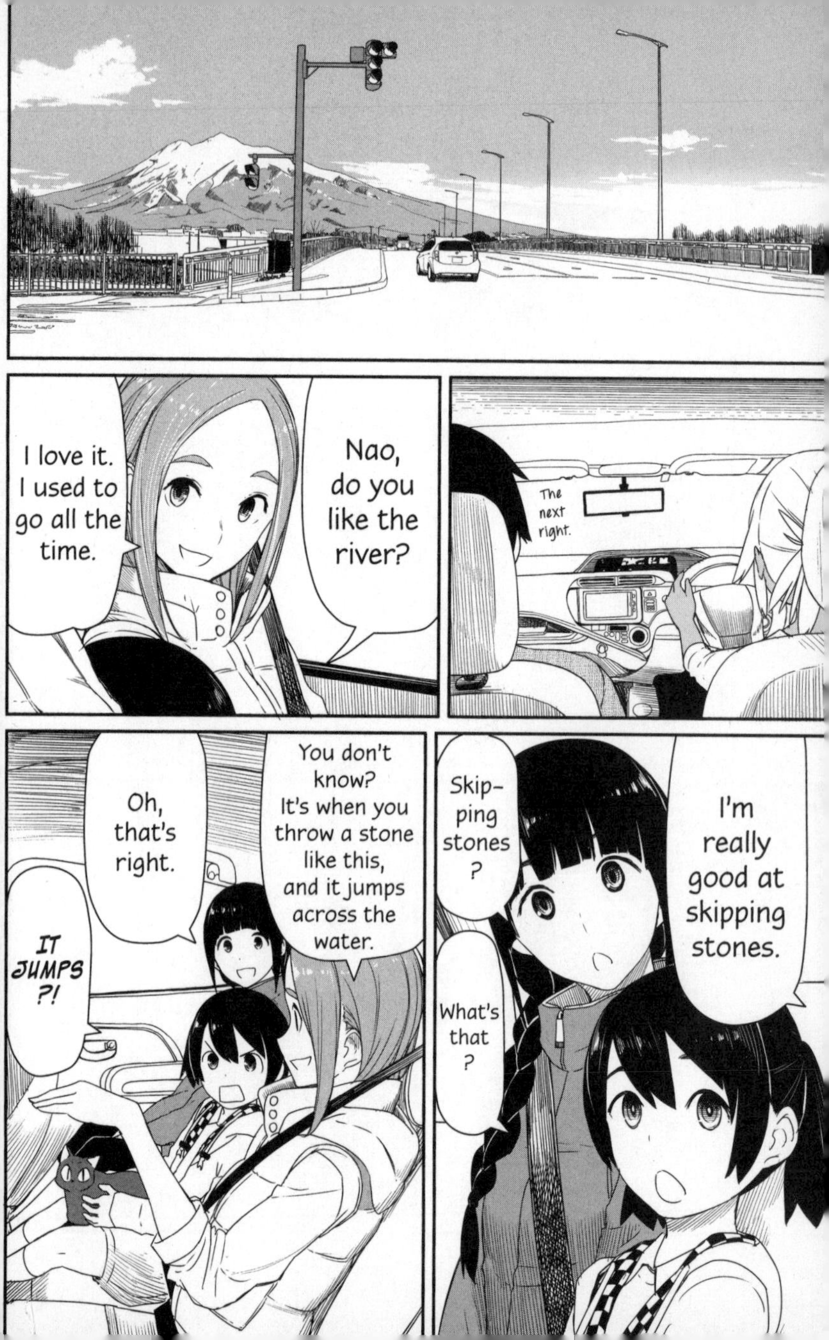
The next right.
Nao, do you like the river?
I love it. I used to go all the time.
I'm really good at skipping stones.
Skip-ping stones?
What's that?
You don't know? It's when you throw a stone like this, and it jumps across the water.
Oh, that's right.
IT JUMPS?!

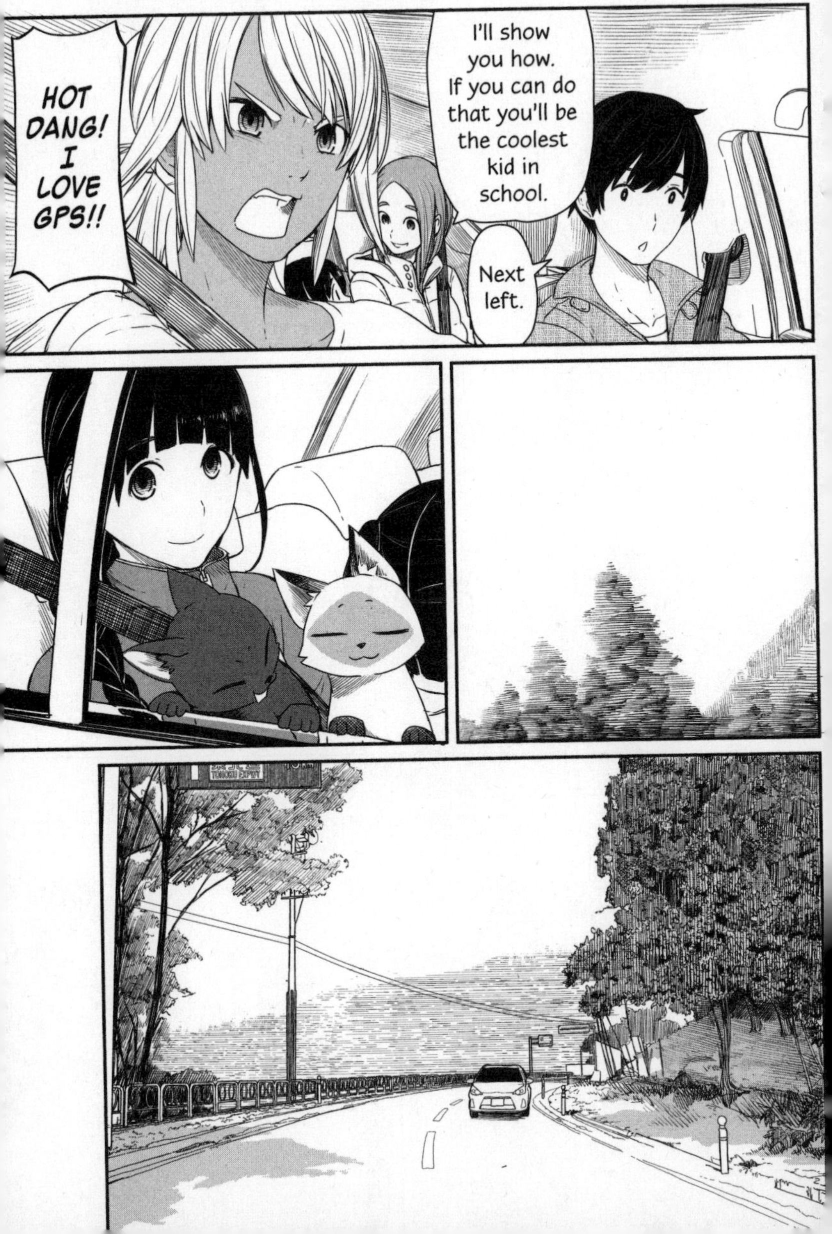
I'll show you how. If you can do that you'll be the coolest kid in school.
Next left.
HOT DANG! I LOVE GPS!!

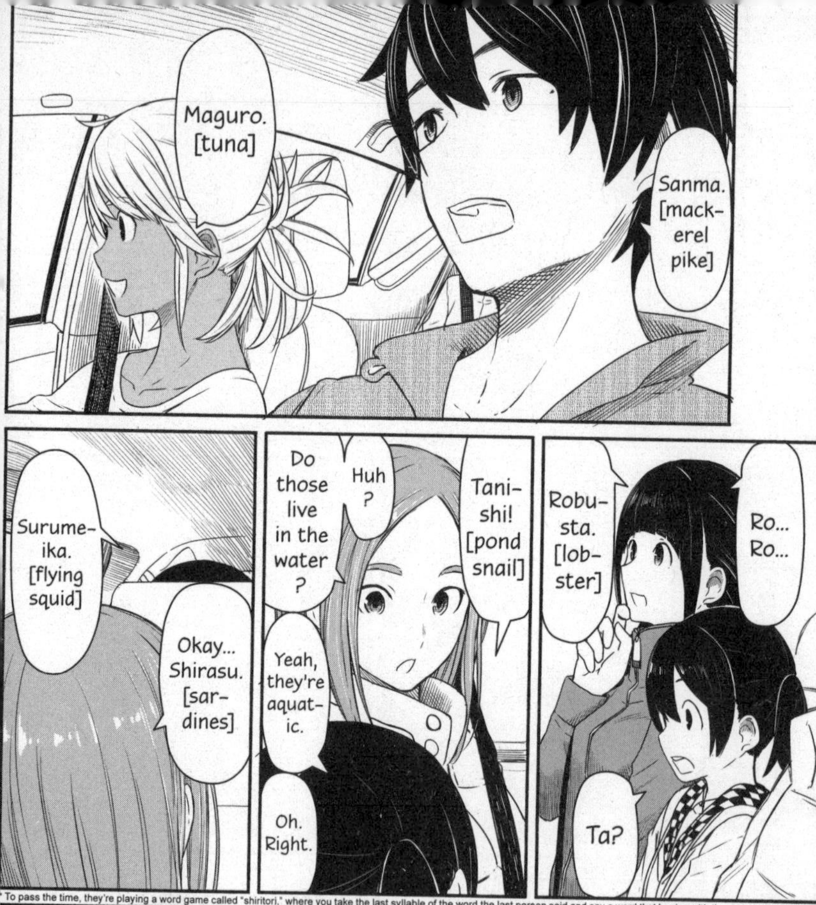
Sanma. [mackerel pike]
Maguro. [tuna]
Ro... Ro...
Robusta. [lobster]
Ta?
Tanishi! [pond snail]
Huh?
Do those live in the water?
Yeah, they're aquatic.
Oh. Right.
Okay... Shirasu. [sardines]
Surumeika. [flying squid]

* To pass the time, they're playing a word game called "shiritori," where you take the last syllable of the word the last person said and say a word that begins with the same syllable.

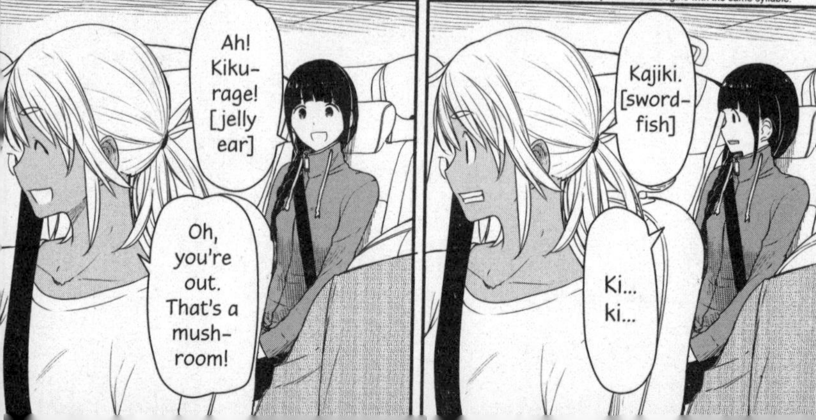
Kajiki. [swordfish]
Ki... ki...
Ah! Kikurage! [jelly ear]
Oh, you're out. That's a mushroom!

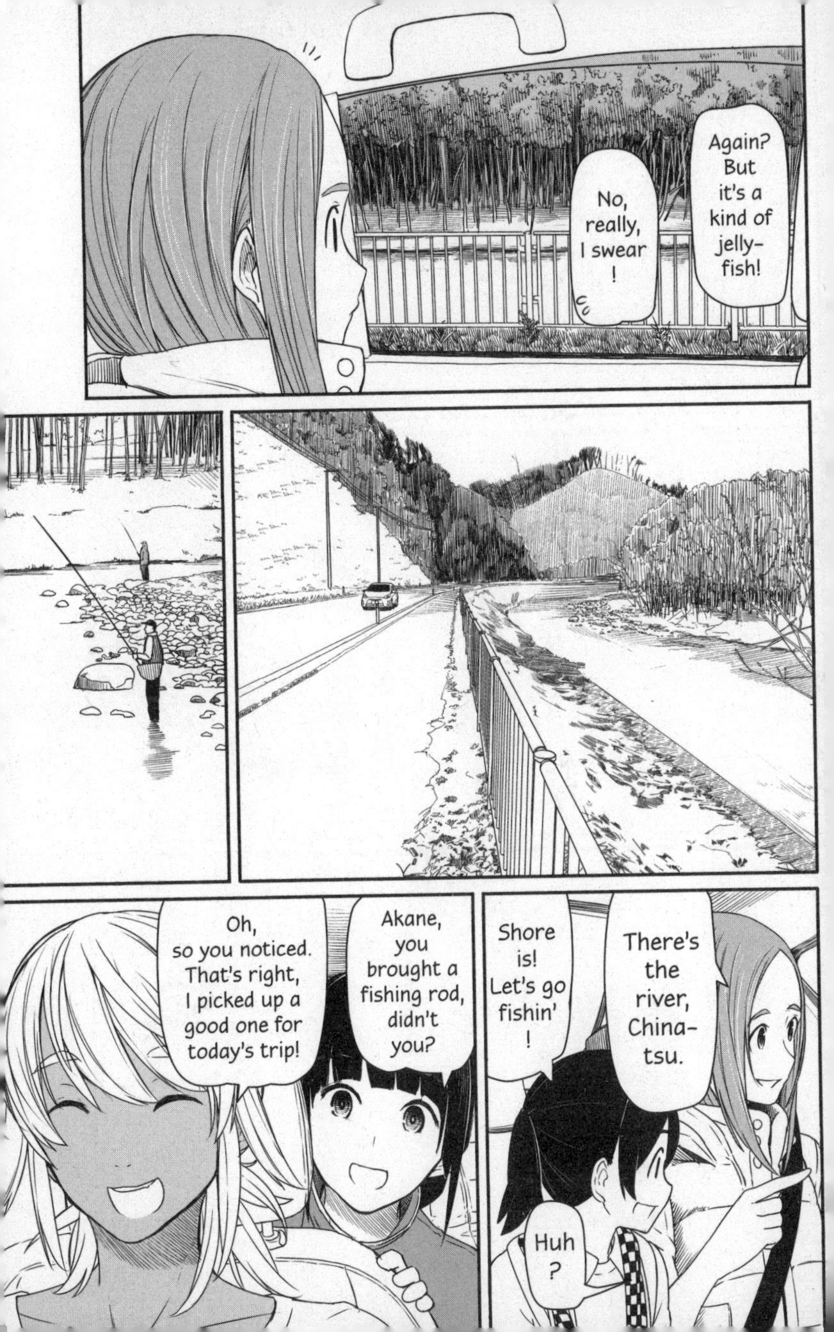
Again? But it's a kind of jelly-fish!
No, really, I swear!
There's the river, China-tsu.
Shore is! Let's go fishin'!
Huh?
Akane, you brought a fishing rod, didn't you?
Oh, so you noticed. That's right, I picked up a good one for today's trip!

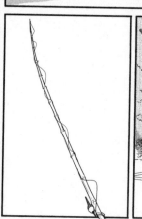

THE LOADS-O'-BITES FISHING ROD!!

TA-DADA-DAAA!

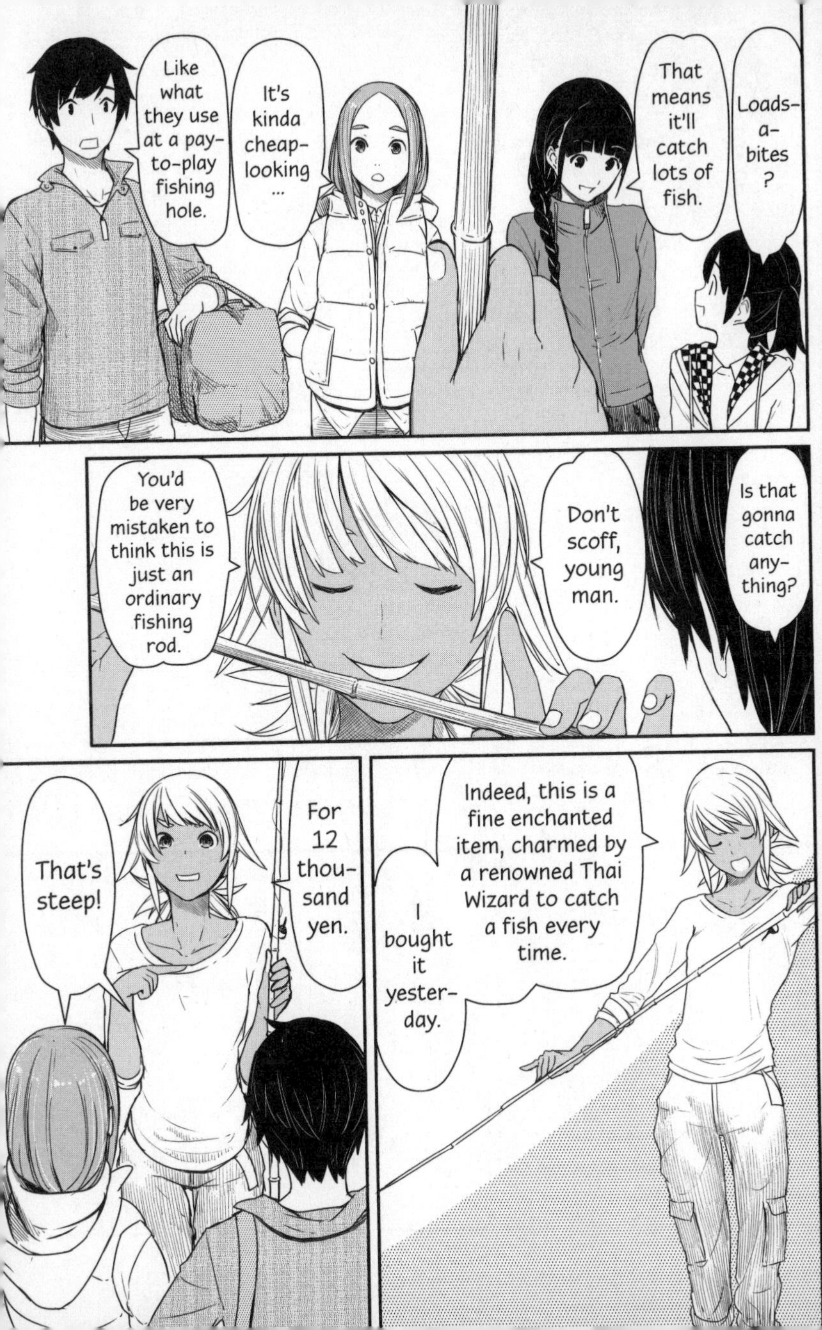
Loads-a-bites?
That means it'll catch lots of fish.
It's kinda cheap-looking...
Like what they use at a pay-to-play fishing hole.
Is that gonna catch anything?
Don't scoff, young man.
You'd be very mistaken to think this is just an ordinary fishing rod.
Indeed, this is a fine enchanted item, charmed by a renowned Thai Wizard to catch a fish every time.
I bought it yesterday.
For 12 thousand yen.
That's steep!

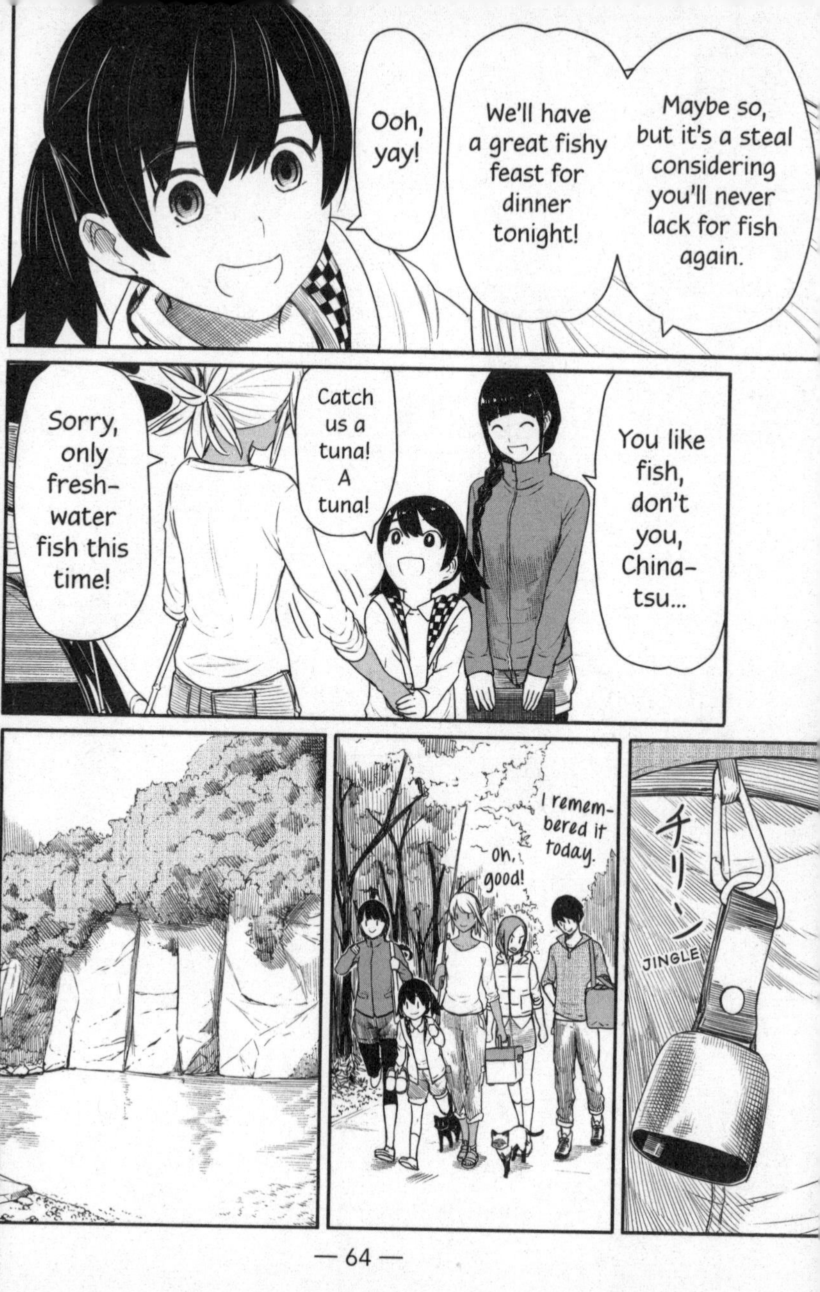
Maybe so, but it's a steal considering you'll never lack for fish again.
We'll have a great fishy feast for dinner tonight!
Ooh, yay!
You like fish, don't you, China-tsu...
Catch us a tuna! A tuna!
Sorry, only fresh-water fish this time!
チリーン
JINGLE
I remem-bered it today.
Oh, good!

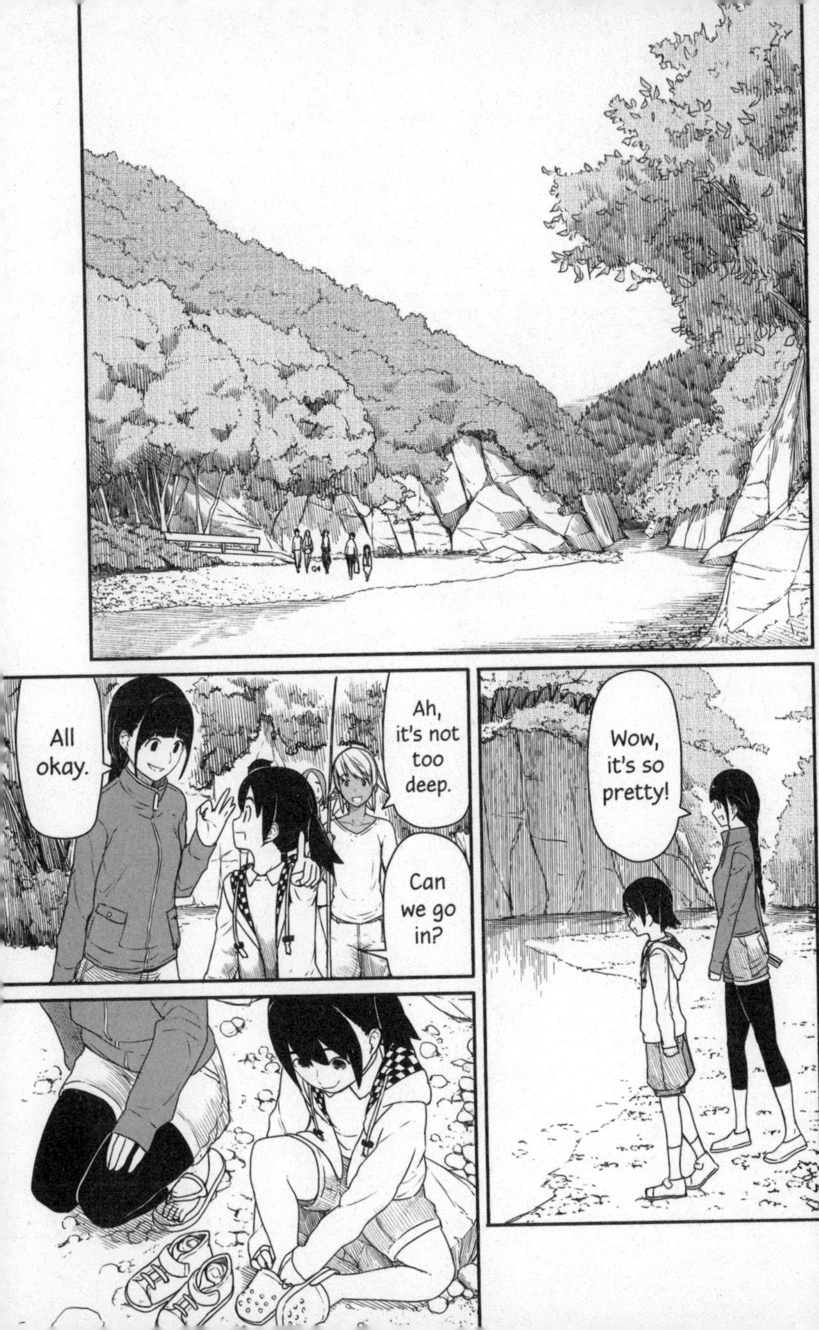
Wow, it's so pretty!
Ah, it's not too deep.
Can we go in?
All okay.

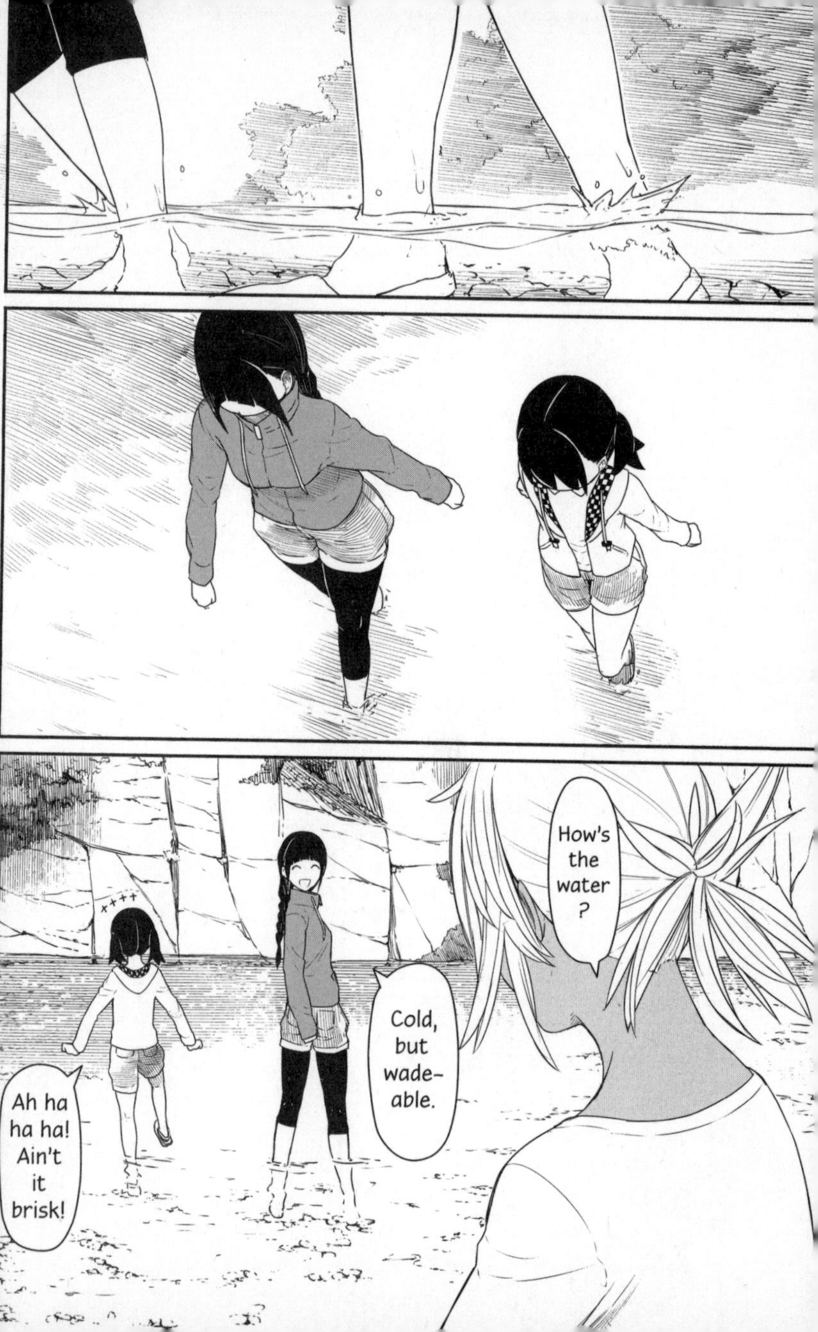
How's the water?
Cold, but wade-able.
Ah ha ha ha! Ain't it brisk!

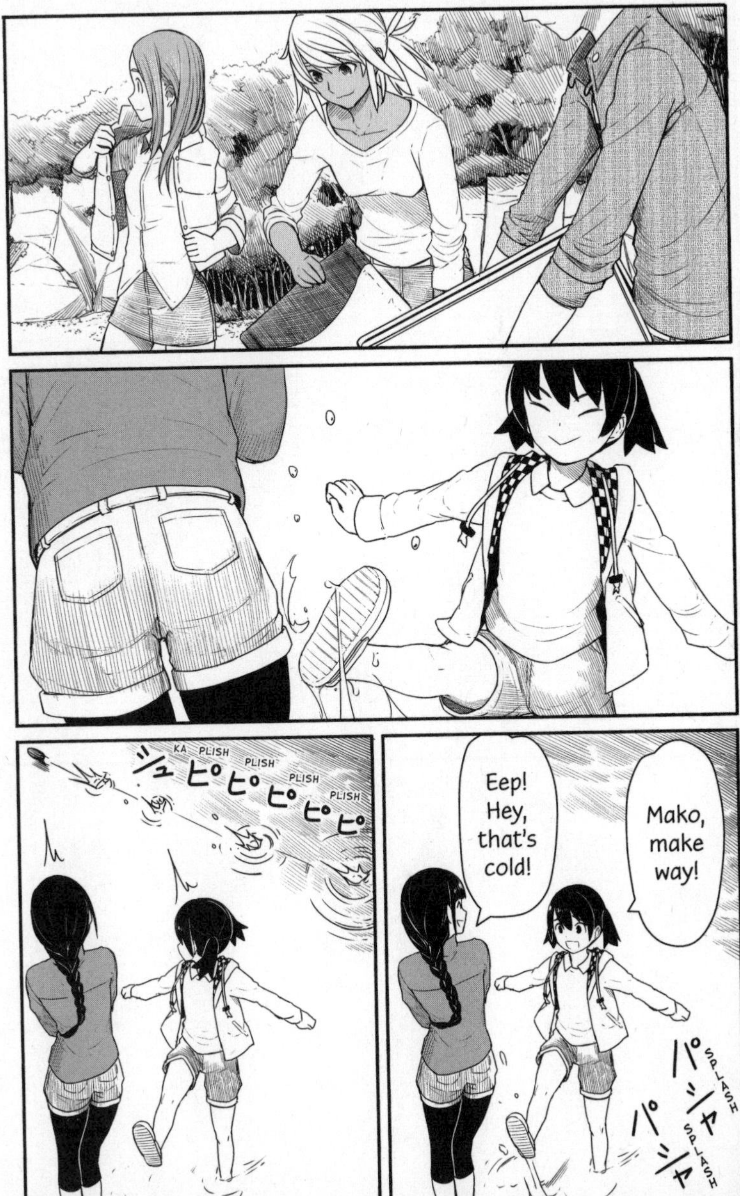

Mako, make way!
Eep! Hey, that's cold!
パシャ SPLASH
パシャ SPLASH
シュ KA
ピ PLISH
ピ PLISH
ピ PLISH
ピ PLISH
ピ

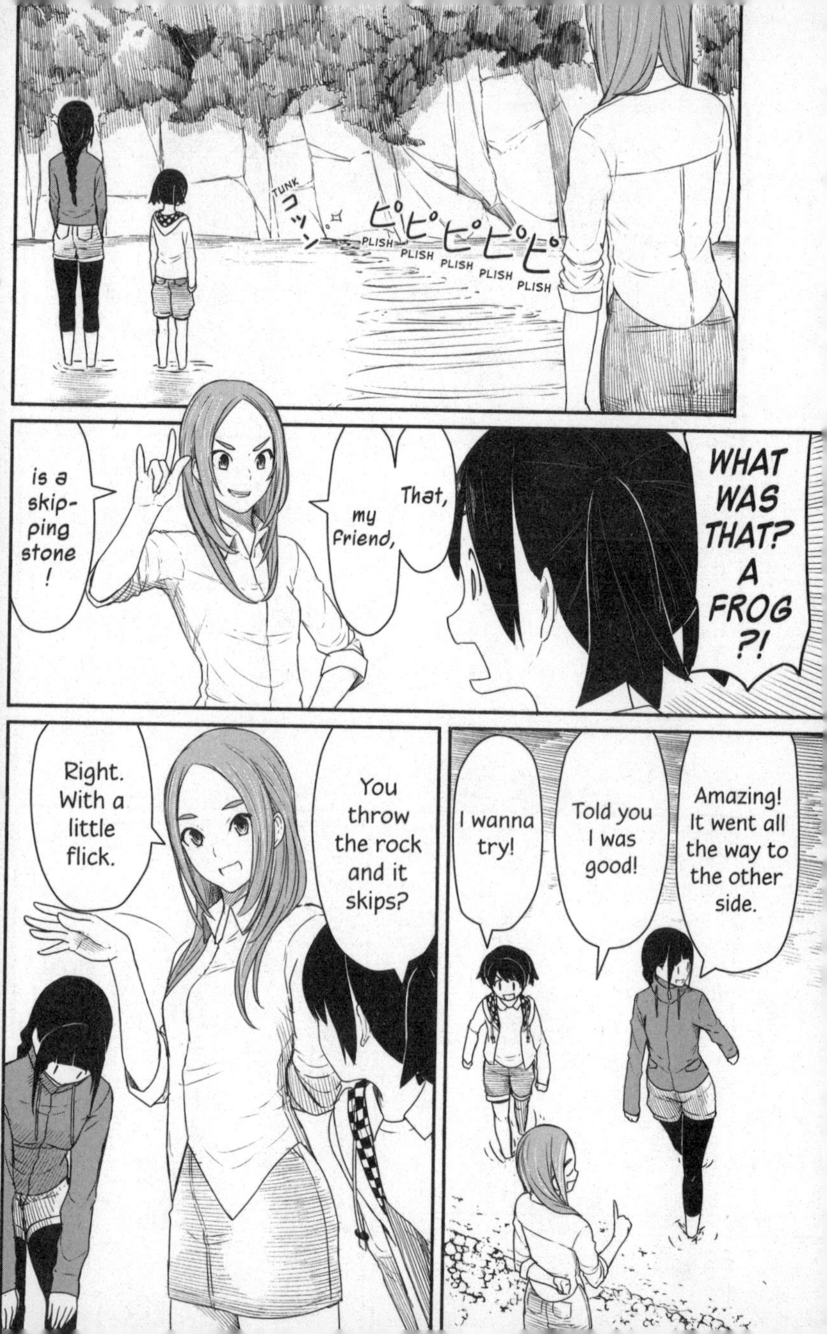

TUNK
コッン
PLISH PLISH PLISH PLISH PLISH
ピピピピピ
WHAT WAS THAT? A FROG ?!
That, my friend,
is a skip-ping stone !
Amazing! It went all the way to the other side.
Told you I was good!
I wanna try!
You throw the rock and it skips?
Right. With a little flick.

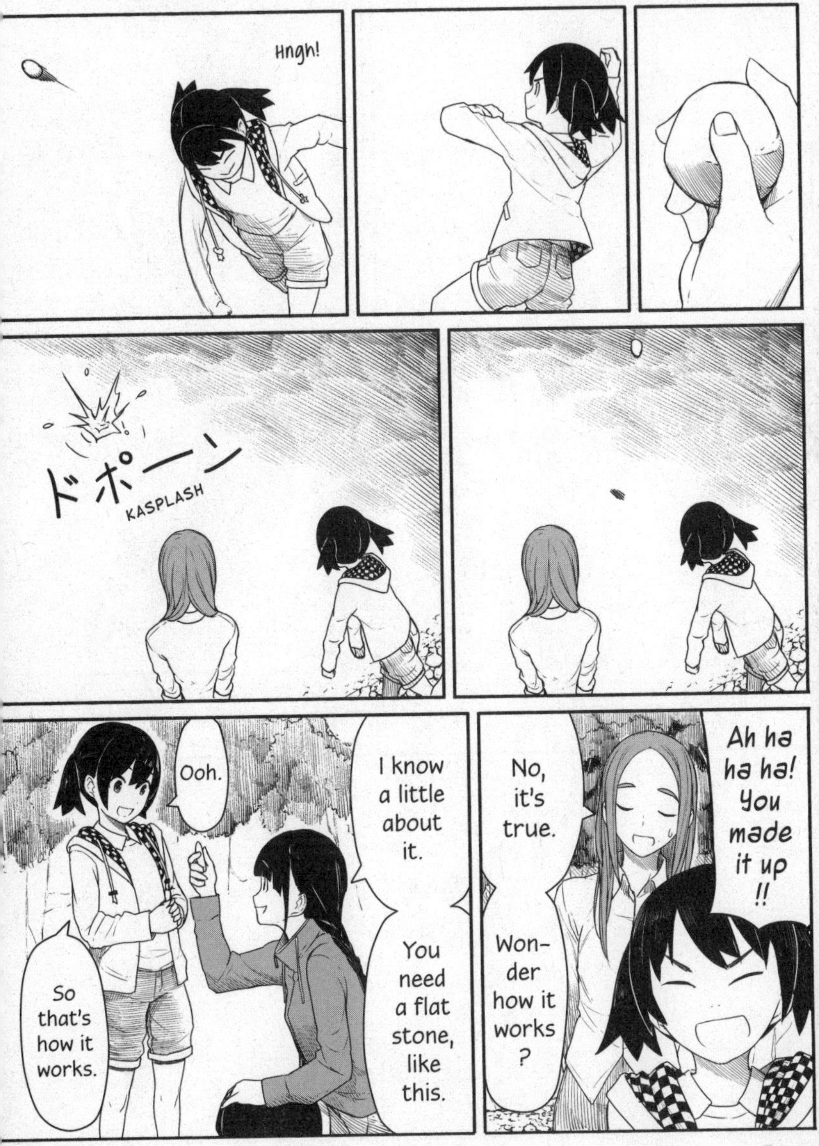
Hngh!
ドポーン
KASPLASH
Ah ha ha ha! You made it up!!
No, it's true.
Wonder how it works?
I know a little about it.
Ooh.
You need a flat stone, like this.
So that's how it works.

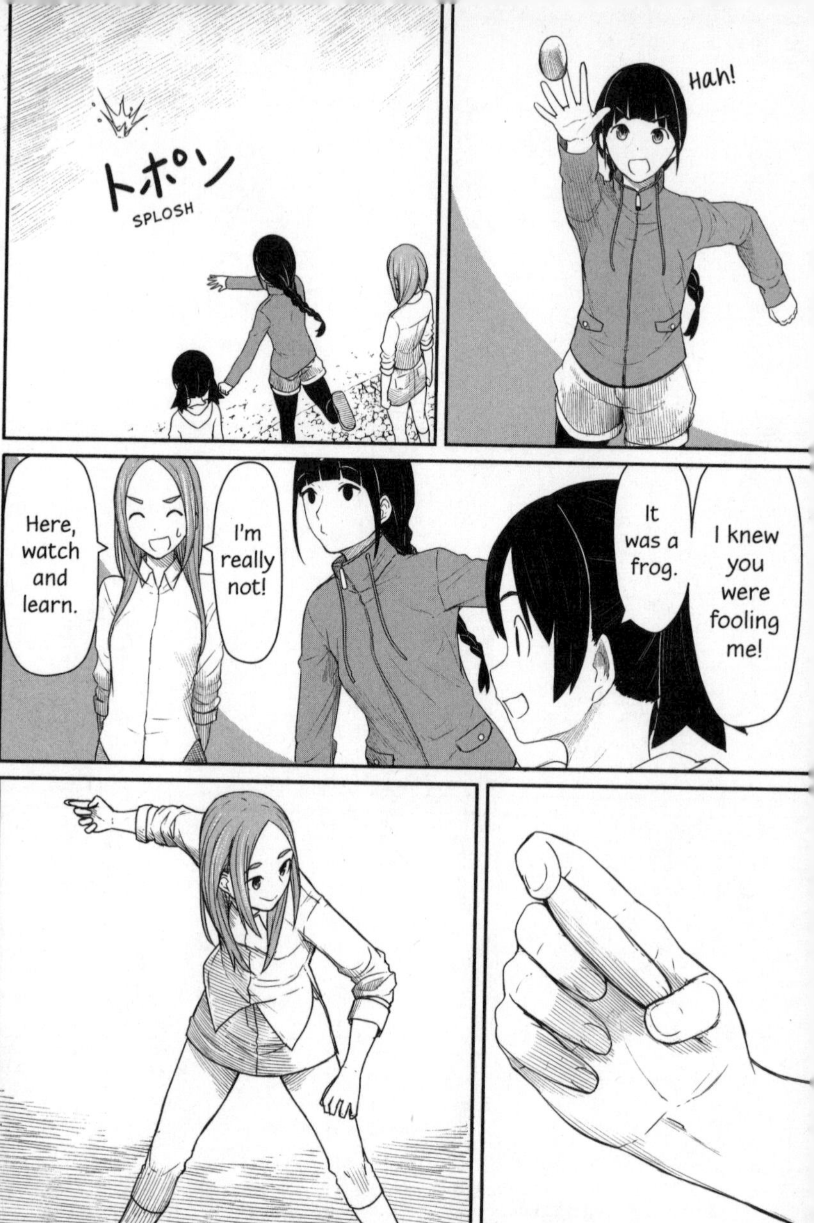
Hah!
トポン
SPLOSH
I knew you were fooling me!
It was a frog.
I'm really not!
Here, watch and learn.

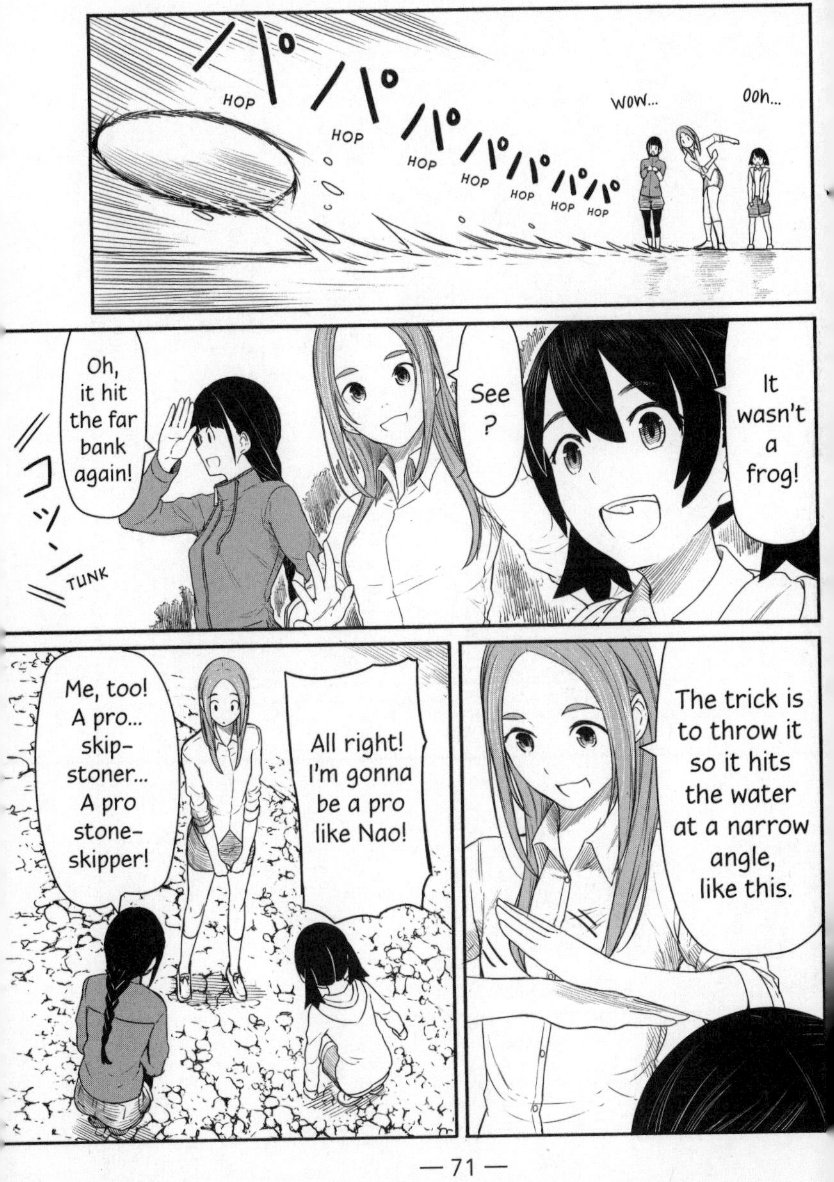
Ooh...
Wow...
HOP
HOP
HOP
HOP
HOP
HOP
HOP
It wasn't a frog!
See?
Oh, it hit the far bank again!
コツーン
TUNK
The trick is to throw it so it hits the water at a narrow angle, like this.
All right! I'm gonna be a pro like Nao!
Me, too! A pro... skip-stoner... A pro stone-skipper!

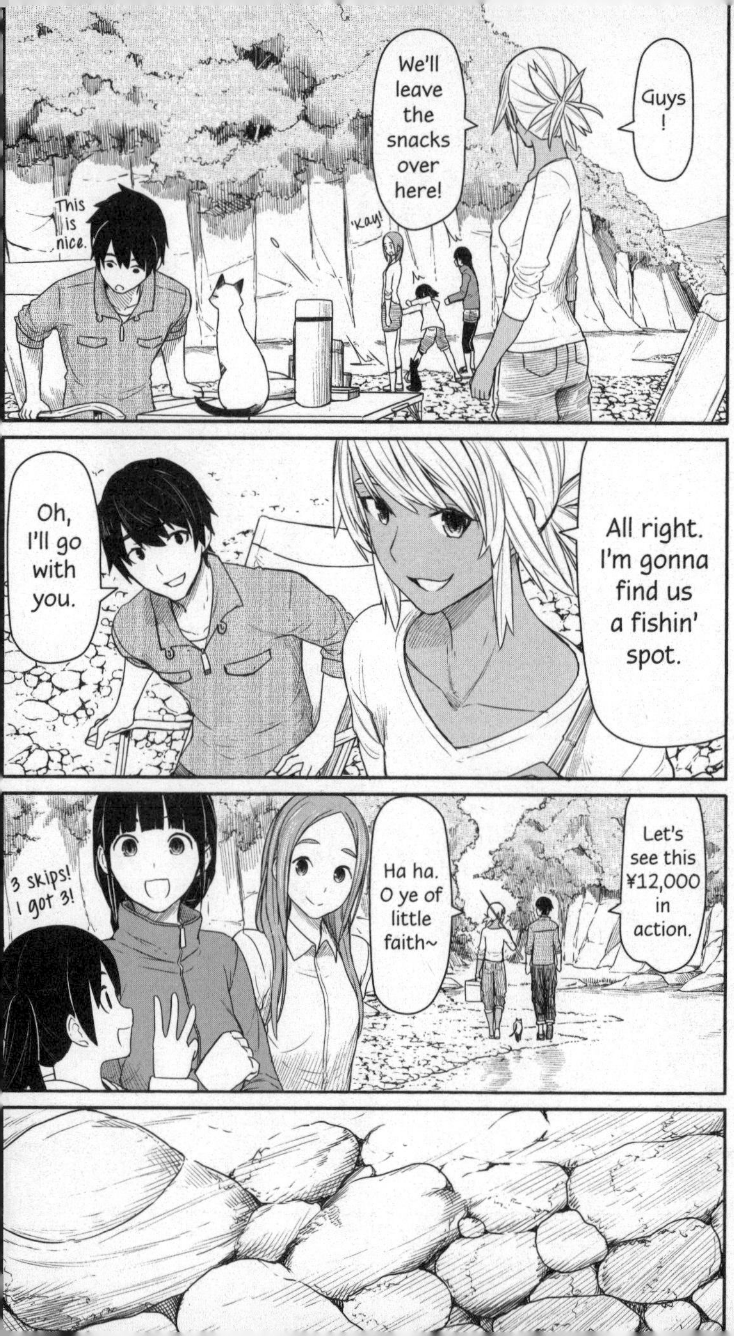
Guys!
We'll leave the snacks over here!
'Kay!
This is nice.
All right. I'm gonna find us a fishin' spot.
Oh, I'll go with you.
Let's see this ¥12,000 in action.
Ha ha. O ye of little faith~
3 skips! I got 3!

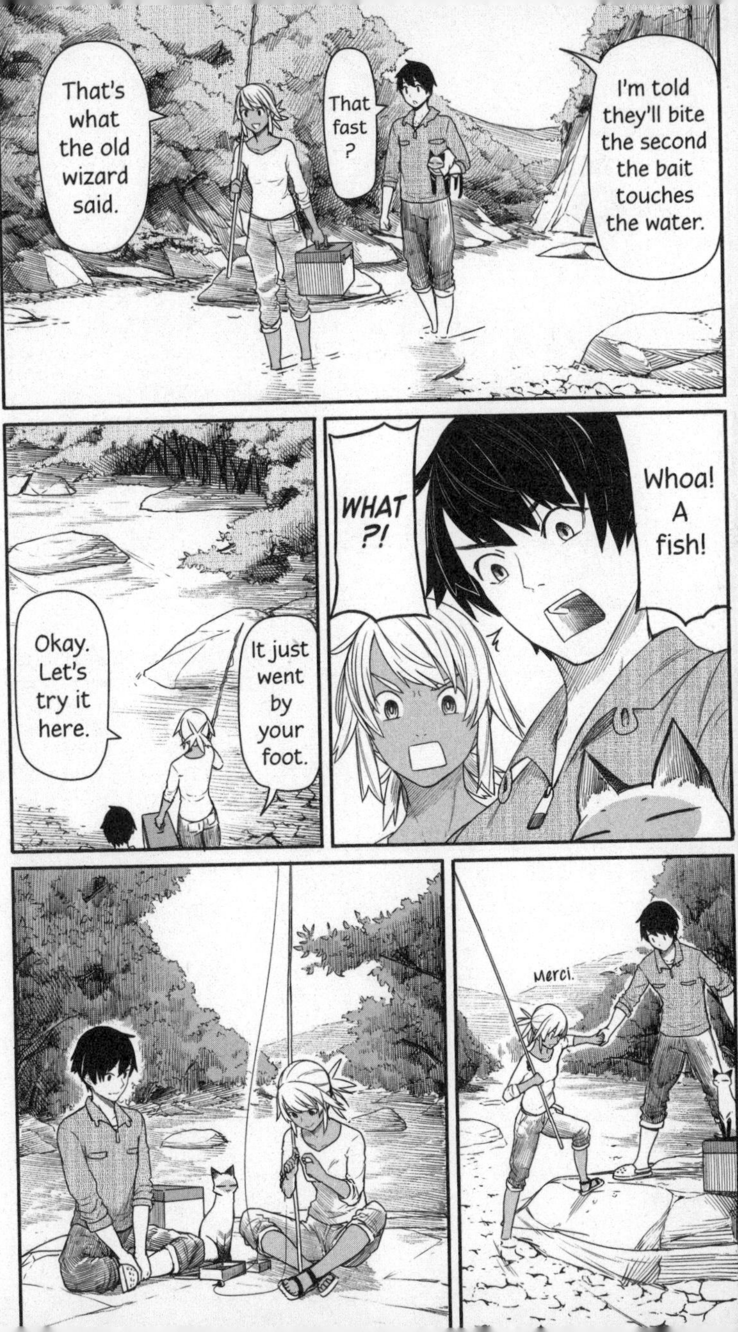
I'm told they'll bite the second the bait touches the water.
That fast?
That's what the old wizard said.
Whoa! A fish!
WHAT?!
It just went by your foot.
Okay. Let's try it here.
Merci.

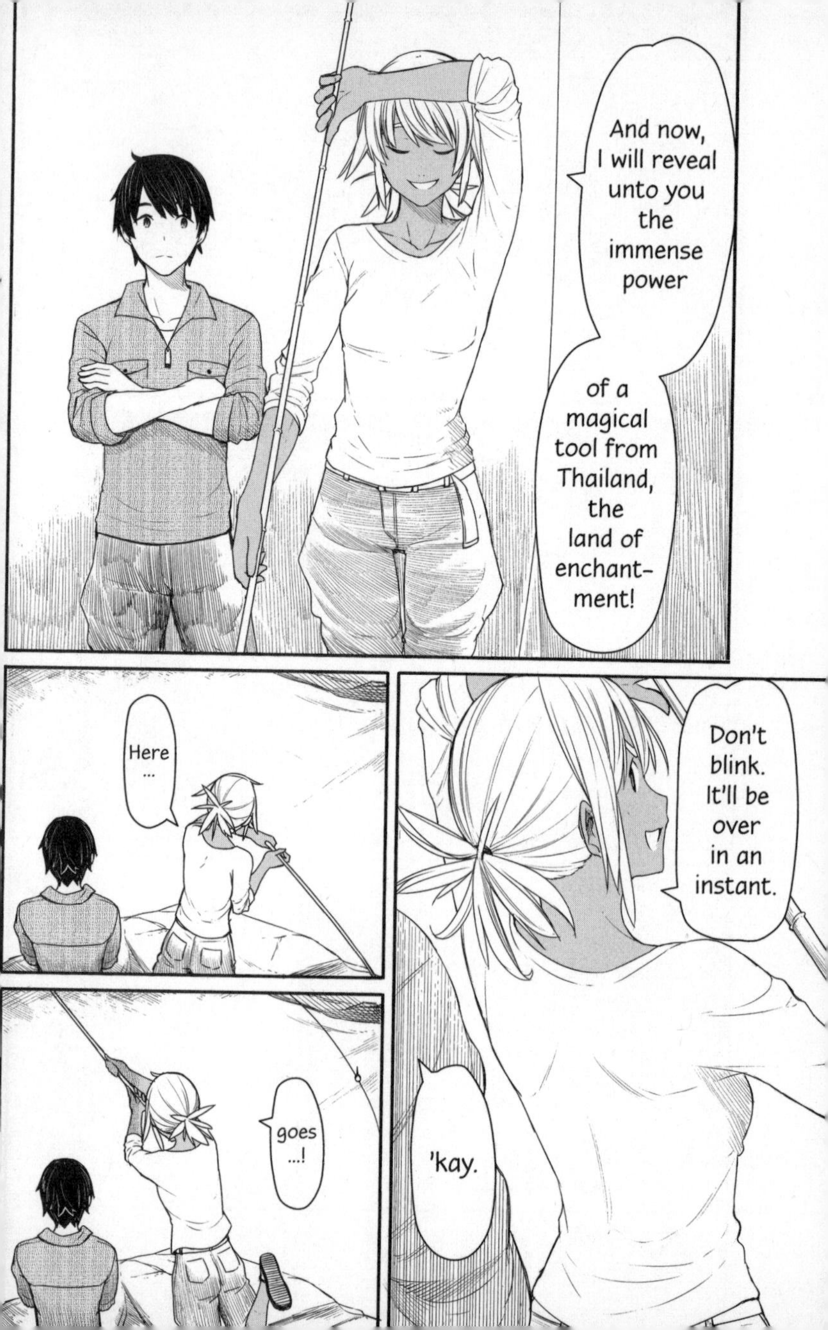
And now, I will reveal unto you the immense power
of a magical tool from Thailand, the land of enchant- ment!
Don't blink. It'll be over in an instant.
'kay.
Here ...
goes ...!

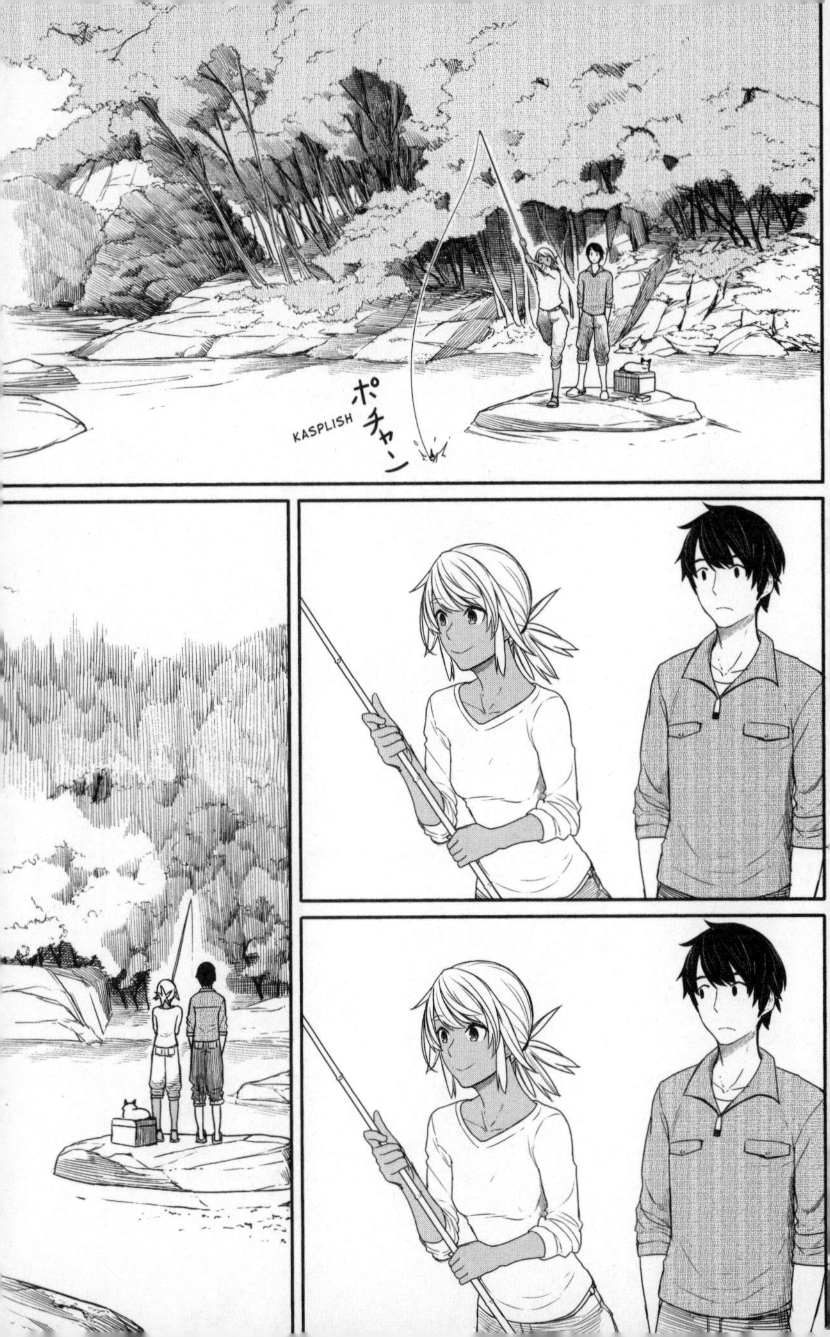
ポチャーン
KASPLISH

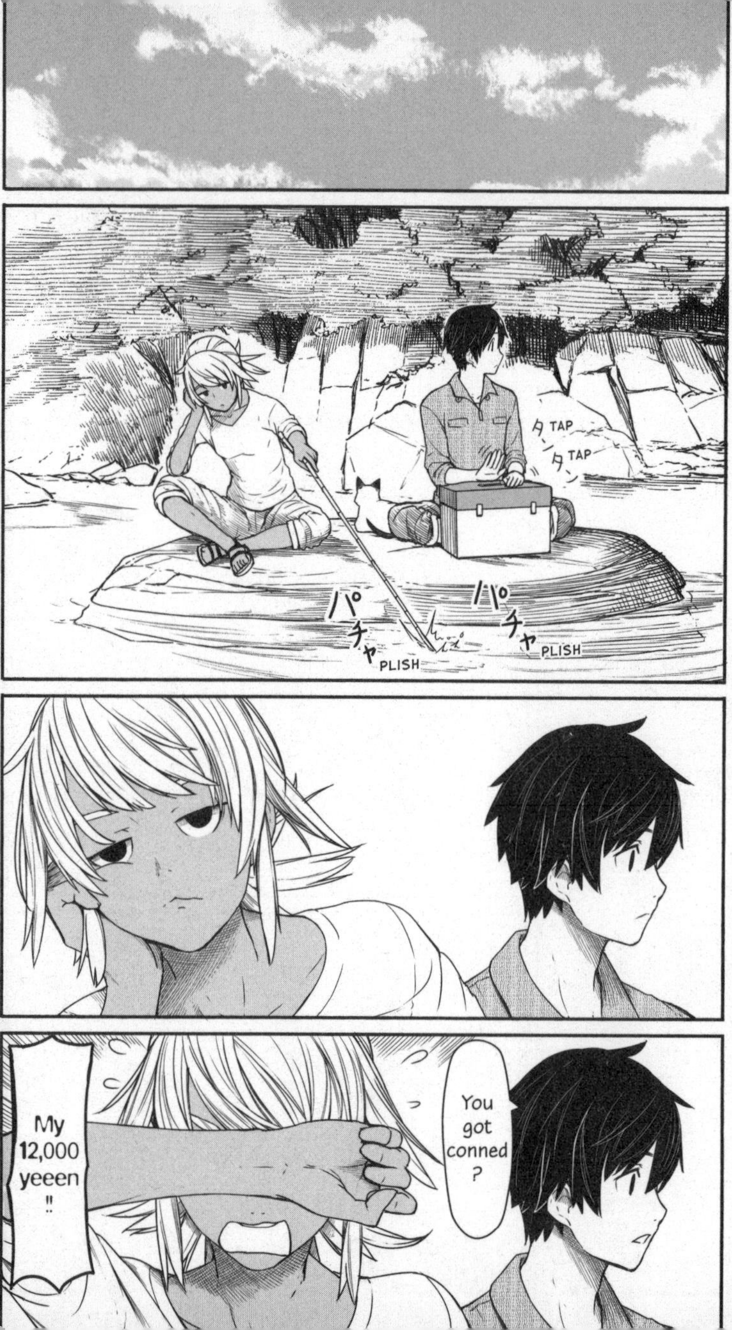
タ TAP
タン TAP
パチャ PLISH
パチャ PLISH
You got conned?
My 12,000 yeeen!!

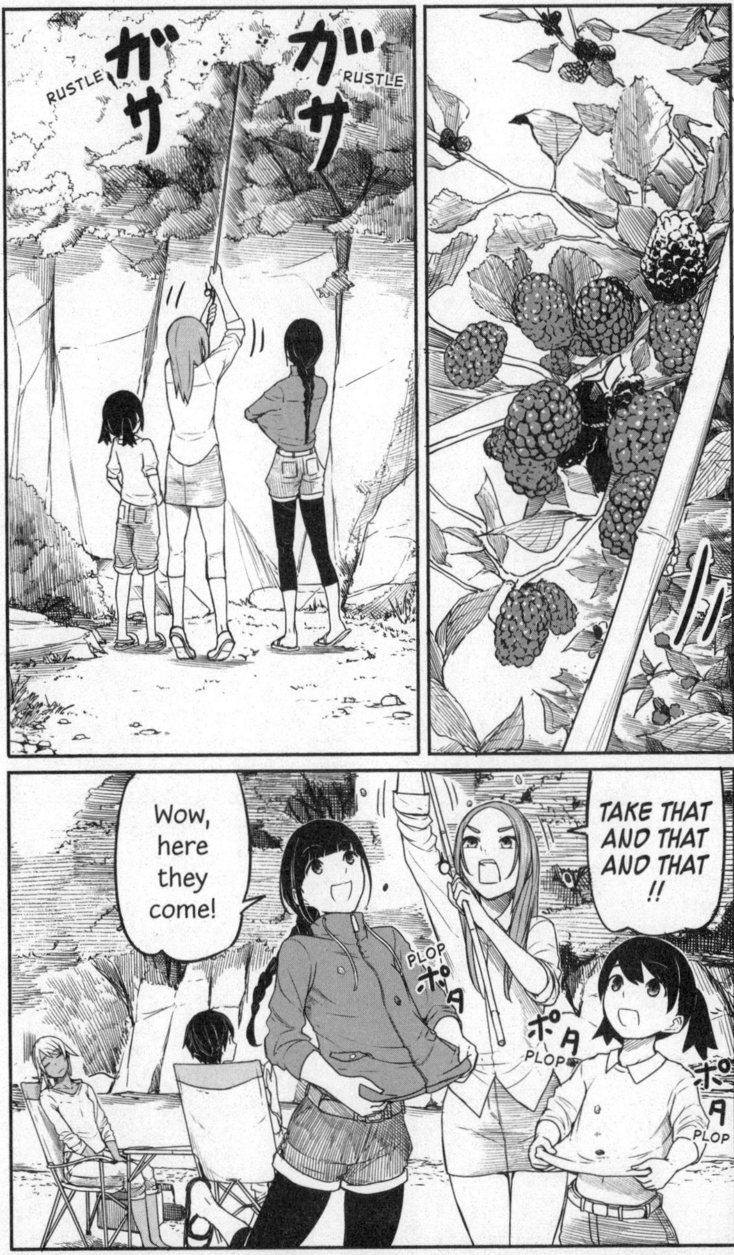
ガサ
RUSTLE
ガサ
RUSTLE
TAKE THAT AND THAT AND THAT !!
Wow, here they come!
ポタ
PLOP
ポタ
PLOP
ポタ
PLOP

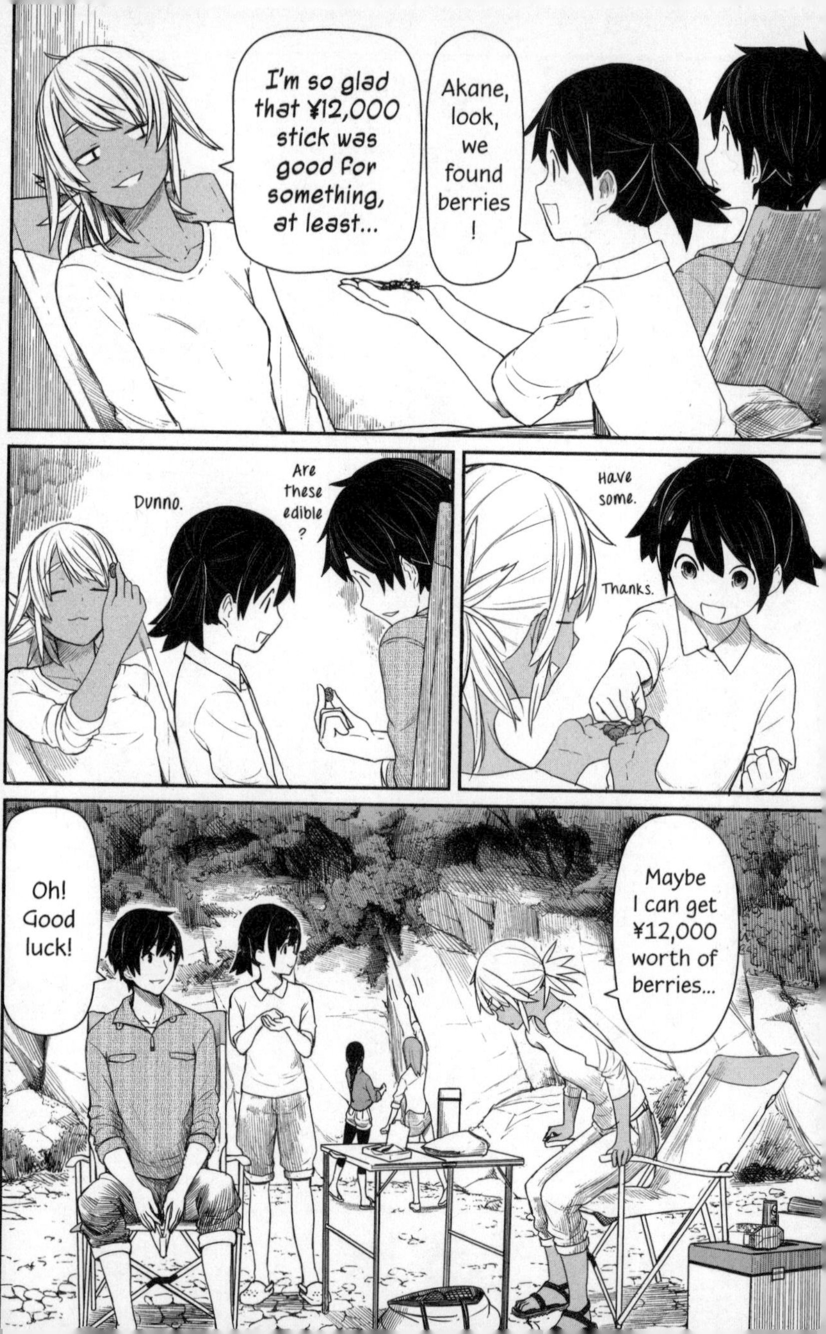

Akane, look, we found berries!
I'm so glad that ¥12,000 stick was good for something, at least...
Have some.
Thanks.
Are these edible?
Dunno.
Maybe I can get ¥12,000 worth of berries...
Oh! Good luck!

Chapter 28
Mouth-Watering Finger Food

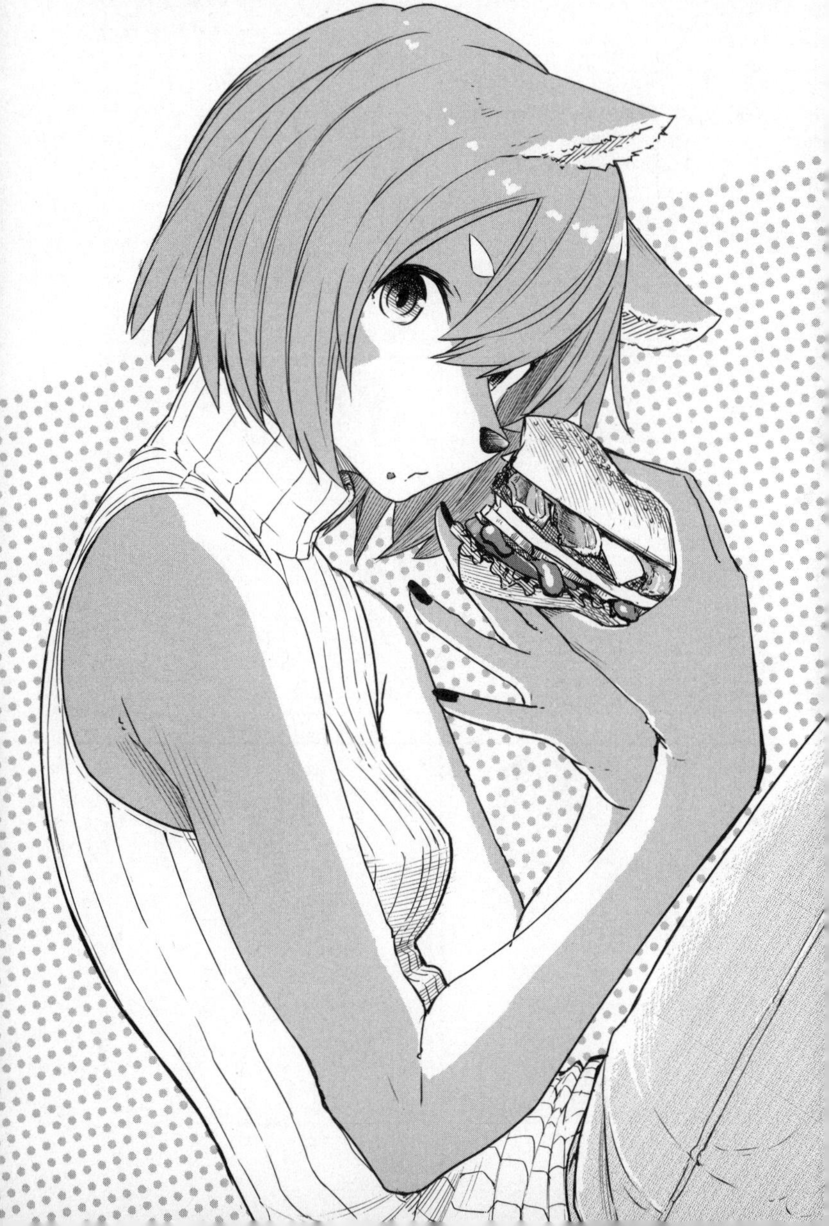

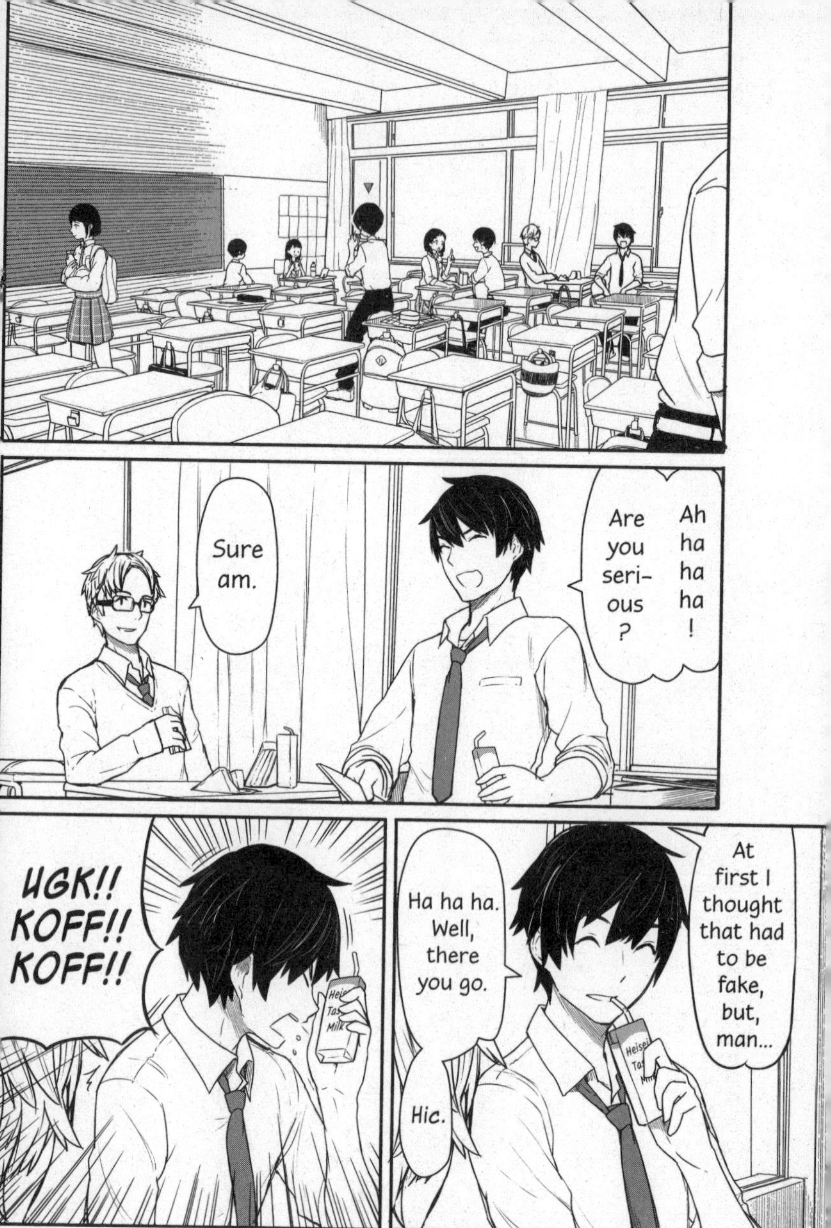
Ah ha ha ha!
Are you seri-ous?
Sure am.
At first I thought that had to be fake, but, man...
Ha ha ha. Well, there you go.
Hic.
UGK!! KOFF!! KOFF!!

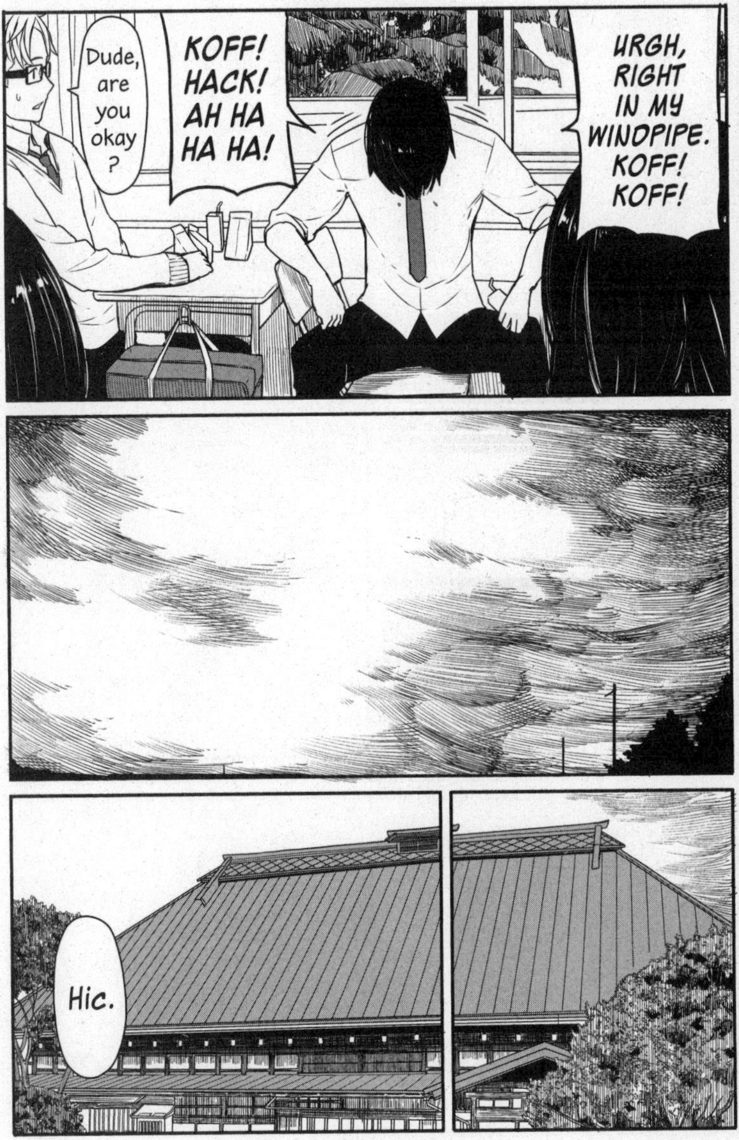
URGH, RIGHT IN MY WINDPIPE. KOFF! KOFF!
KOFF! HACK! AH HA HA HA!
Dude, are you okay?
Hic.

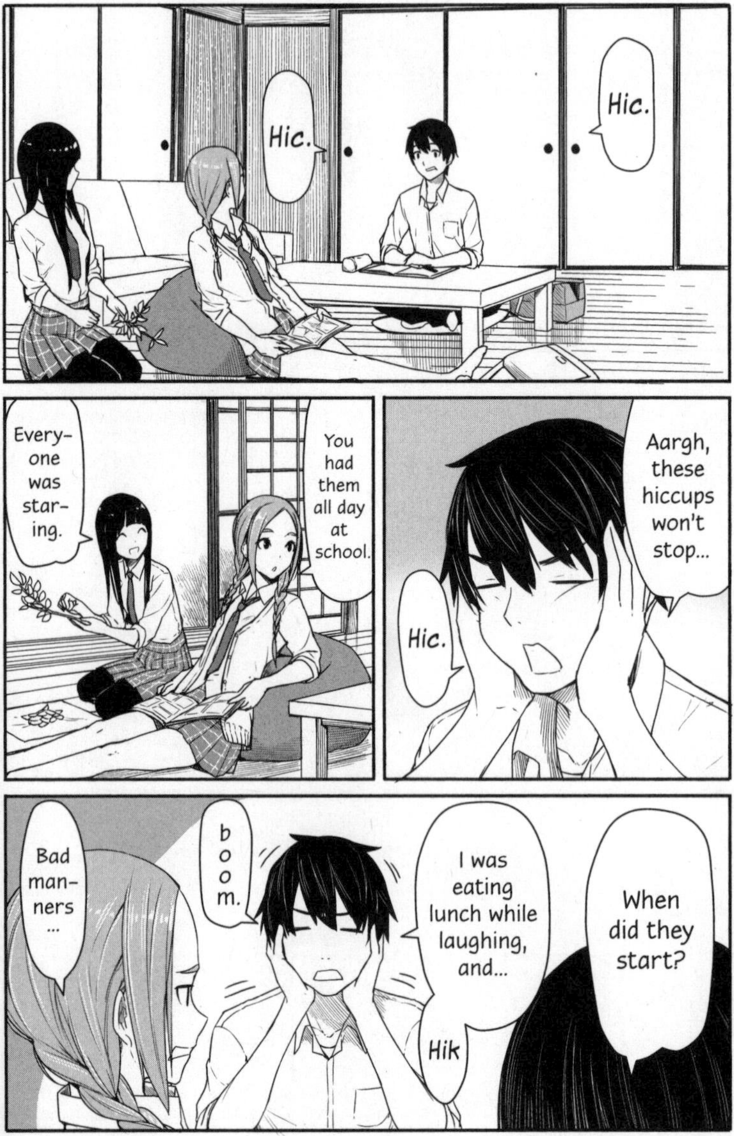
Hic.
Hic.
Aargh, these hiccups won't stop...
Hic.
You had them all day at school.
Every-one was star-ing.
When did they start?
I was eating lunch while laughing, and...
Hik
boom.
Bad man-ners...

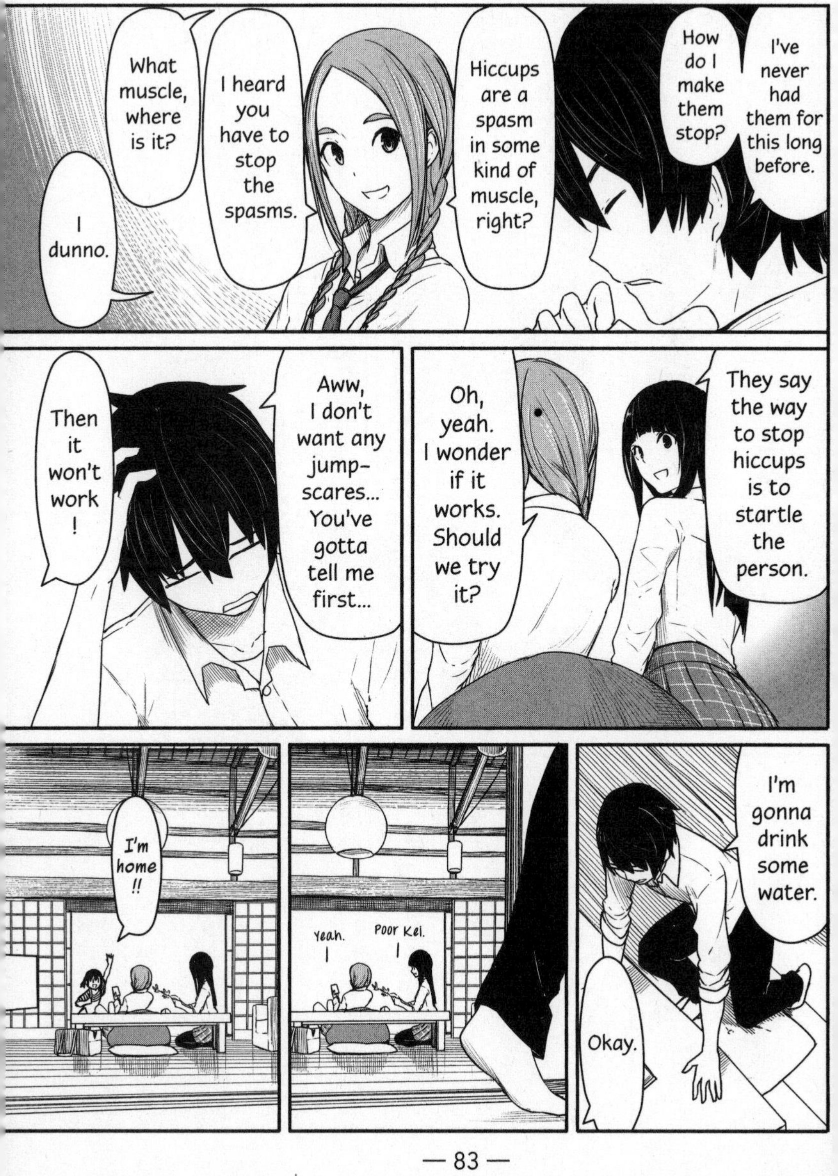
I've never had them for this long before.
How do I make them stop?
Hiccups are a spasm in some kind of muscle, right?
I heard you have to stop the spasms.
What muscle, where is it?
I dunno.
They say the way to stop hiccups is to startle the person.
Oh, yeah. I wonder if it works. Should we try it?
Aww, I don't want any jump-scares... You've gotta tell me first...
Then it won't work!
I'm gonna drink some water.
Okay.
Poor Kei.
Yeah.
I'm home!!

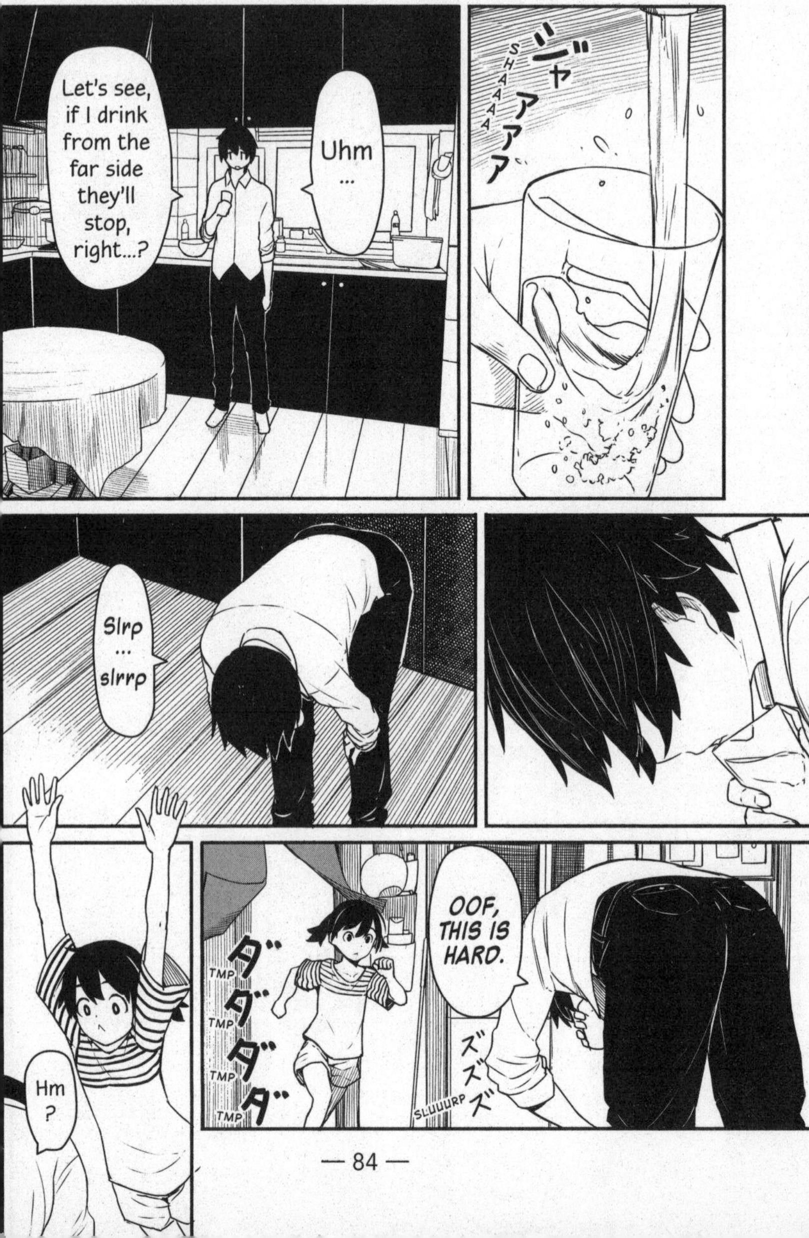
ジャアアア
SHAAAAA
Uhm ...
Let's see, if I drink from the far side they'll stop, right...?
Slrp ... slrrp
OOF, THIS IS HARD.
ズズズ
SLUUURP
ダダダダ
TMP TMP TMP TMP
Hm ?

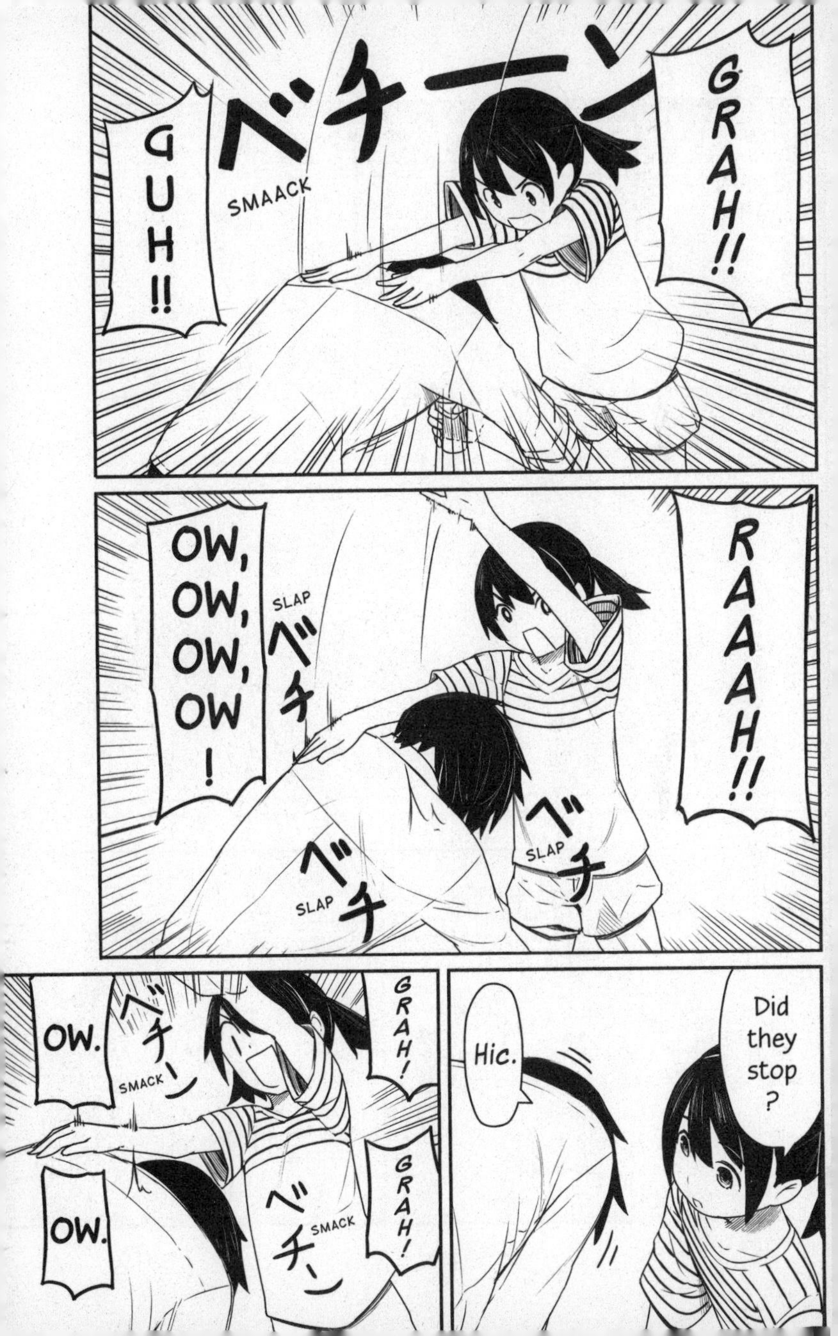
GRAH!!
ベチーン
SMAACK
GUH!!
RAAAAH!!
ベチ
SLAP
ベチ
SLAP
ベチ
SLAP
OW, OW, OW, OW!
Did they stop?
Hic.
GRAH!
ベチーン
SMACK
OW.
GRAH!
ベチーン
SMACK
OW.

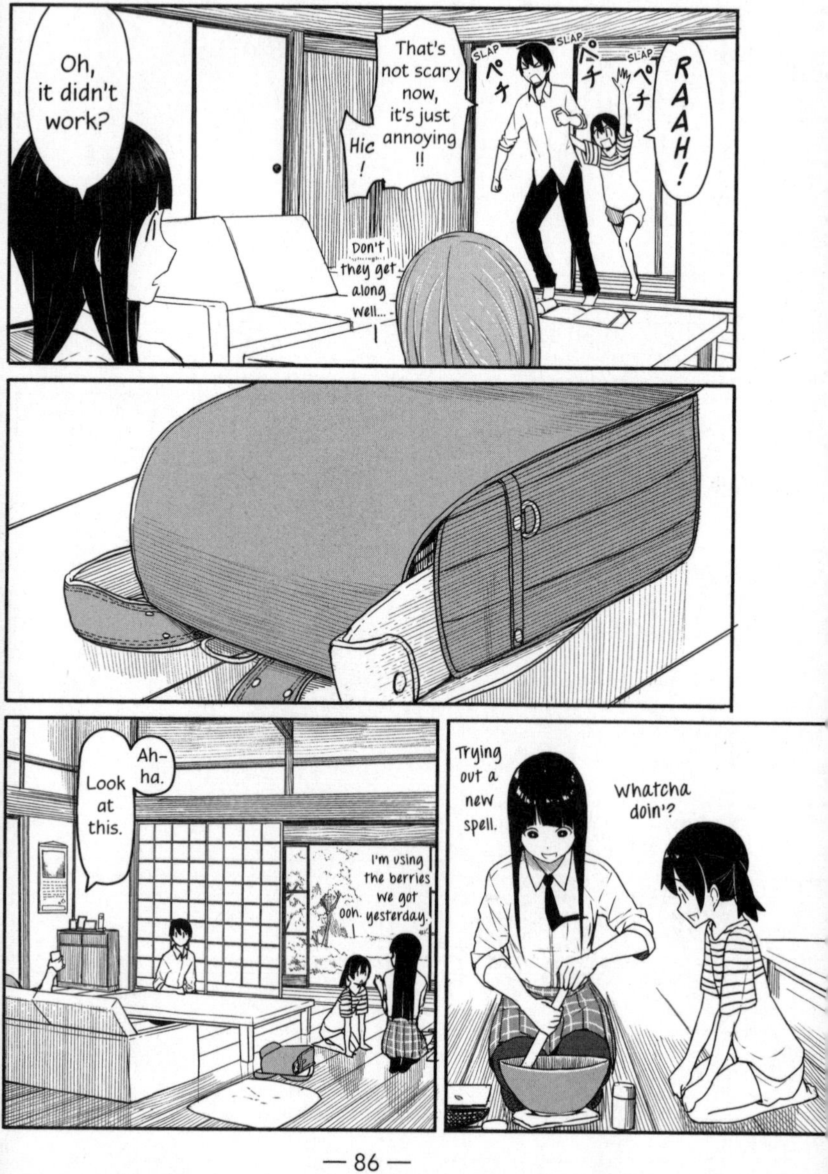
RAAH!
SLAP
ペチ
SLAP
ペチ
SLAP
ペチ
That's not scary now, it's just annoying!!
Hic!
Don't they get along well...!
Oh, it didn't work?
Whatcha doin'?
Trying out a new spell.
Ah-ha.
Look at this.
I'm using the berries we got yesterday.
Ooh.

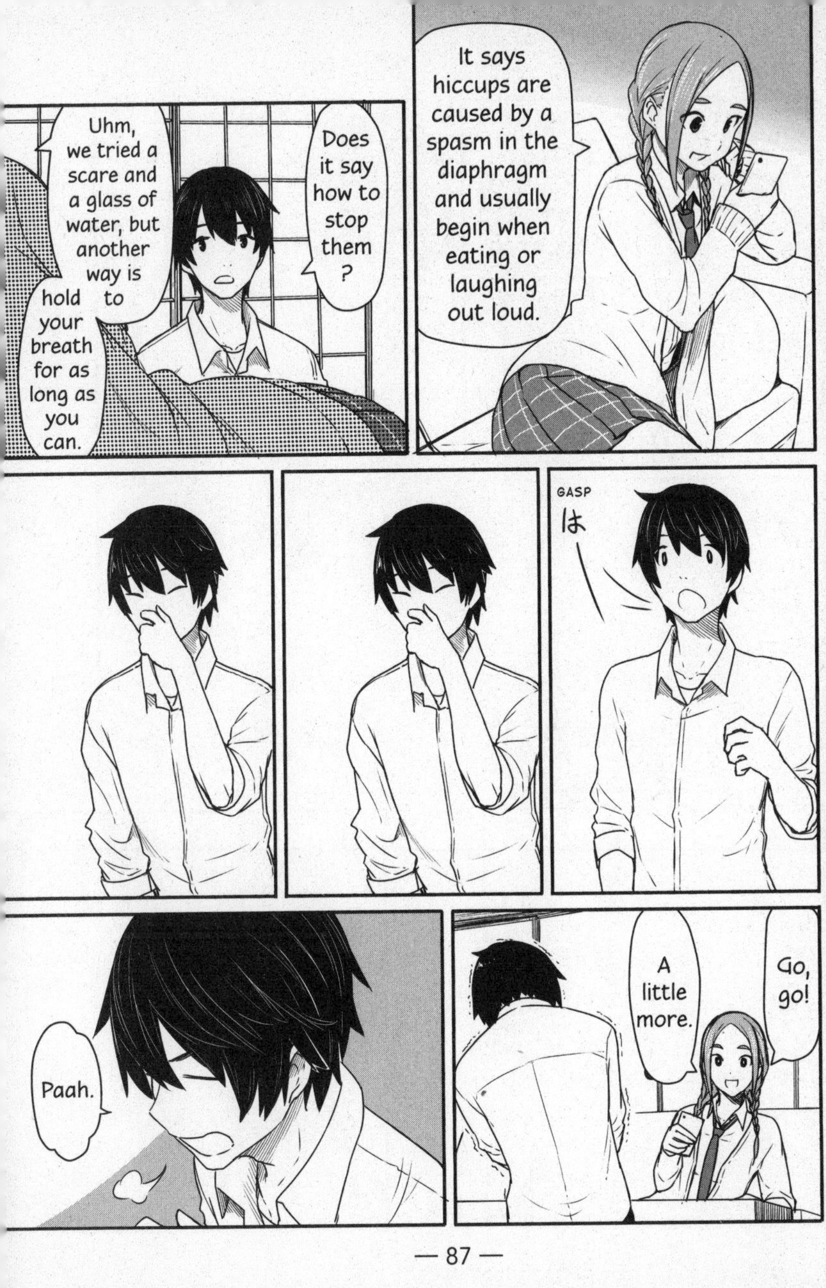

It says hiccups are caused by a spasm in the diaphragm and usually begin when eating or laughing out loud.
Does it say how to stop them?
Uhm, we tried a scare and a glass of water, but another way is to hold your breath for as long as you can.
GASP
は
Go, go!
A little more.
Paah.

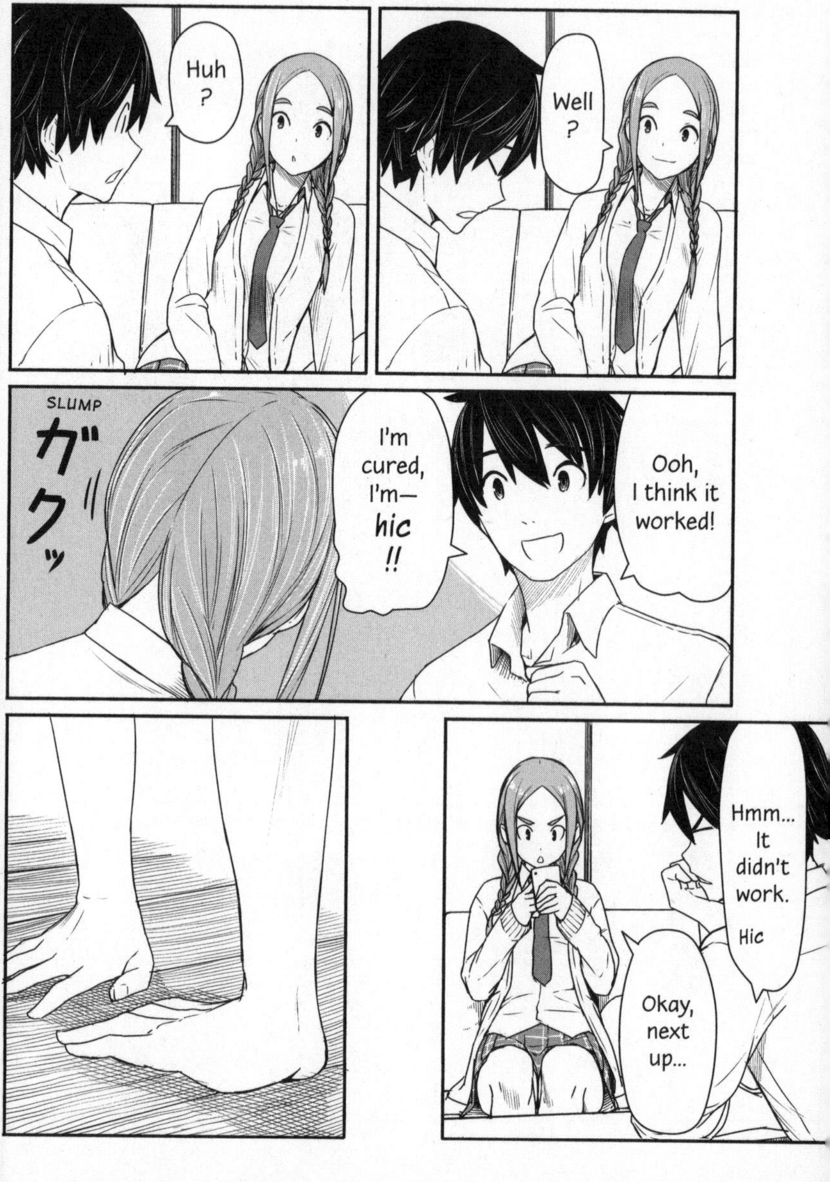
Well ?
Huh ?
Ooh, I think it worked!
I'm cured, I'm— hic !!
SLUMP
ガクッ
Hmm... It didn't work.
Hic
Okay, next up...

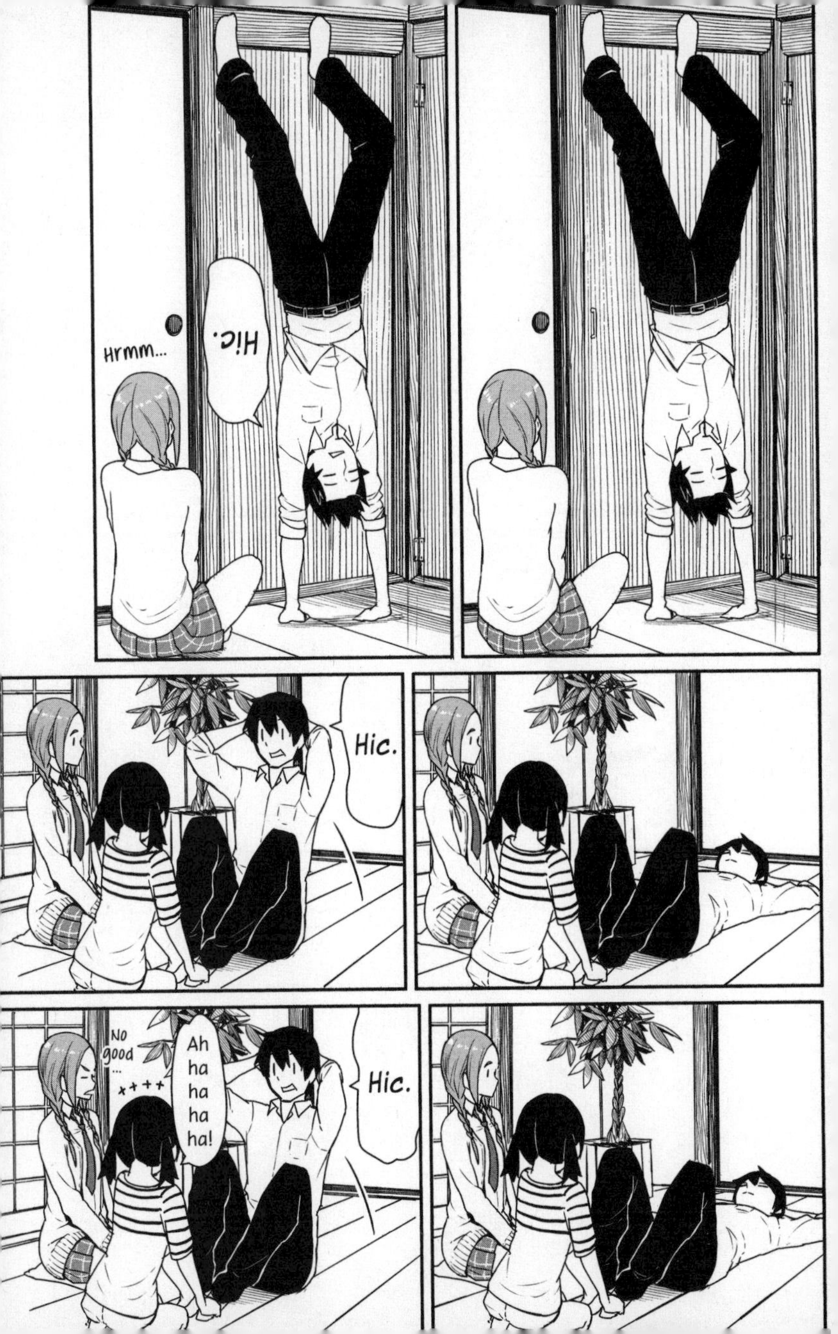
Hic.
Hrmm...
Hic.
Hic.
Ah ha ha ha ha!
No good...

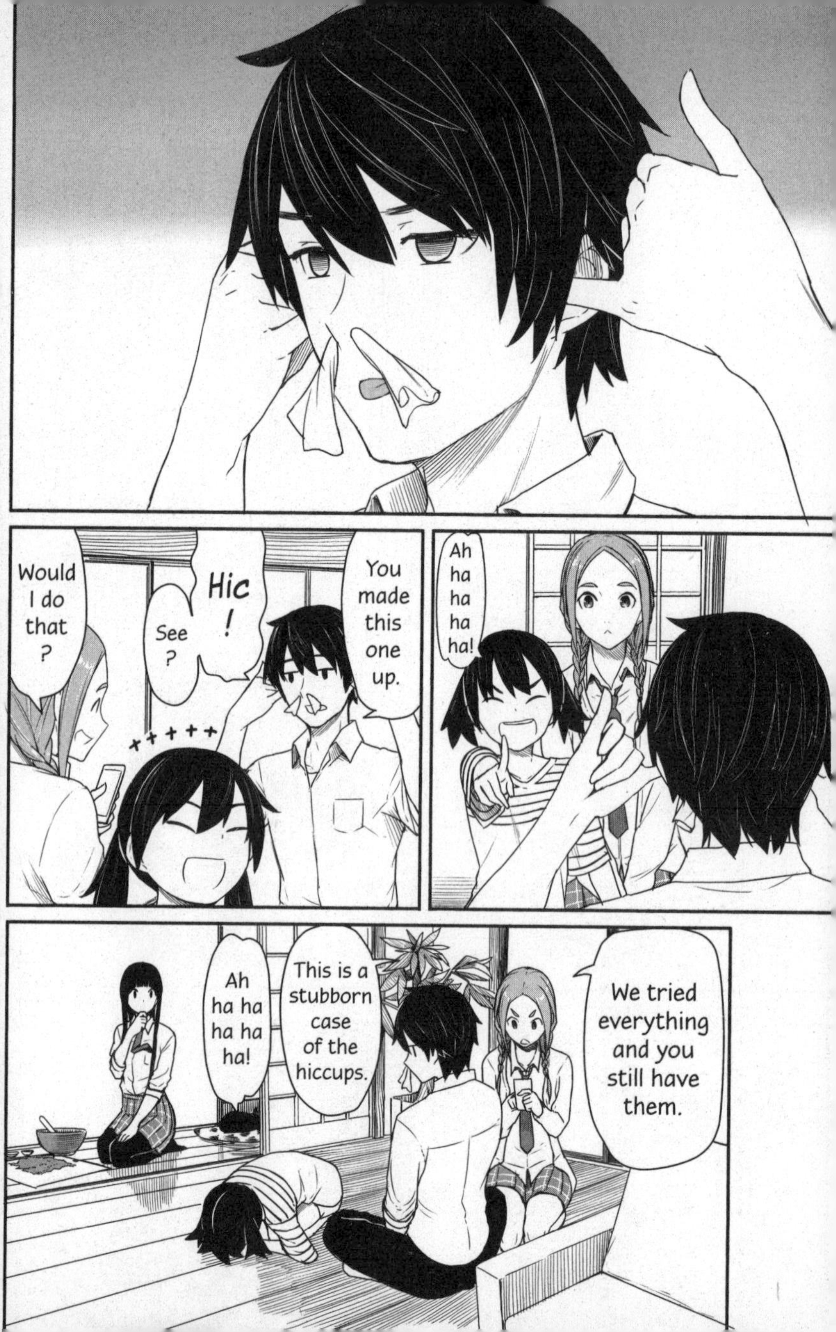
Ah ha ha ha ha!
You made this one up.
Hic!
See?
Would I do that?
We tried everything and you still have them.
This is a stubborn case of the hiccups.
Ah ha ha ha ha ha!

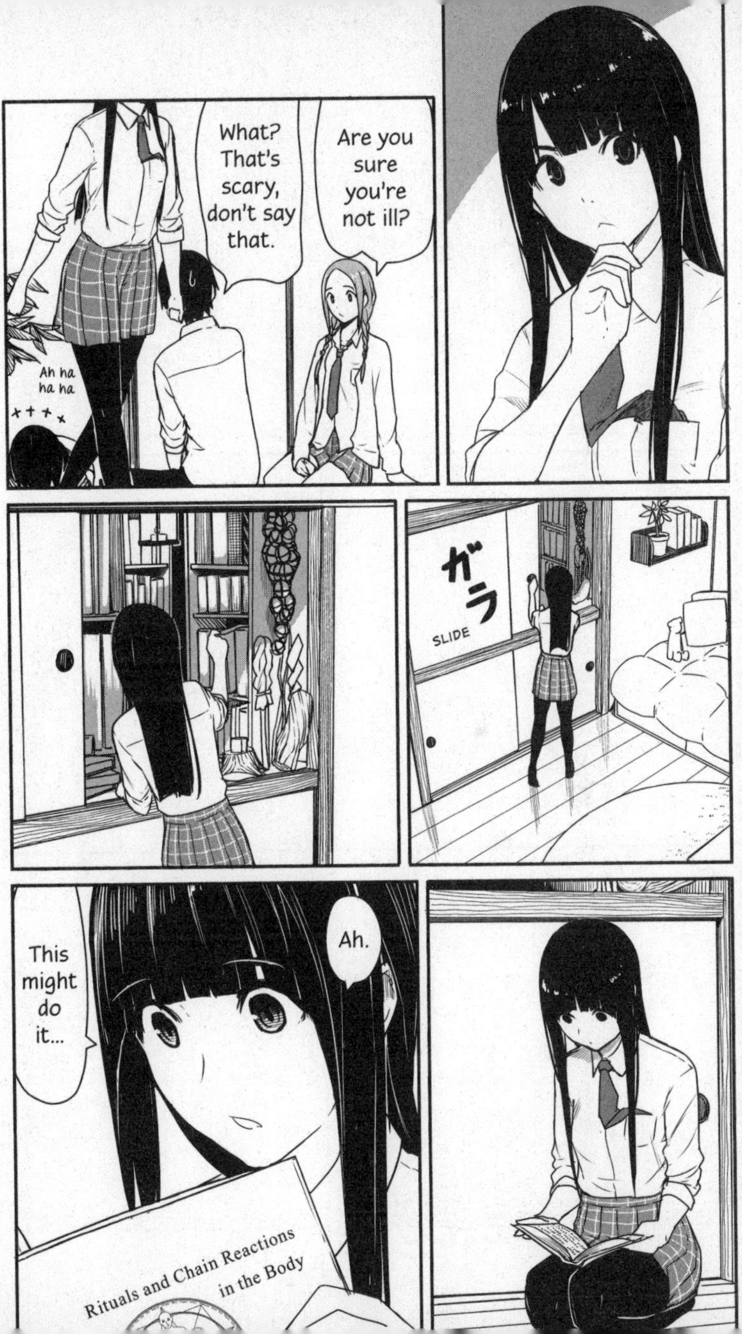
Are you sure you're not ill?
What? That's scary, don't say that.
Ah ha ha ha
ガラ
SLIDE
Ah.
This might do it...
Rituals and Chain Reactions in the Body

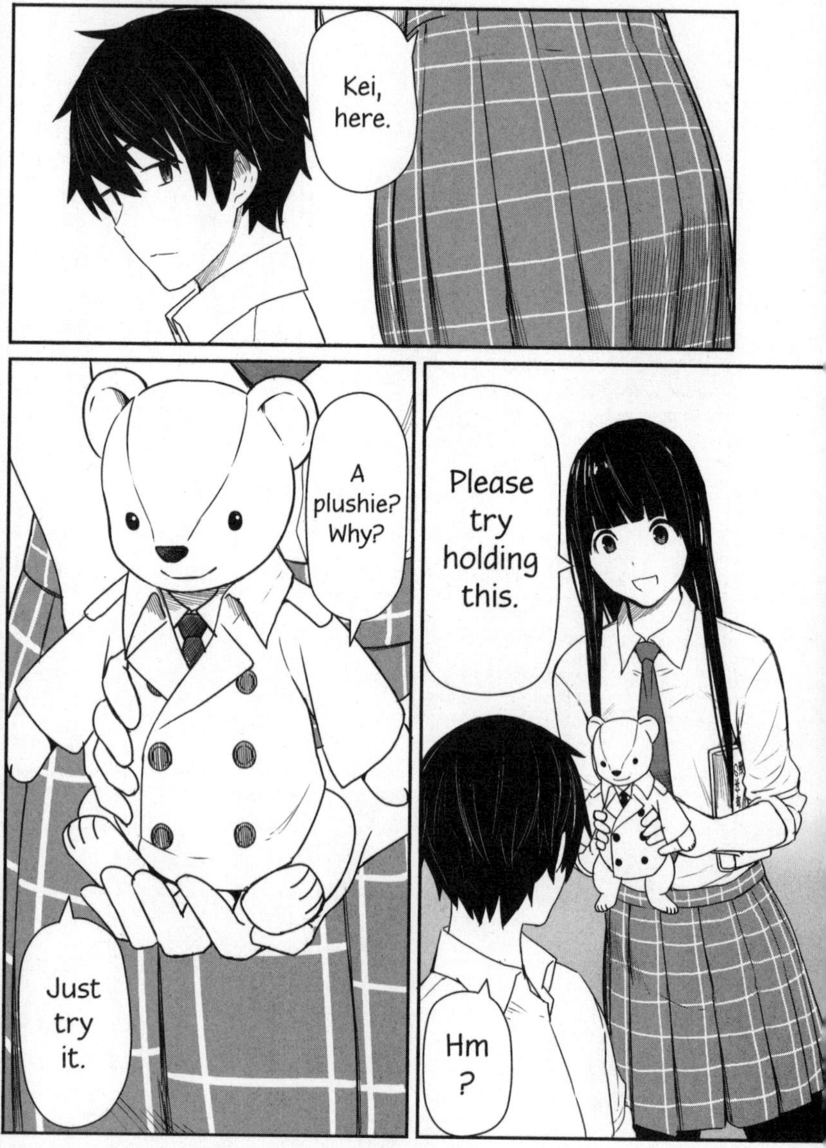
Kei, here.
Please try holding this.
Hm?
A plushie? Why?
Just try it.

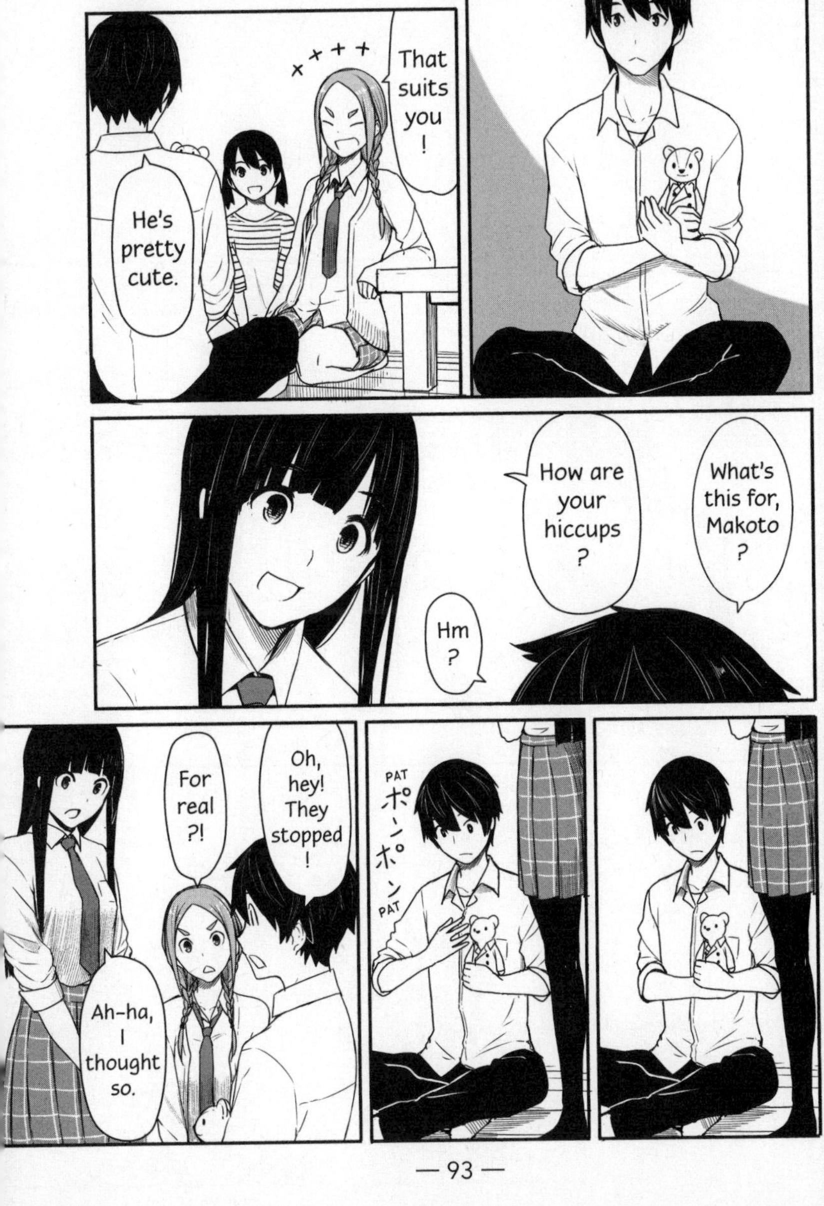
That suits you!
He's pretty cute.
What's this for, Makoto?
How are your hiccups?
Hm?
PAT
ポンポン
PAT
Oh, hey! They stopped!
For real?!
Ah-ha, I thought so.

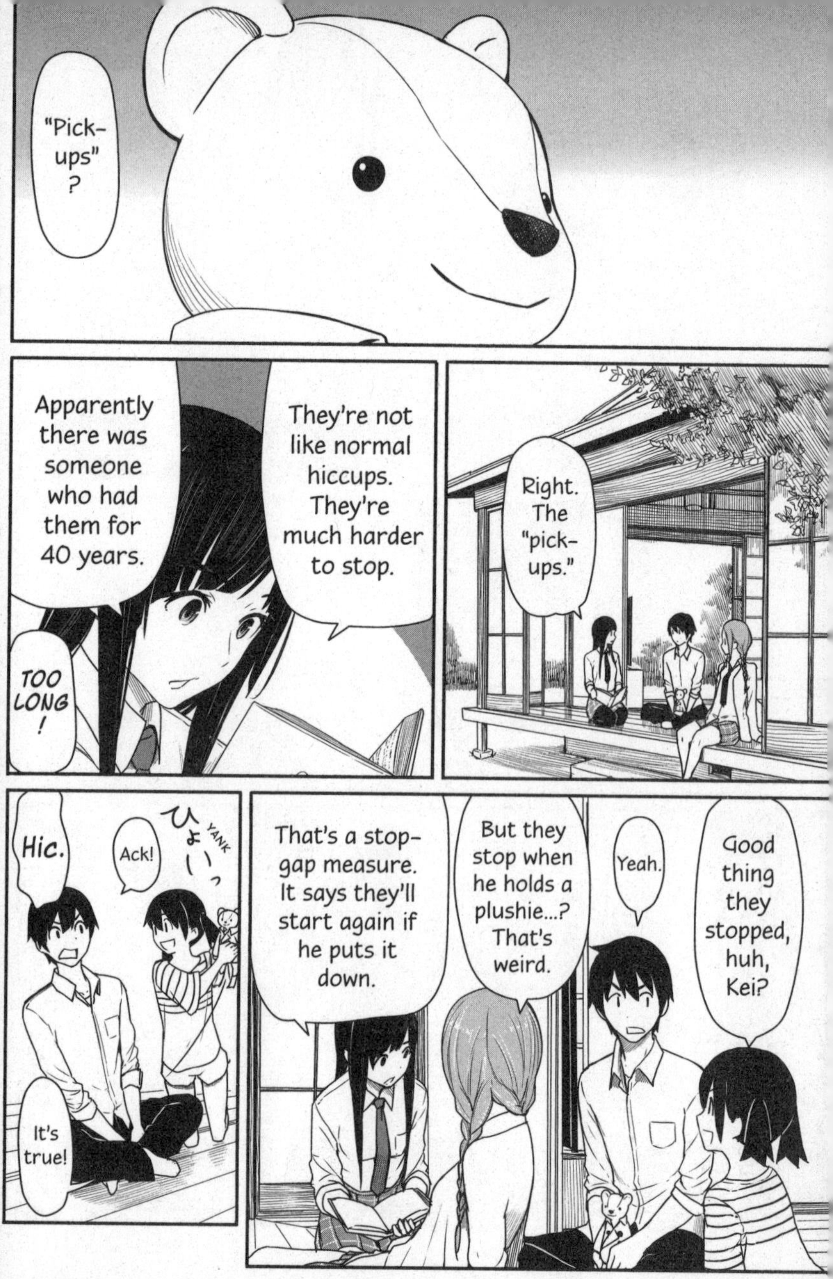
"Pick-ups"?
Right. The "pick-ups."
They're not like normal hiccups. They're much harder to stop.
Apparently there was someone who had them for 40 years.
TOO LONG!
Good thing they stopped, huh, Kei?
Yeah.
But they stop when he holds a plushie...? That's weird.
That's a stop-gap measure. It says they'll start again if he puts it down.
ひょいっ
YANK
Ack!
Hic.
It's true!

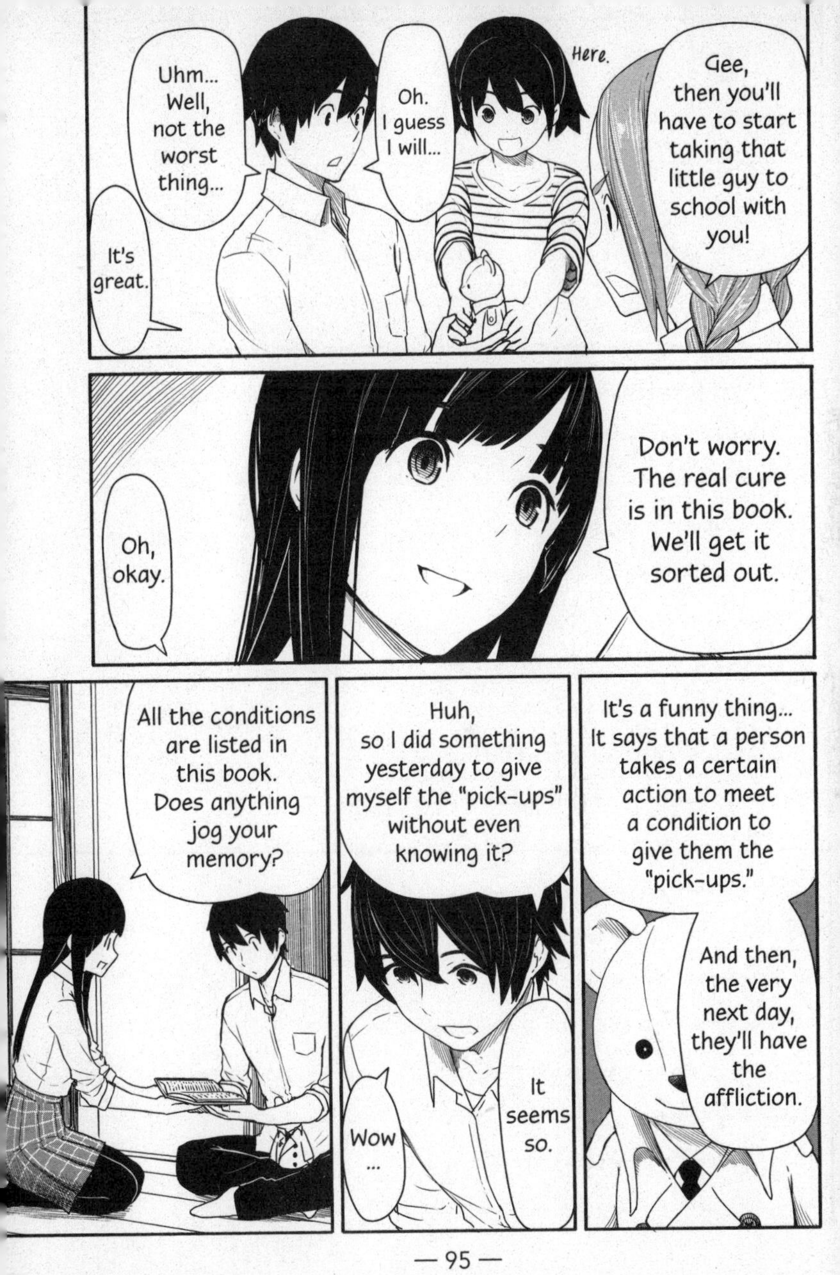
Gee, then you'll have to start taking that little guy to school with you!
Here.
Oh. I guess I will...
Uhm... Well, not the worst thing...
It's great.
Don't worry. The real cure is in this book. We'll get it sorted out.
Oh, okay.
It's a funny thing... It says that a person takes a certain action to meet a condition to give them the "pick-ups."
And then, the very next day, they'll have the affliction.
Huh, so I did something yesterday to give myself the "pick-ups" without even knowing it?
It seems so.
Wow ...
All the conditions are listed in this book. Does anything jog your memory?

21. In the living room, fall asleep with static on the radio

22. In the living room, squeeze a tomato and draw a picture with the juice

23. In the bathroom, let 5 eels swim in the bathtub

24. From the bathroom, stare at a cloud for 3 hours and 26 minutes

25. In the bathroom, use an entire bar of soap in one day

26. Fill the bath with cold water and get in while wearing one's favorite outfit

27. In the bathroom, play with a remote-controlled toy

28. In the bathroom, break a watermelon with one's fist

29. In the bathroom, eat 5 hot peppers

30. In the bathroom, spread sawdust on the floor

31. In the bathroom, wash a writing utensil

32. In the bathroom, place a hydrangea petal on the back of one's hand

33. Place cedar charcoal in the corners of the bathroom

34. In the bathroom, eat clams steamed with sake

35. In the kitchen, make 184 sushi rolls in one day

36. In the kitchen, put down a sea bream and let a stray cat steal it

37. In the kitchen, wrap up tangerines in a purple handkerchief

38. In the kitchen, put sunblock on the window glass

39. In the kitchen, take 15 deep breaths

40. In the kitchen, burn 11⅔ lbs. of pork

41. In the kitchen, lose a ruby ring down the drain

42. In the kitchen, set down a mochi grinder and walk in a circle around it 6 times
    counter-clockwise

43. In the kitchen, finely slice maitake mushrooms with a knife in each hand

44. In the kitchen, put a mortar bowl on one's head and spin around 3 times

2053 Conditions
That Can Cause "Pick-ups"
Household Edition

1. At the front door, spin 7 times and jump 5 times

2. At the front door, open and close the door 15 times in 10 seconds

3. At the front door, stack 4 shoes and throw them outside

4. At the front door, poke the ceiling with a shoehorn

5. At the front door, let a bird that came inside perch on one's left shoulder

6. At the front door, release 8 woodlice

7. At the front door, break a brand-new glass

8. In the living room, sprinkle heated seawater

9. In the living room, stare at a clock for 34 minutes

10. In the living room, sleep with a feather placed on one's head

11. In the living room, drop a lucky cat on one's foot

12. In the living room, hold water in one's mouth for 1 hour and 28 minutes

13. In the living room, put up a picture of an elephant, then remove it 3 minutes later

14. In the living room, eat Dolls' Festival rice cakes with a woman of 57 years and 6 month

15. In the living room, eat Dolls' Festival rice cakes with a man of 34 years and 7 months

16. In the living room, dismantle and reassemble an automobile engine

17. In the living room, talk on the phone with a friend for 5 hours, 30 minutes, 12 seconds

18. In the center of the living room, make a stack of 10 dictionaries

19. In the living room, walk in a circle 5 times clockwise around a bottle of vinegar

20. In the living room, tie old clothing around one's calves

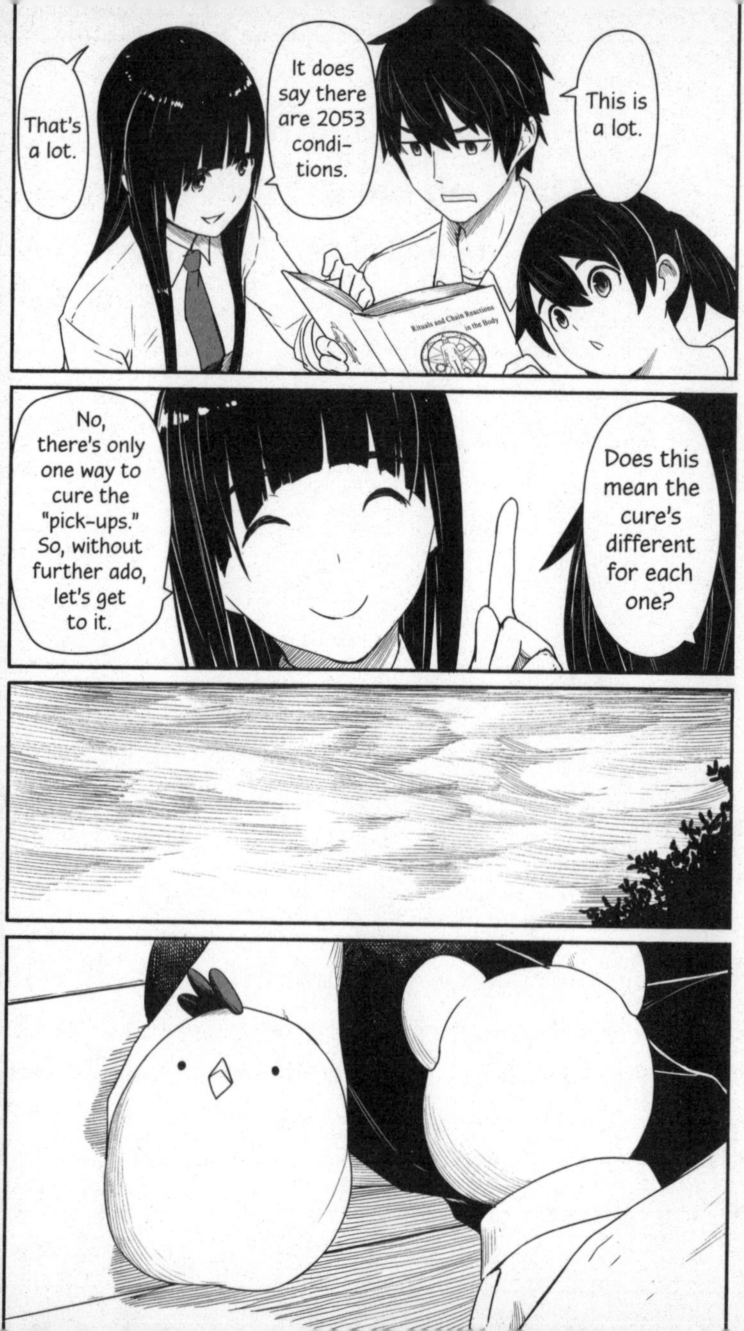
This is a lot.
It does say there are 2053 conditions.
That's a lot.
Rituals and Chain Reactions in the Body
Does this mean the cure's different for each one?
No, there's only one way to cure the "pick-ups." So, without further ado, let's get to it.

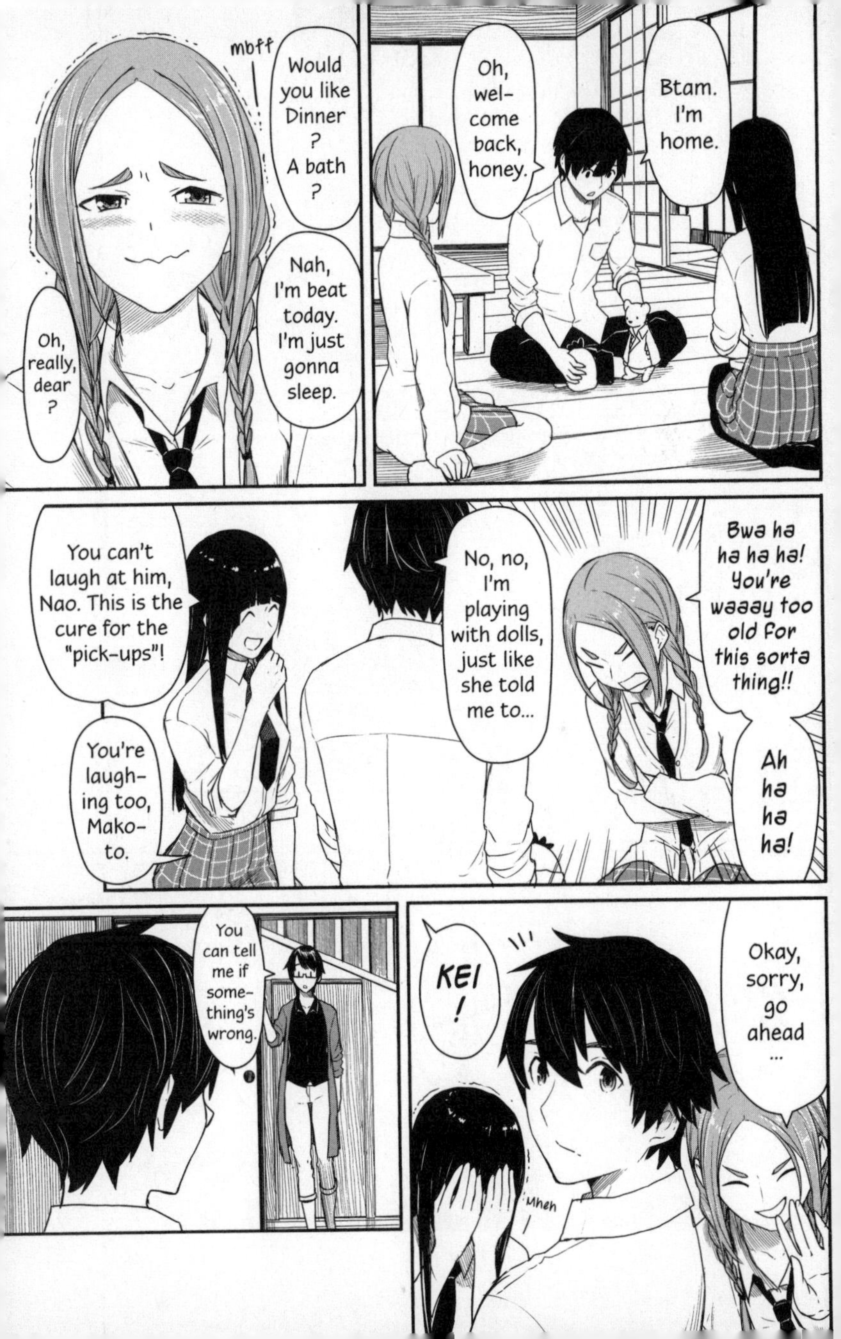
Btam. I'm home.
Oh, welcome back, honey.
Would you like Dinner? A bath?
mbff
Nah, I'm beat today. I'm just gonna sleep.
Oh, really, dear?
Bwa ha ha ha ha! You're waaay too old for this sorta thing!!
Ah ha ha ha!
No, no, I'm playing with dolls, just like she told me to...
You can't laugh at him, Nao. This is the cure for the "pick-ups"!
You're laughing too, Makoto.
Okay, sorry, go ahead...
KEI!
Mheh
You can tell me if something's wrong.

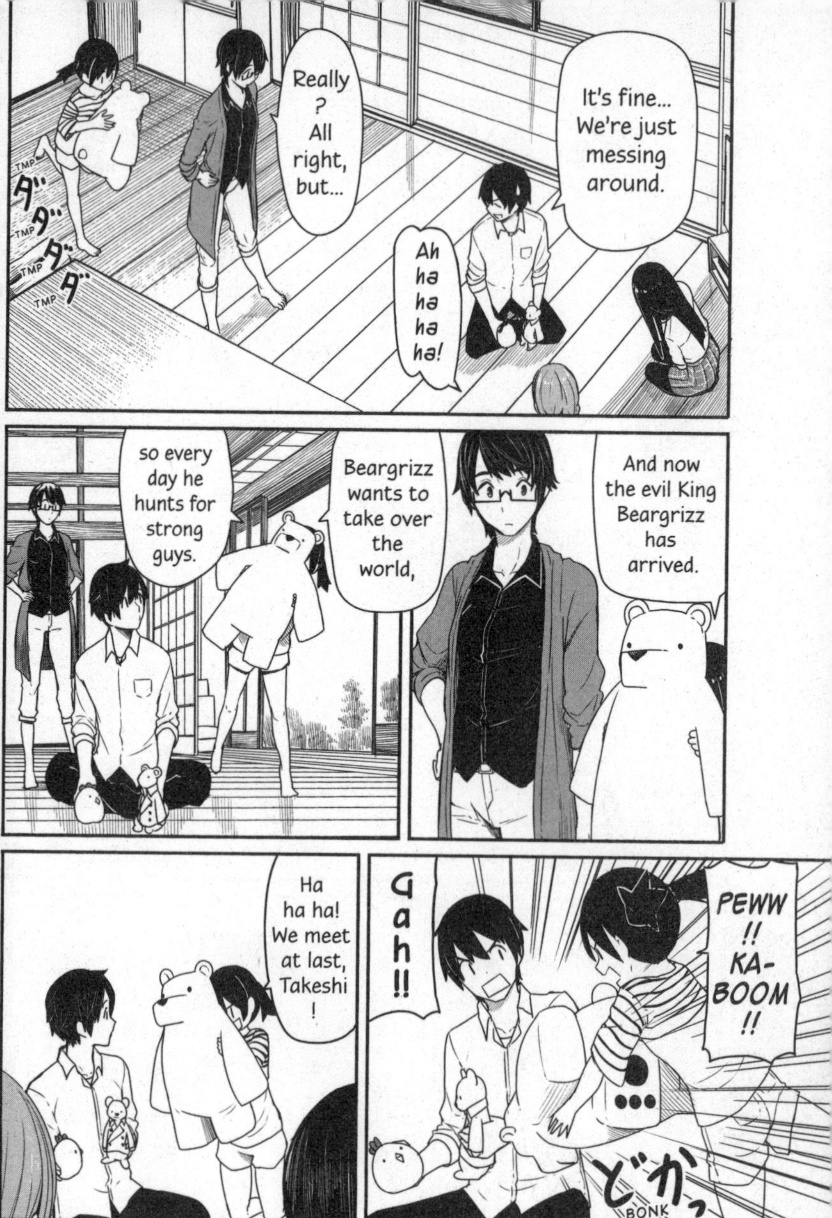
It's fine... We're just messing around.
Really? All right, but...
Ah ha ha ha ha!
ダ TMP ダ TMP ダ TMP ダ TMP
And now the evil King Beargrizz has arrived.
Beargrizz wants to take over the world,
so every day he hunts for strong guys.
PEWW!! KA-BOOM!!
Gah!!
どかっ BONK
Ha ha ha! We meet at last, Takeshi!

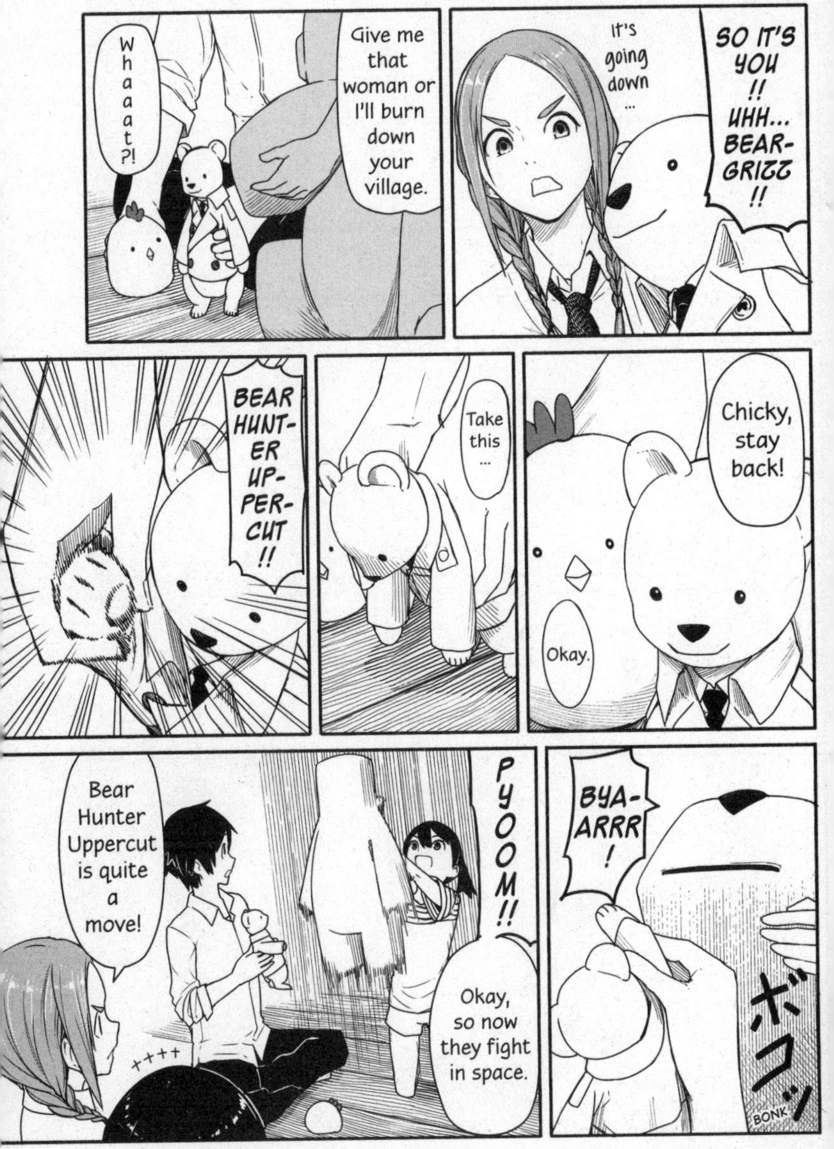
SO IT'S YOU!! UHH... BEAR-GRIZZ!!
It's going down ...
Give me that woman or I'll burn down your village.
Whaaaat?!
Chicky, stay back!
Okay.
Take this ...
BEAR HUNTER UPPERCUT!!
BYA-ARRR!
ボコッ
BONK
PYOOOM!!
Okay, so now they fight in space.
Bear Hunter Uppercut is quite a move!

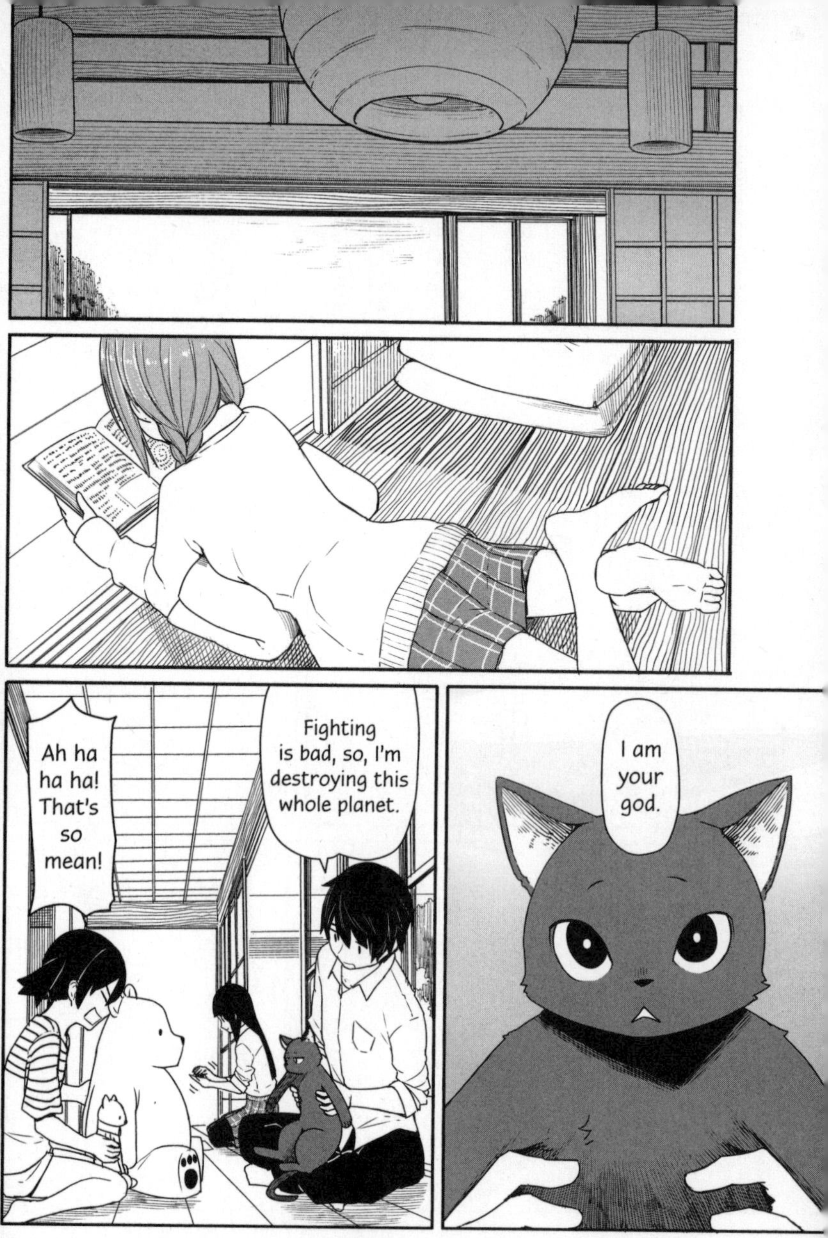
I am your god.
Fighting is bad, so, I'm destroying this whole planet.
Ah ha ha ha! That's so mean!

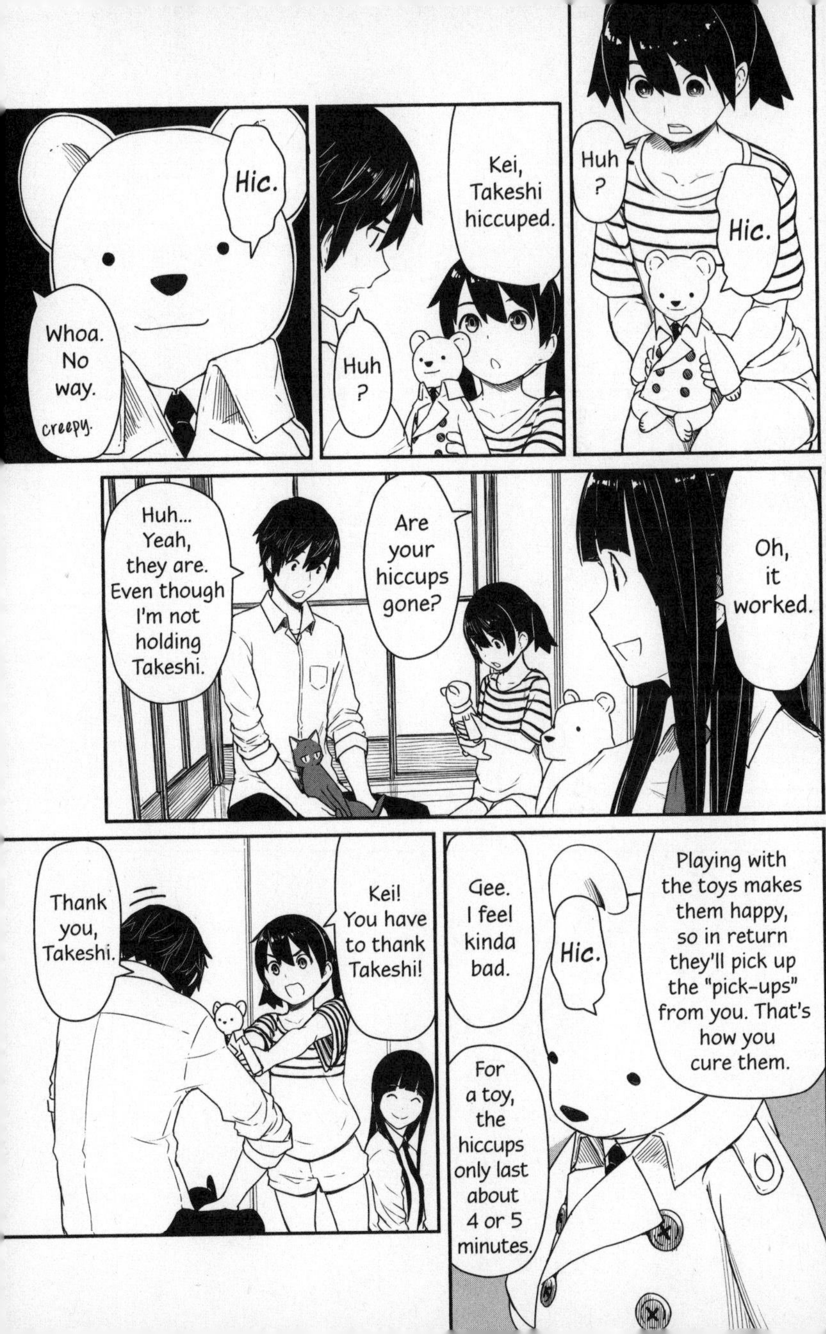
Huh?
Hic.
Kei, Takeshi hiccuped.
Huh?
Hic.
Whoa. No way.
creepy.
Oh, it worked.
Are your hiccups gone?
Huh... Yeah, they are. Even though I'm not holding Takeshi.
Playing with the toys makes them happy, so in return they'll pick up the "pick-ups" from you. That's how you cure them.
Hic.
Gee. I feel kinda bad.
For a toy, the hiccups only last about 4 or 5 minutes.
Kei! You have to thank Takeshi!
Thank you, Takeshi.

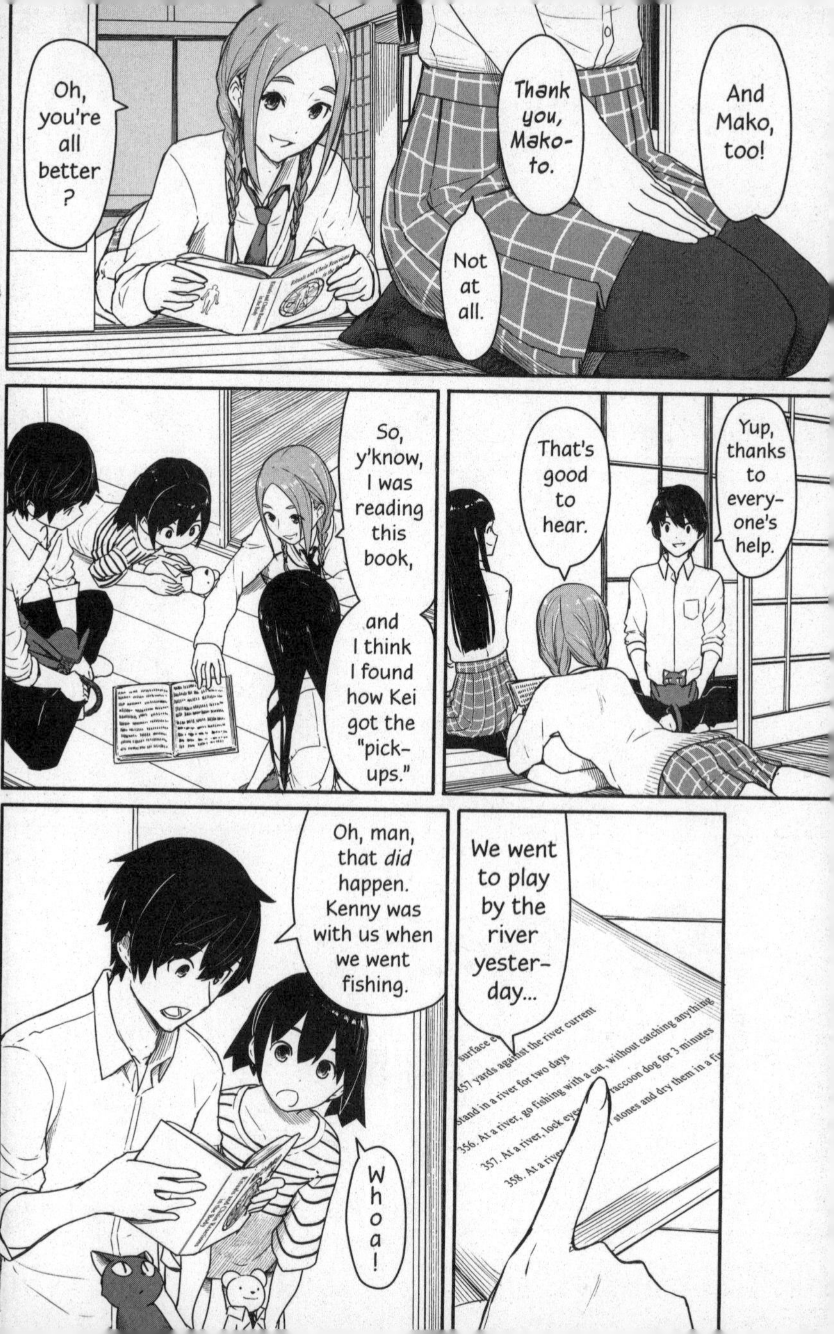

And Mako, too!
Thank you, Mako-to.
Oh, you're all better?
Not at all.
Yup, thanks to every-one's help.
That's good to hear.
So, y'know, I was reading this book,
and I think I found how Kei got the "pick-ups."
We went to play by the river yesterday...
surface e
857 yards against the river current
Stand in a river for two days
356. At a river, go fishing with a cat, without catching anything
357. At a river, lock eye raccoon dog for 3 minutes
358. At a rive stones and dry them in a fi
Oh, man, that *did* happen. Kenny was with us when we went fishing.
Whoa!

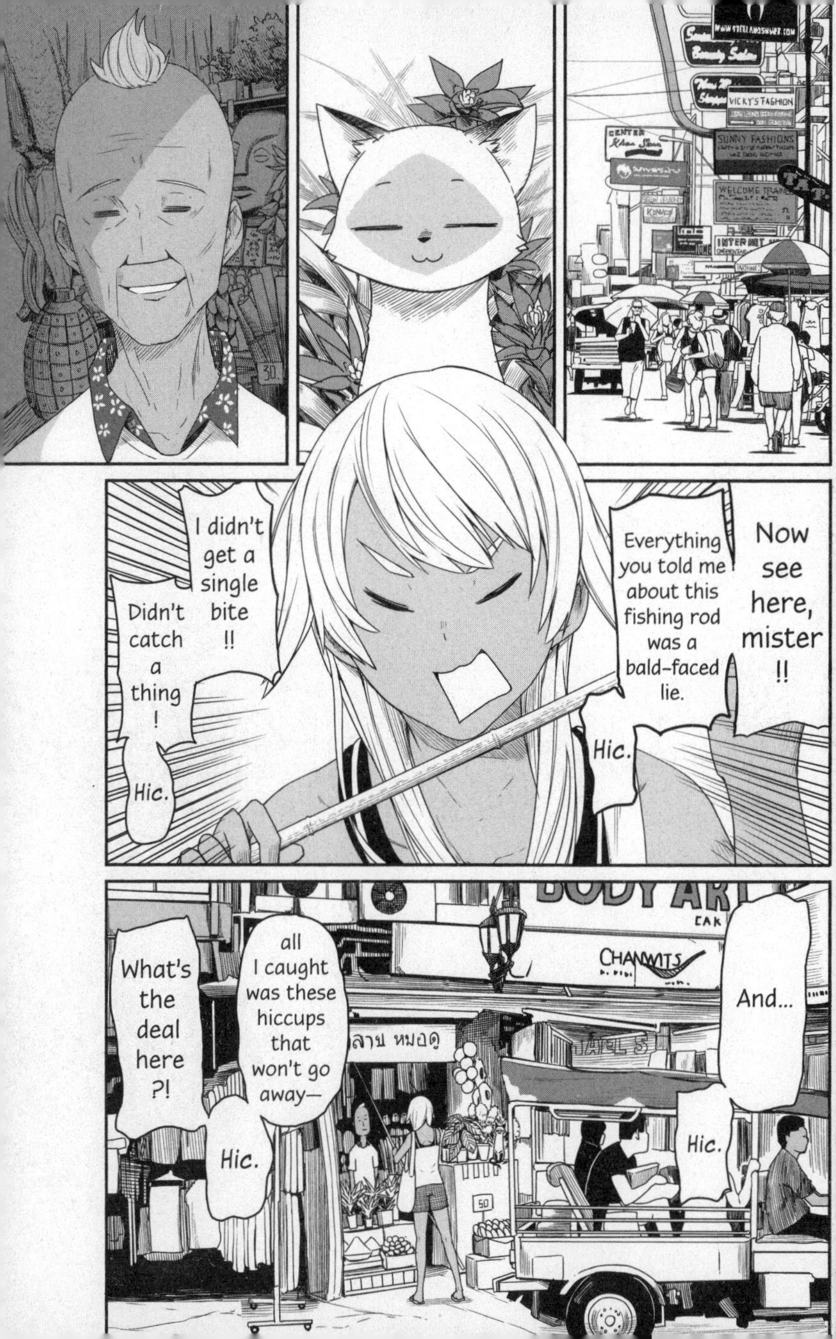
VICKY'S FASHION
SUNNY FASHIONS
Now see here, mister !!
Everything you told me about this fishing rod was a bald-faced lie.
Hic.
I didn't get a single bite !!
Didn't catch a thing !
Hic.
BODY ART
CHANWITS
And...
Hic.
all I caught was these hiccups that won't go away—
What's the deal here ?!
Hic.

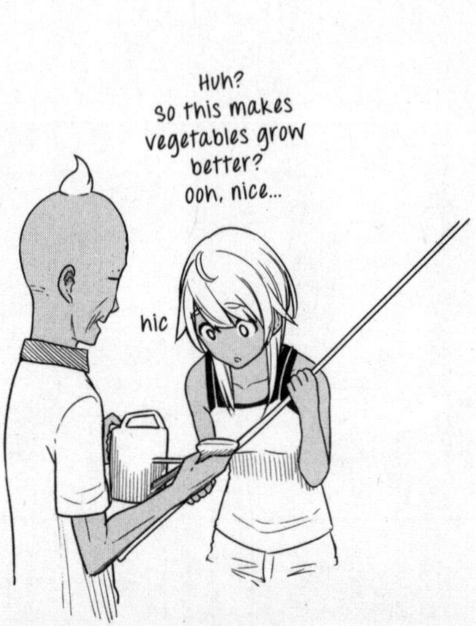
Huh? So this makes vegetables grow better? Ooh, nice...
hic

Chapter 29
Flying Puddles

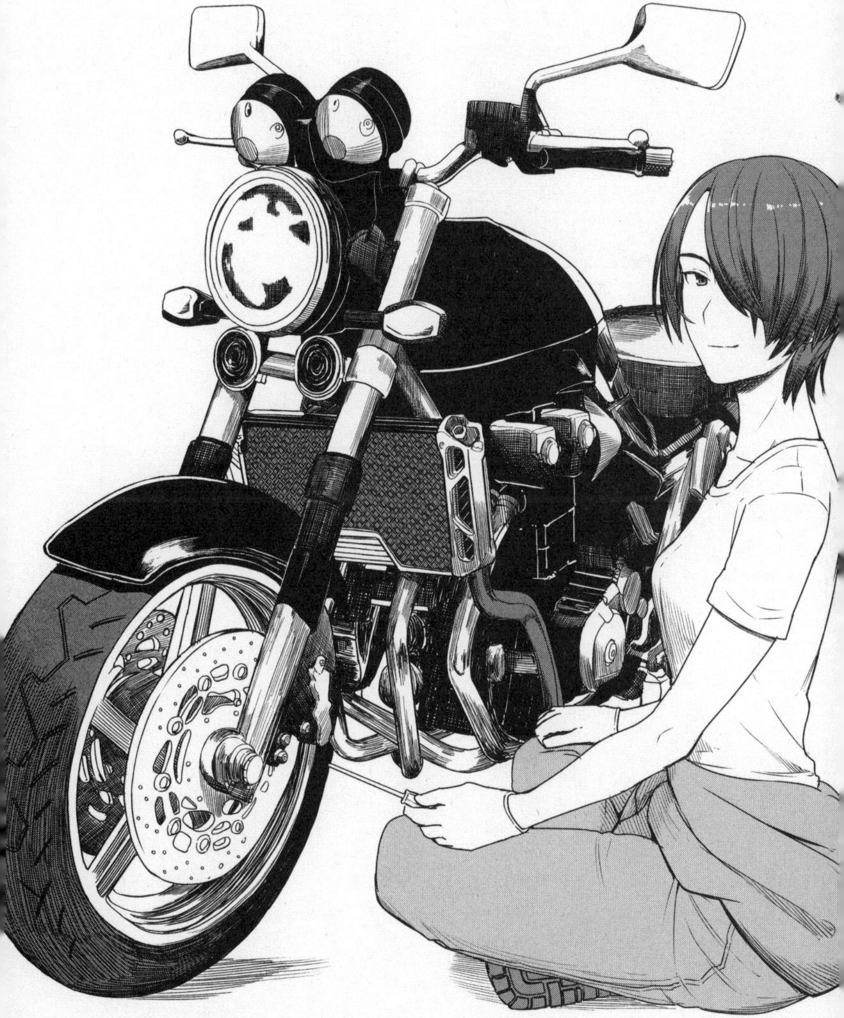

アイスクリーム店
Ice Cream

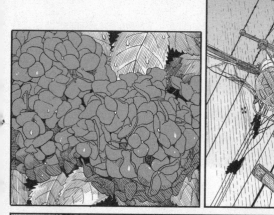

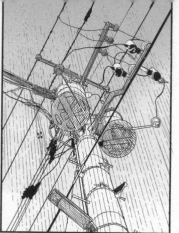

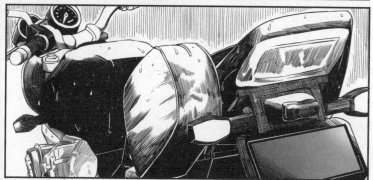

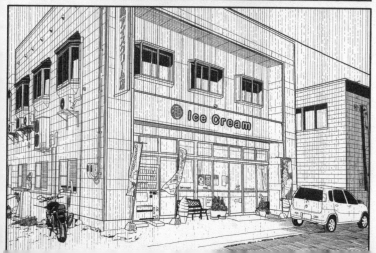

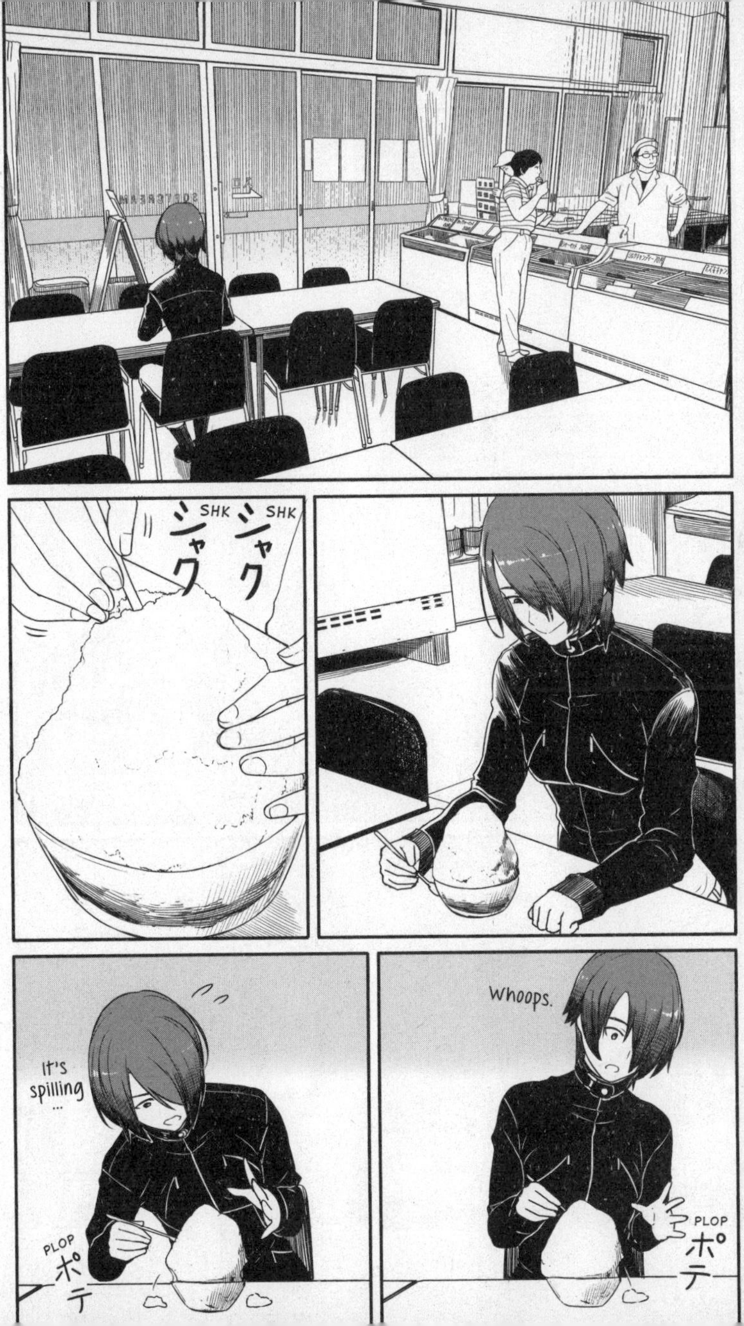
SHK
シャク
SHK
シャク
Whoops.
PLOP
ポテ
It's spilling ...
PLOP
ポテ

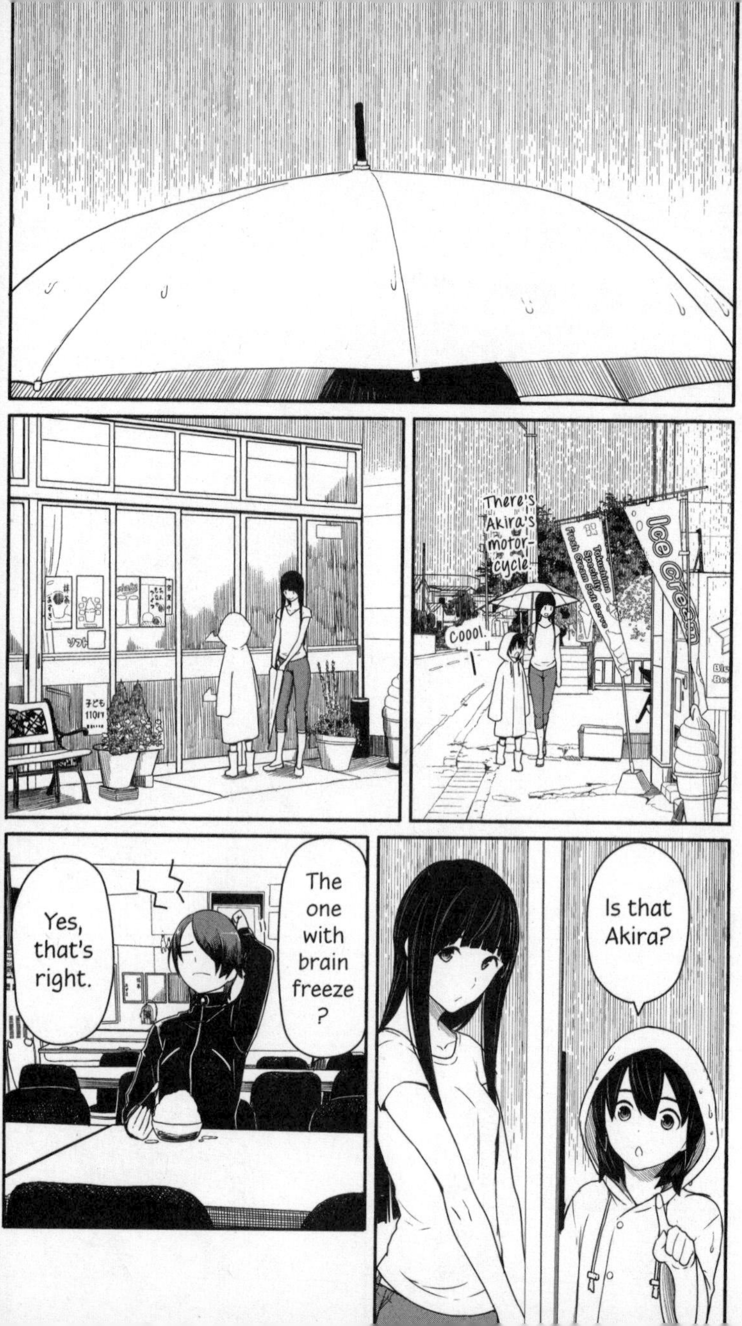
Ice Cream
Tokushima Specialty Fresh Cream Soft Serve
There's Akira's motor-cycle!
Coool.
子ども110番
ソフト
Is that Akira?
The one with brain freeze?
Yes, that's right.

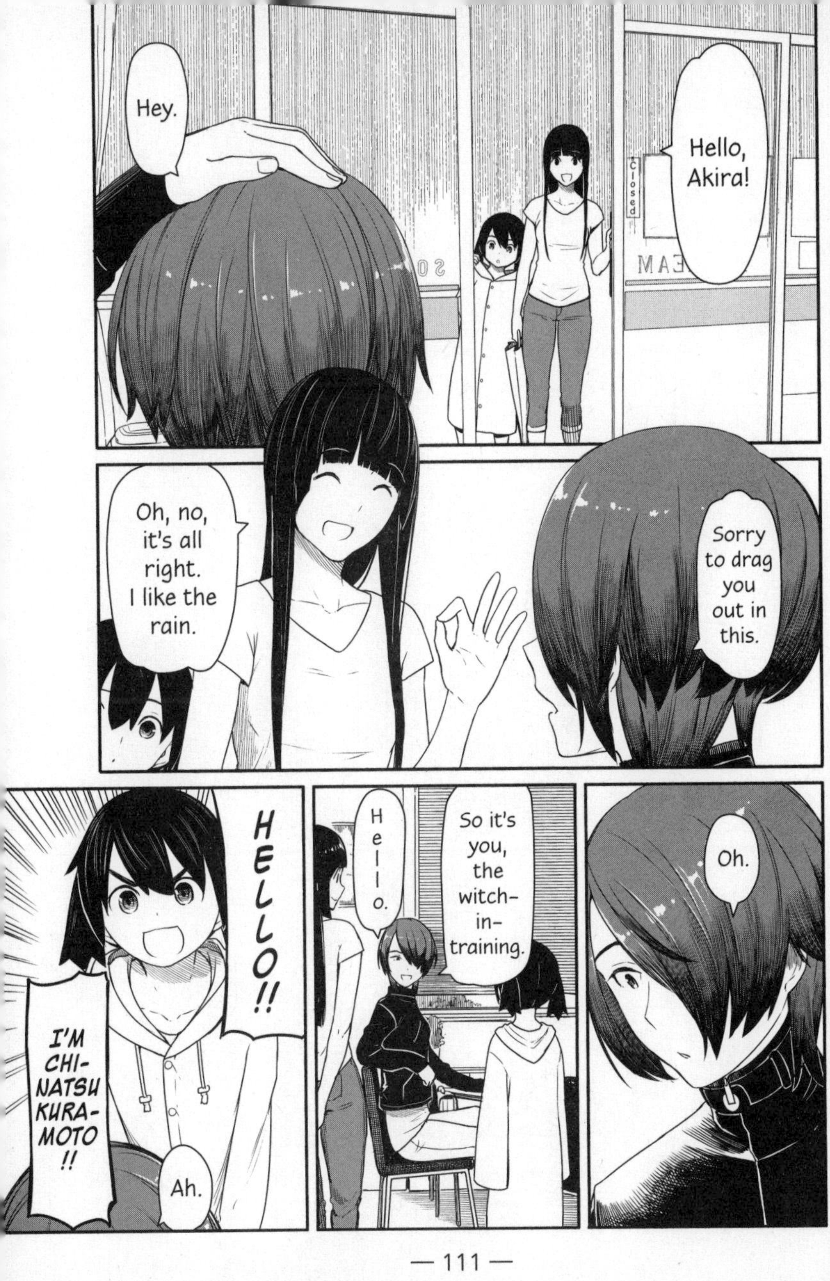
Hello, Akira!
Closed
Hey.
Sorry to drag you out in this.
Oh, no, it's all right. I like the rain.
Oh.
So it's you, the witch-in-training.
Hello.
HELLO!!
I'M CHINATSU KURAMOTO!!
Ah.

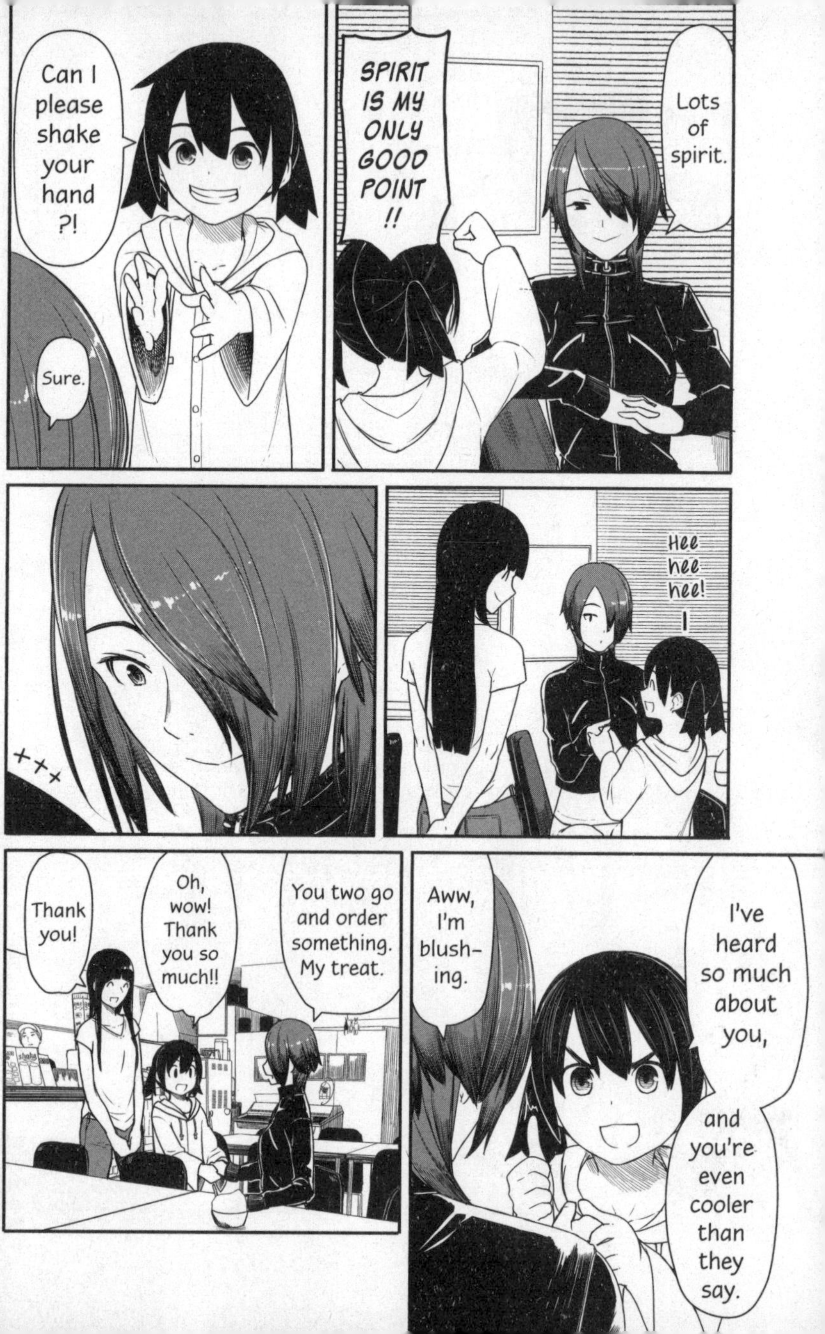
Lots of spirit.
SPIRIT IS MY ONLY GOOD POINT!!
Can I please shake your hand?!
Sure.
Hee hee hee!
I've heard so much about you,
and you're even cooler than they say.
Aww, I'm blush-ing.
You two go and order something. My treat.
Oh, wow! Thank you so much!!
Thank you!

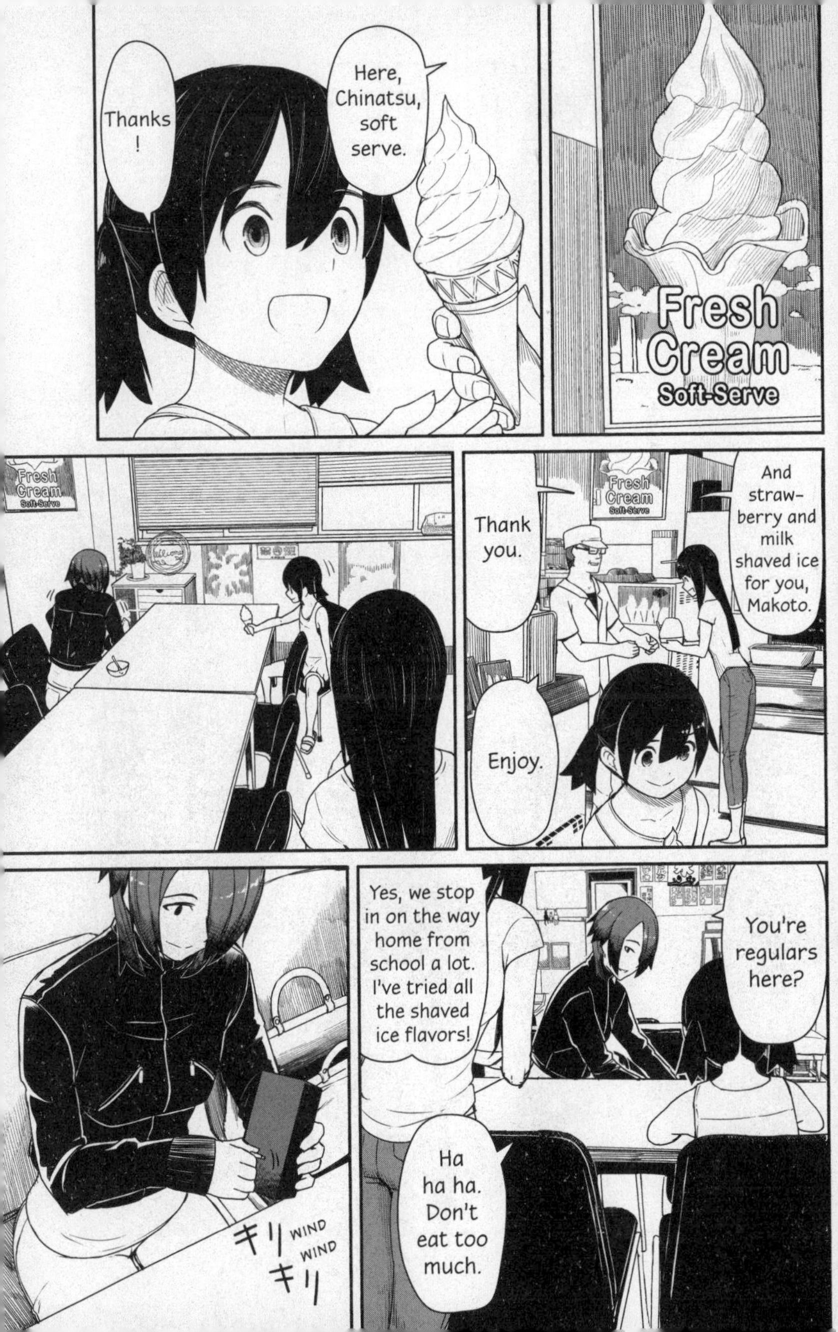
Fresh Cream
Soft-Serve
Here, Chinatsu, soft serve.
Thanks!
And strawberry and milk shaved ice for you, Makoto.
Fresh Cream
Soft-Serve
Thank you.
Enjoy.
Fresh Cream
Soft-Serve
You're regulars here?
Yes, we stop in on the way home from school a lot. I've tried all the shaved ice flavors!
Ha ha ha. Don't eat too much.
キリ WIND
キリ WIND

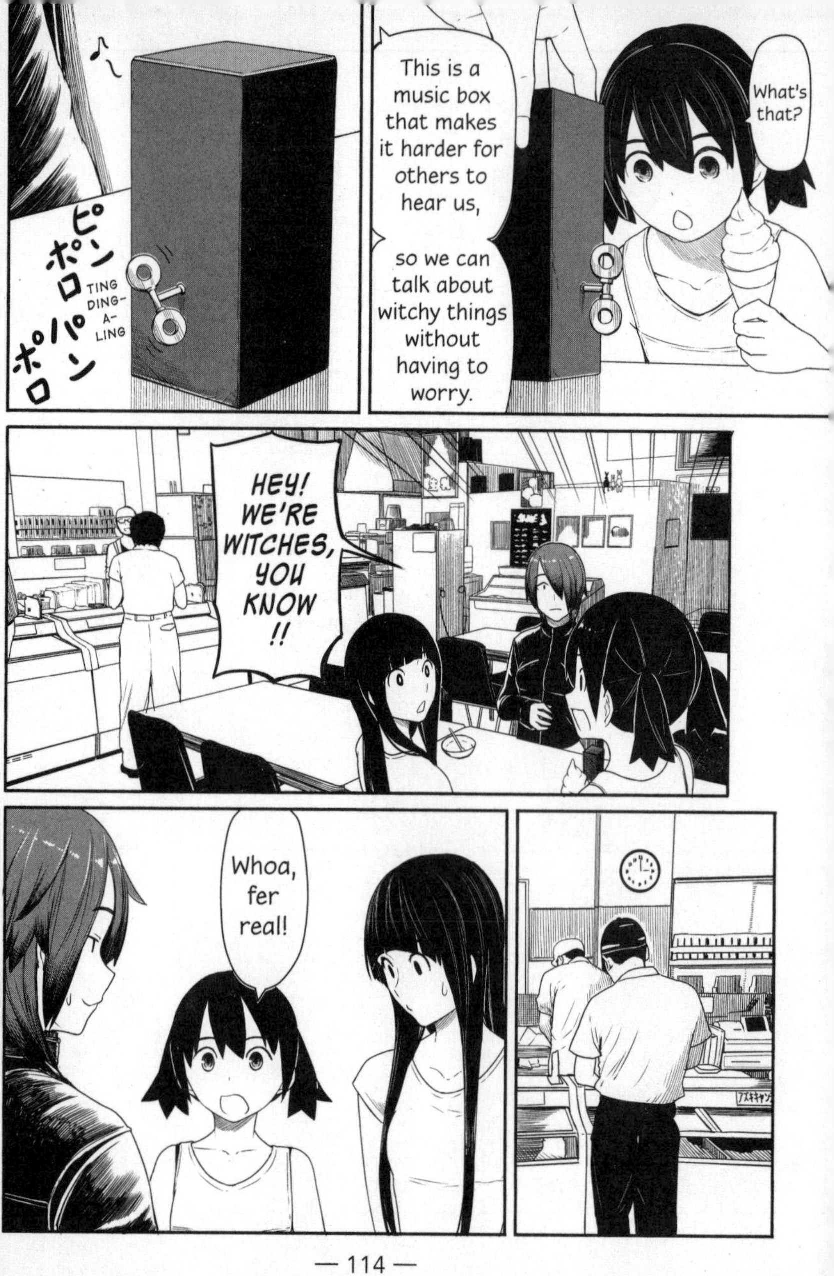
What's that?
This is a music box that makes it harder for others to hear us,
so we can talk about witchy things without having to worry.
ピン ポロ パン ポロ
TING DING-A-LING
HEY! WE'RE WITCHES, YOU KNOW!!
Whoa, fer real!

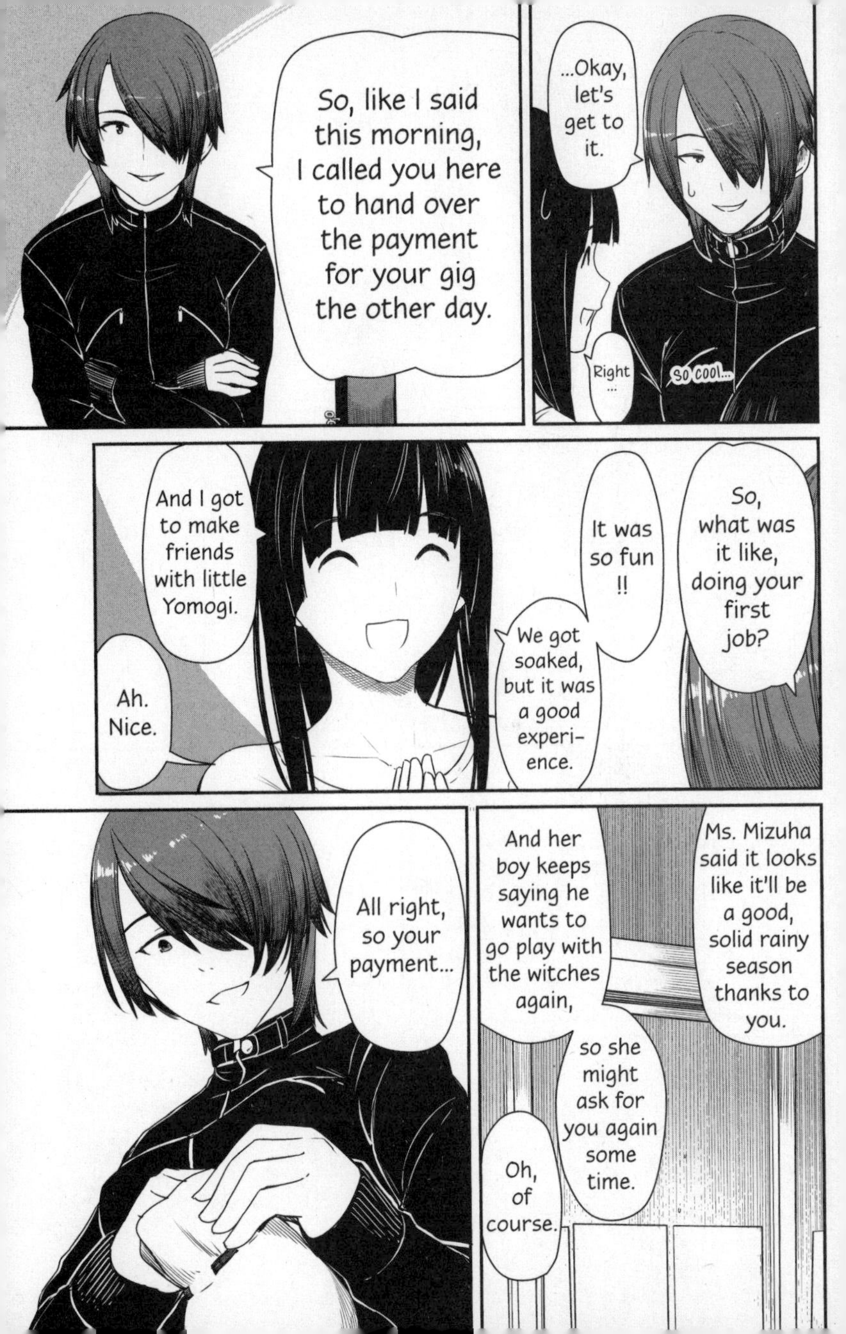
...Okay, let's get to it.
Right...
So cool...
So, like I said this morning, I called you here to hand over the payment for your gig the other day.
So, what was it like, doing your first job?
It was so fun!!
We got soaked, but it was a good experi-ence.
And I got to make friends with little Yomogi.
Ah. Nice.
Ms. Mizuha said it looks like it'll be a good, solid rainy season thanks to you.
And her boy keeps saying he wants to go play with the witches again,
so she might ask for you again some time.
Oh, of course.
All right, so your payment...

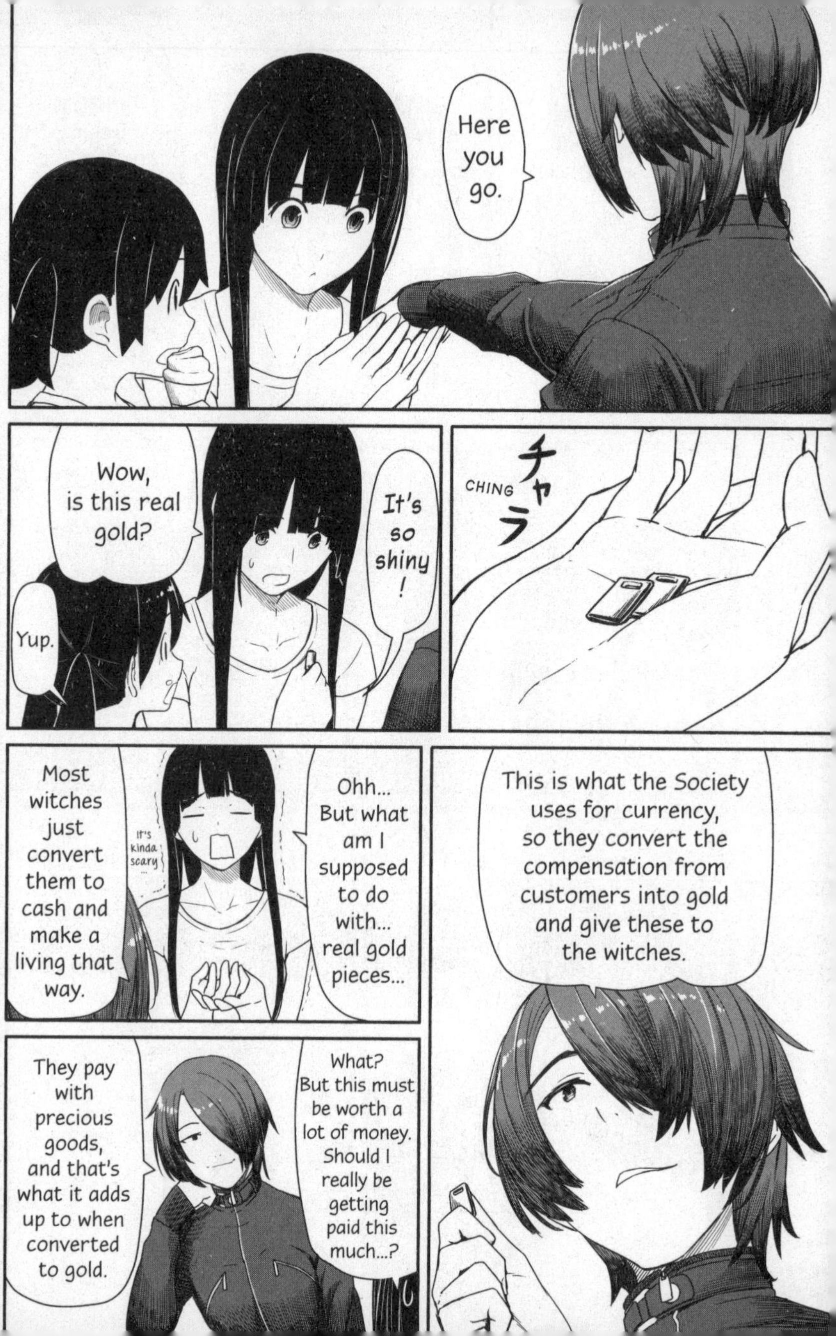
Here you go.
CHING
チャラ
Wow, is this real gold?
It's so shiny!
Yup.
This is what the Society uses for currency, so they convert the compensation from customers into gold and give these to the witches.
Ohh... But what am I supposed to do with... real gold pieces...
It's kinda scary...
Most witches just convert them to cash and make a living that way.
What? But this must be worth a lot of money. Should I really be getting paid this much...?
They pay with precious goods, and that's what it adds up to when converted to gold.

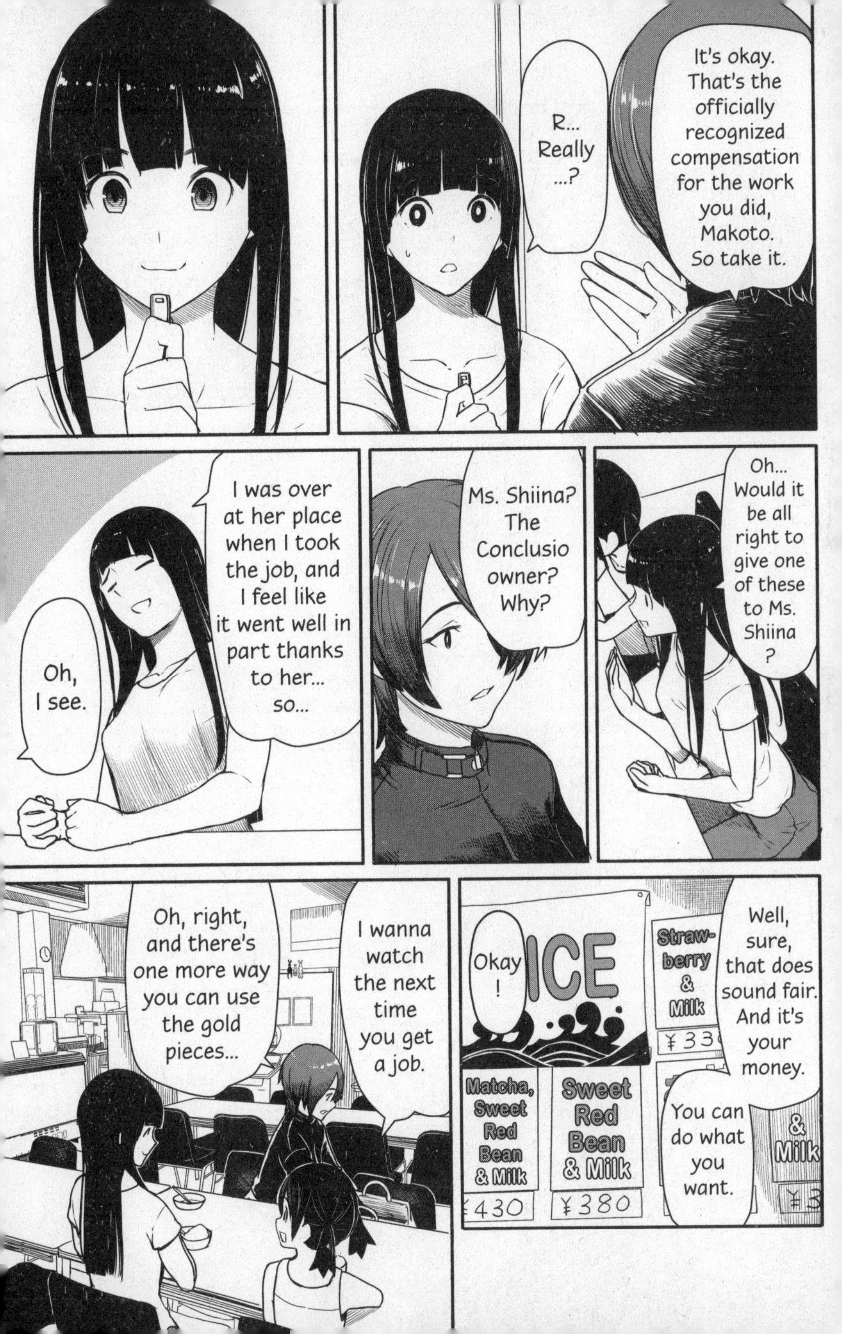
It's okay. That's the officially recognized compensation for the work you did, Makoto. So take it.
R... Really ...?
Oh... Would it be all right to give one of these to Ms. Shiina ?
Ms. Shiina? The Conclusio owner? Why?
I was over at her place when I took the job, and I feel like it went well in part thanks to her... so...
Oh, I see.
Well, sure, that does sound fair. And it's your money.
You can do what you want.
Okay !
ICE
Straw-berry & Milk
Sweet Red Bean & Milk
¥380
Matcha, Sweet Red Bean & Milk
¥430
& Milk
I wanna watch the next time you get a job.
Oh, right, and there's one more way you can use the gold pieces...

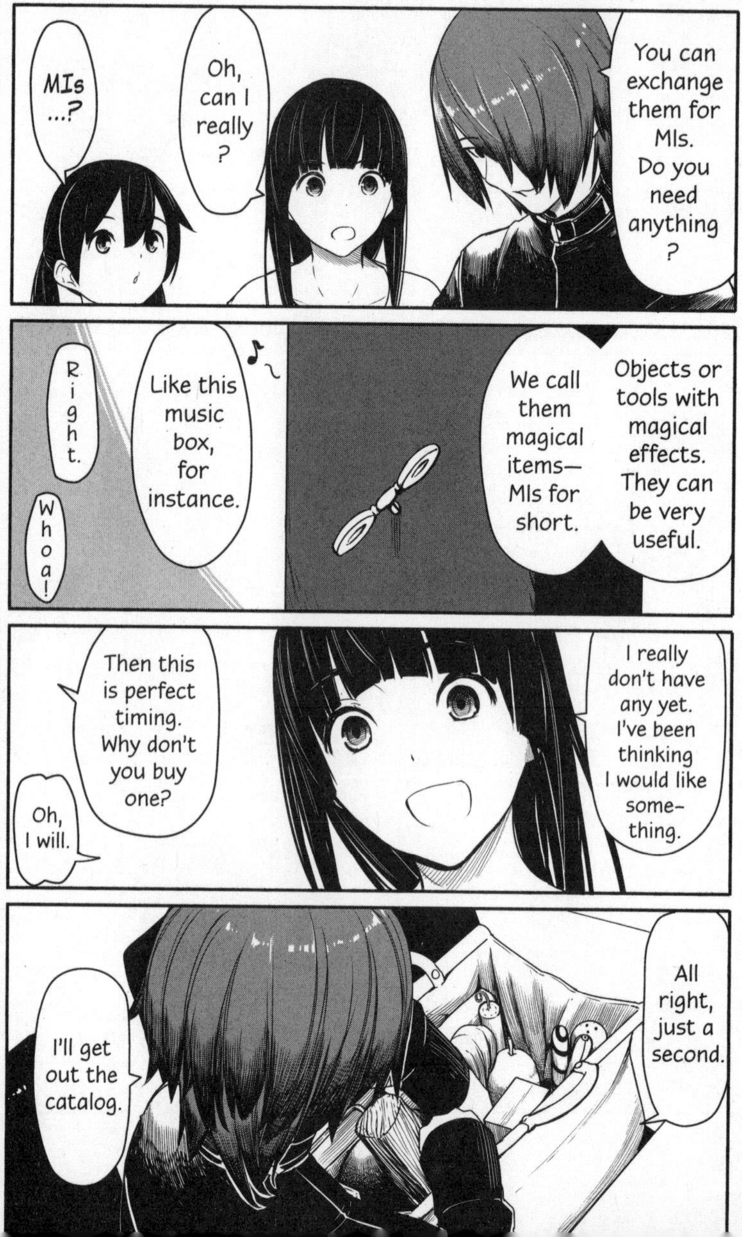
You can exchange them for MIs. Do you need anything?
Oh, can I really?
MIs ...?
Objects or tools with magical effects. They can be very useful.
We call them magical items—MIs for short.
Like this music box, for instance.
Right.
Whoa!
I really don't have any yet. I've been thinking I would like some-thing.
Then this is perfect timing. Why don't you buy one?
Oh, I will.
All right, just a second.
I'll get out the catalog.

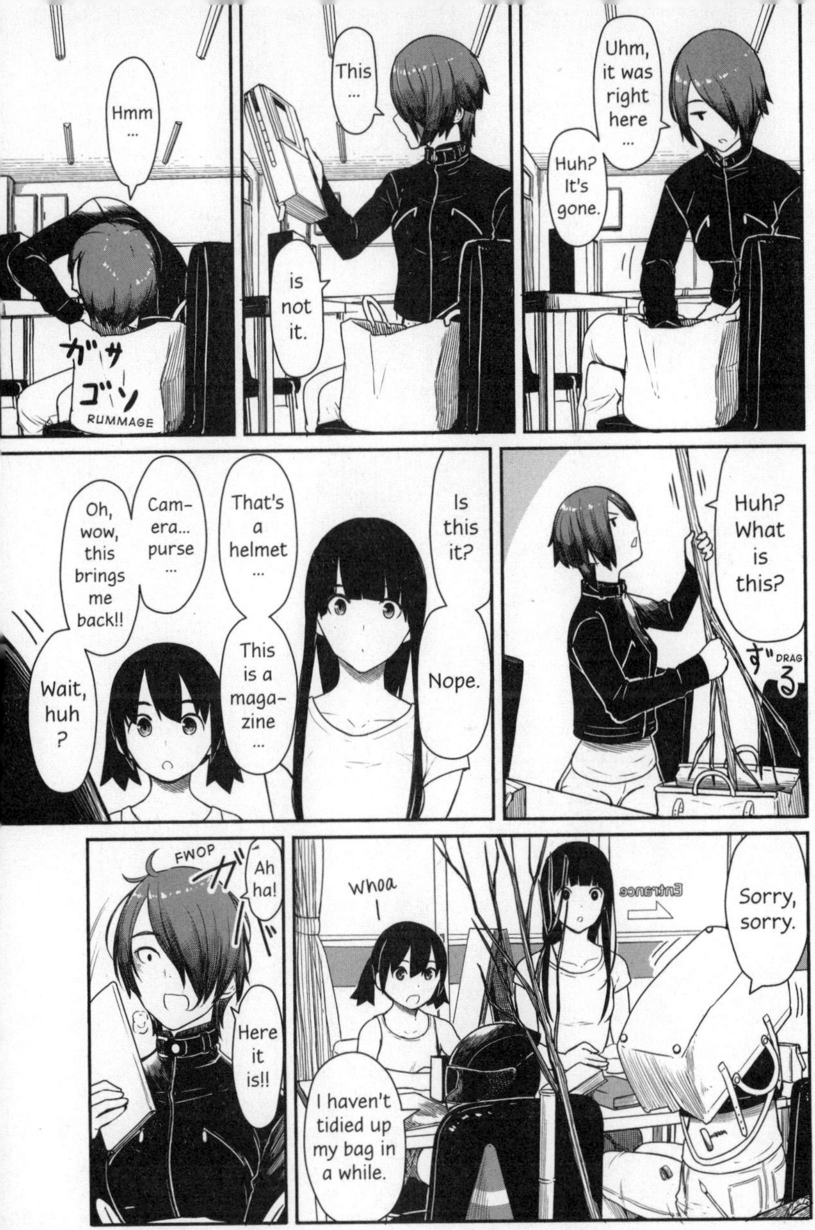
Uhm, it was right here ...
Huh? It's gone.
This ...
is not it.
Hmm ...
ガサ ゴソ
RUMMAGE
Huh? What is this?
ずる
DRAG
Is this it?
Nope.
That's a helmet ...
This is a magazine ...
Cam-era... purse ...
Oh, wow, this brings me back!!
Wait, huh ?
Sorry, sorry.
Whoa !
I haven't tidied up my bag in a while.
Ah ha!
ガ
FWOP
Here it is!!

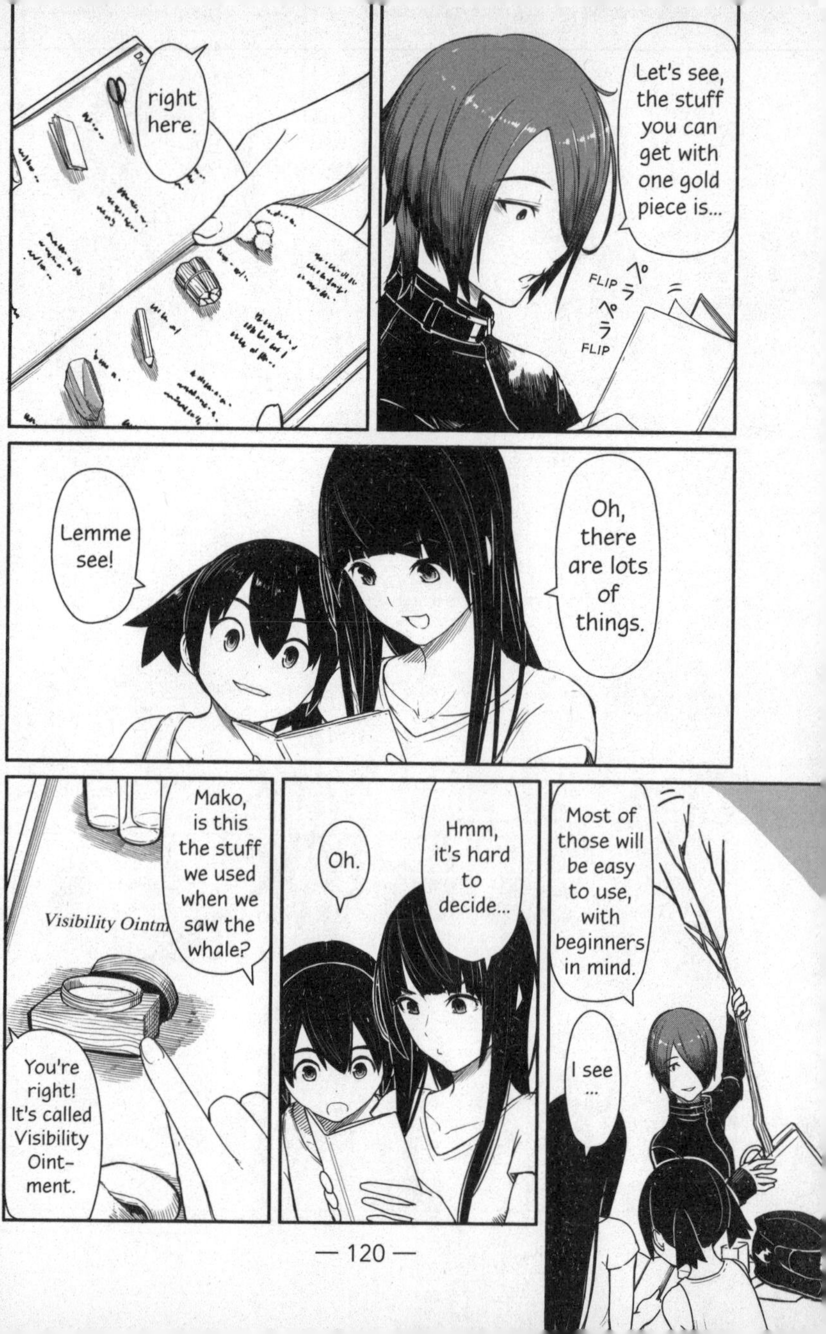
Let's see, the stuff you can get with one gold piece is...
ペラ FLIP
ペラ FLIP
right here.
Oh, there are lots of things.
Lemme see!
Most of those will be easy to use, with beginners in mind.
I see ...
Hmm, it's hard to decide...
Oh.
Mako, is this the stuff we used when we saw the whale?
Visibility Ointm
You're right! It's called Visibility Oint-ment.

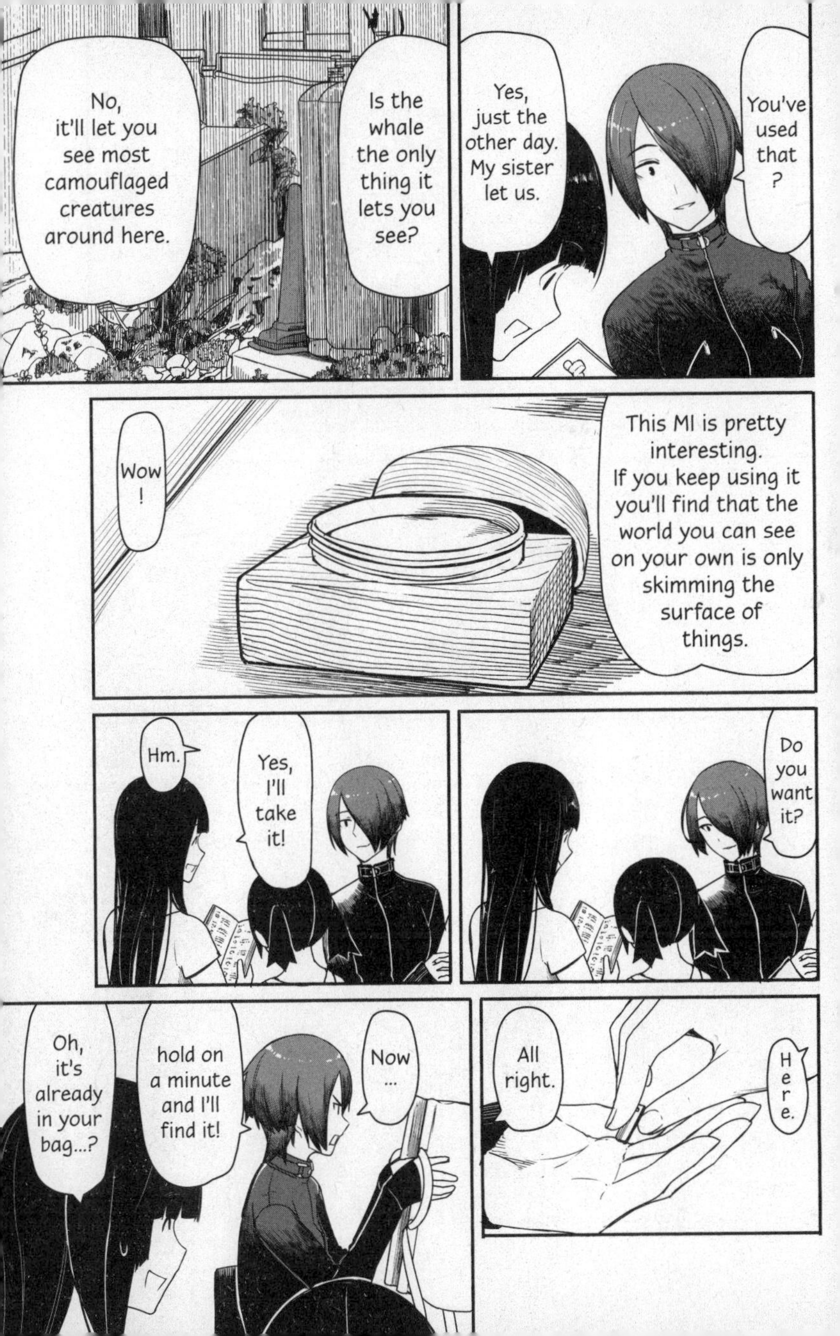
You've used that?
Yes, just the other day. My sister let us.
Is the whale the only thing it lets you see?
No, it'll let you see most camouflaged creatures around here.
This MI is pretty interesting. If you keep using it you'll find that the world you can see on your own is only skimming the surface of things.
Wow!
Do you want it?
Yes, I'll take it!
Hm.
Here.
All right.
Now...
hold on a minute and I'll find it!
Oh, it's already in your bag...?

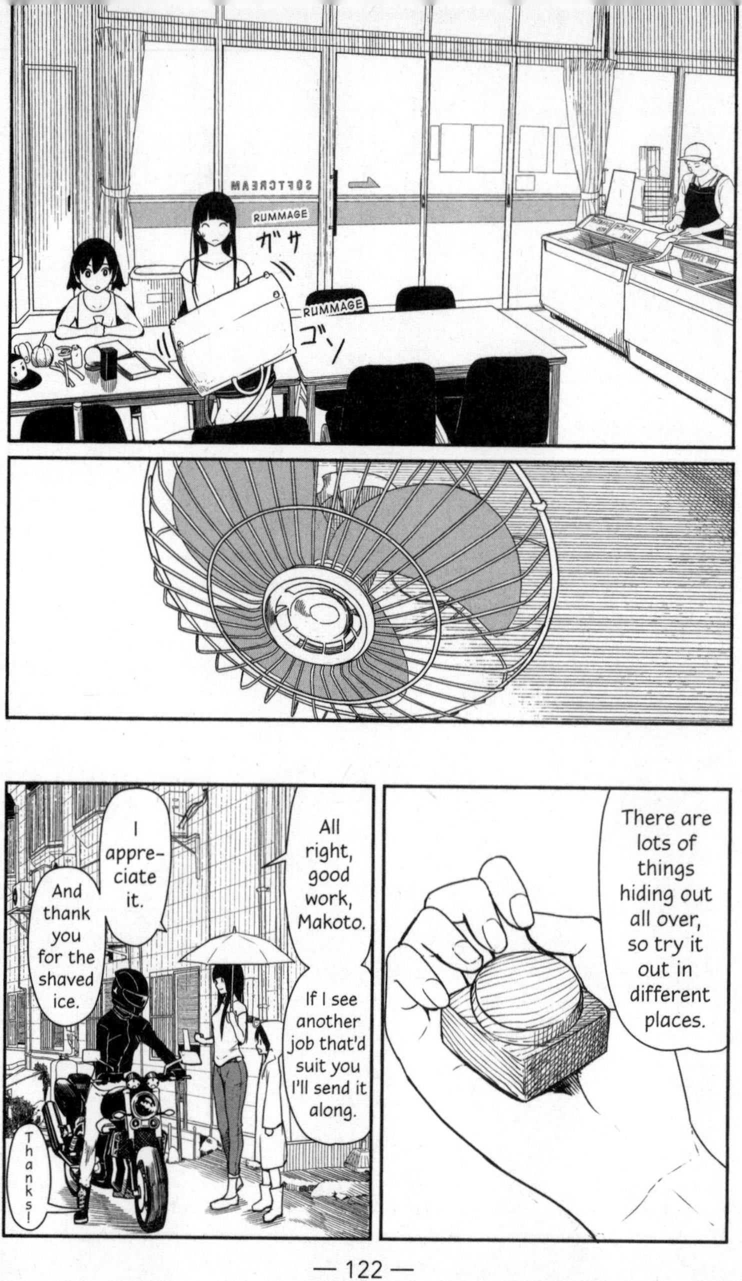
RUMMAGE
ガサ
RUMMAGE
ゴソ
There are lots of things hiding out all over, so try it out in different places.
All right, good work, Makoto.
If I see another job that'd suit you I'll send it along.
I appreciate it.
And thank you for the shaved ice.
Thanks!

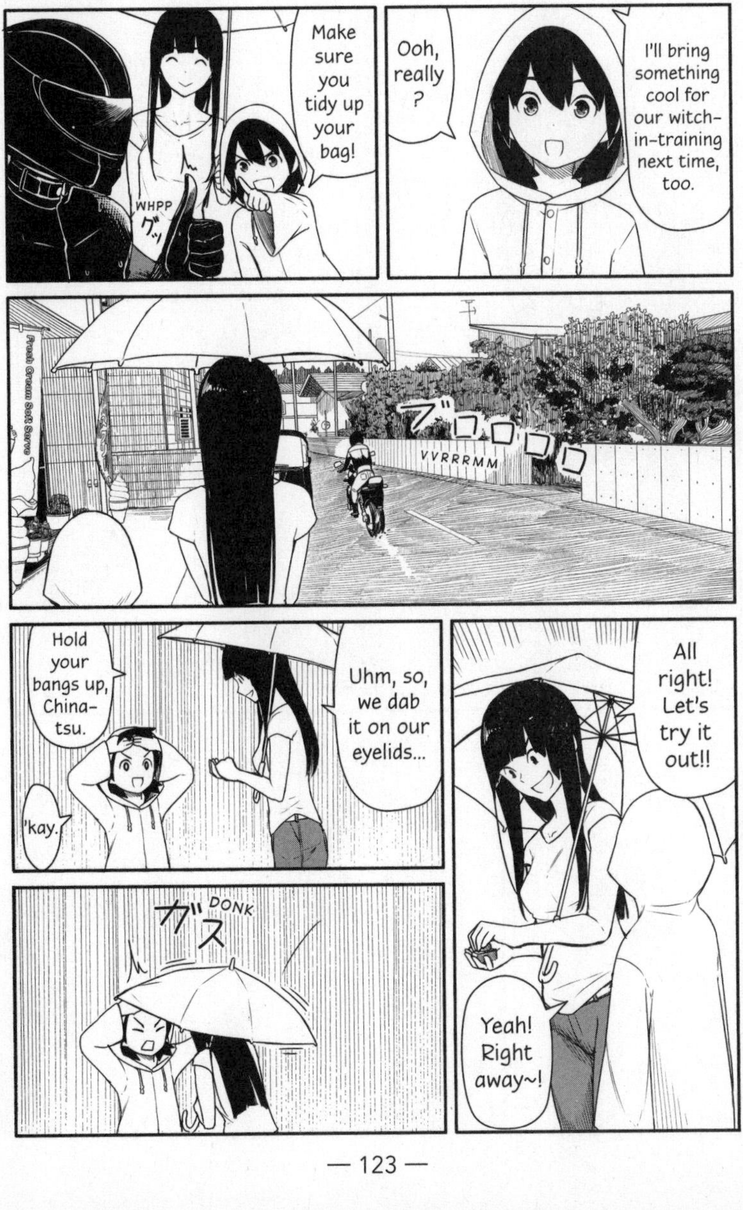
I'll bring something cool for our witch-in-training next time, too.
Ooh, really?
Make sure you tidy up your bag!
WHPP
グッ
ブロロロロ
VVRRRMM
Fresh Cream Soft Serve
All right! Let's try it out!!
Yeah! Right away~!
Uhm, so, we dab it on our eyelids...
Hold your bangs up, China-tsu.
'kay.
ガス
DONK

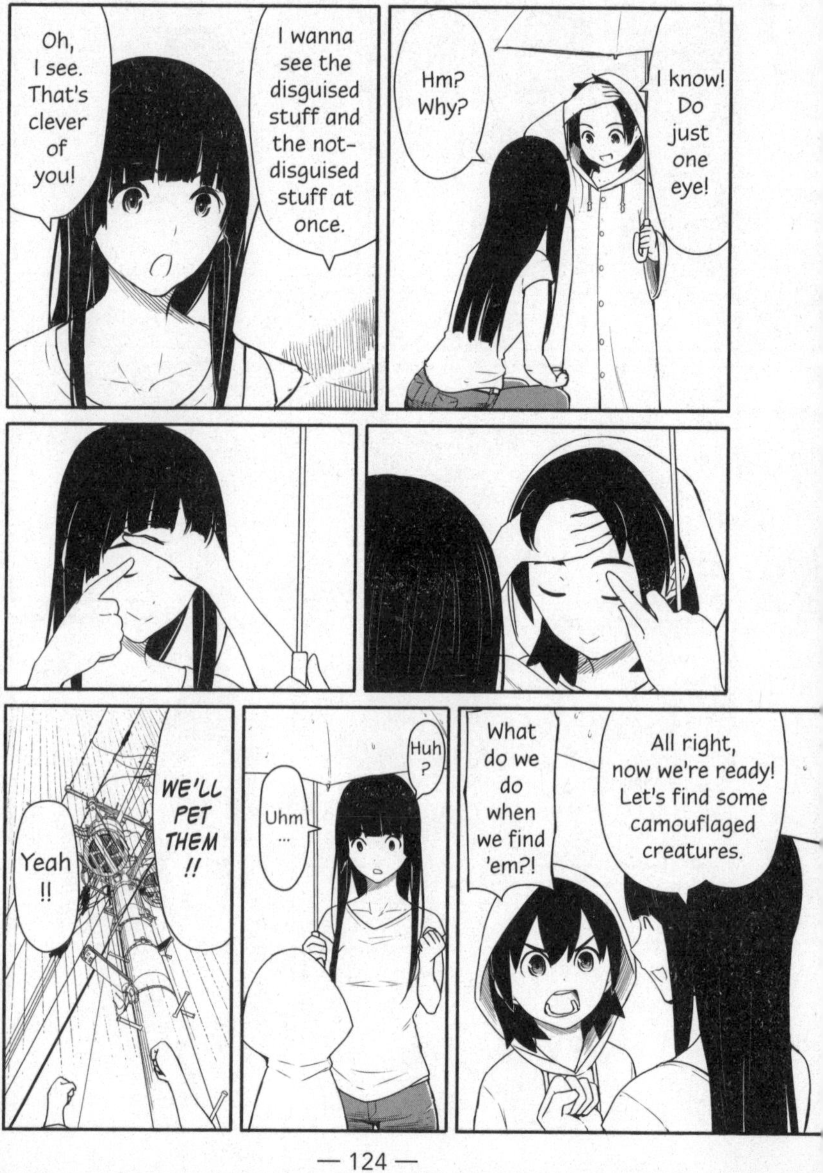
I know! Do just one eye!
Hm? Why?
I wanna see the disguised stuff and the not-disguised stuff at once.
Oh, I see. That's clever of you!
All right, now we're ready! Let's find some camouflaged creatures.
What do we do when we find 'em?!
Huh?
Uhm ...
WE'LL PET THEM!!
Yeah!!

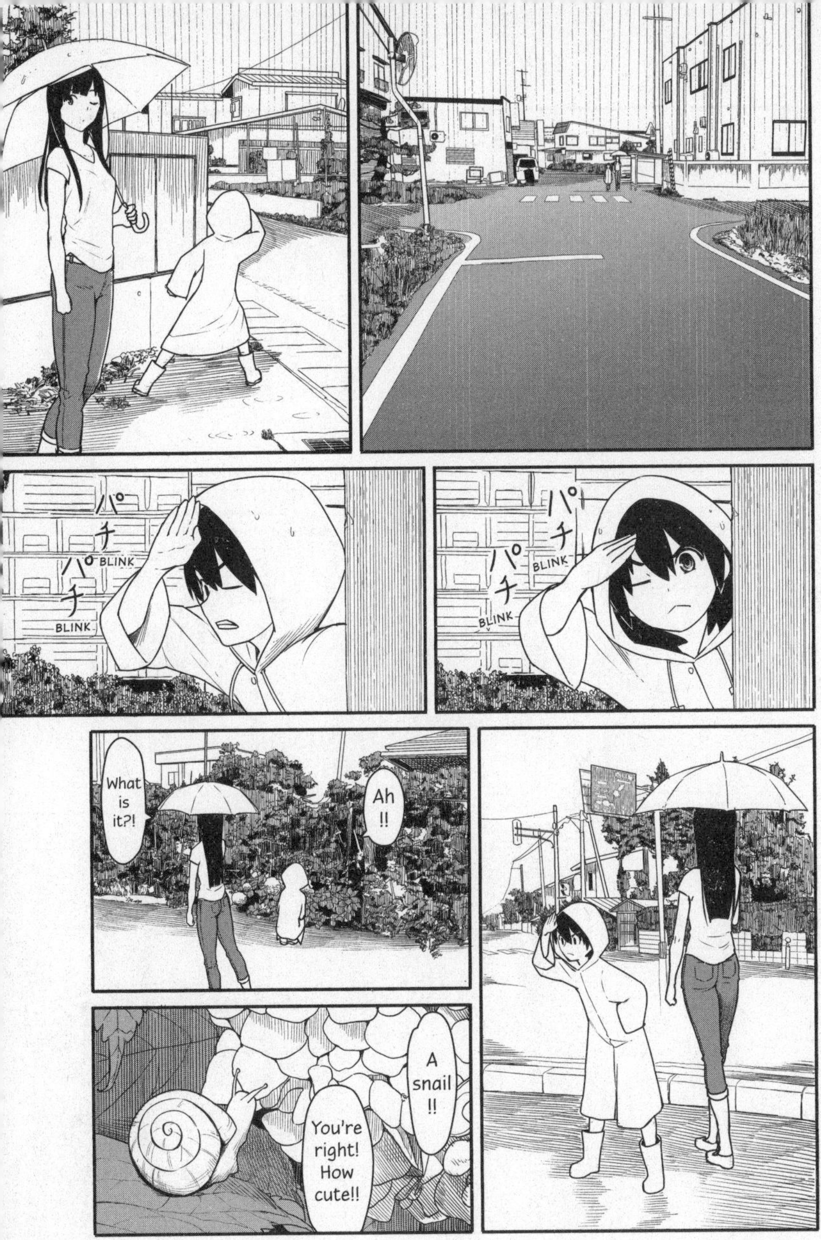
パチ
BLINK
パチ
BLINK
パチ
BLINK
パチ
BLINK
Ah !!
What is it?!
A snail !!
You're right! How cute!!

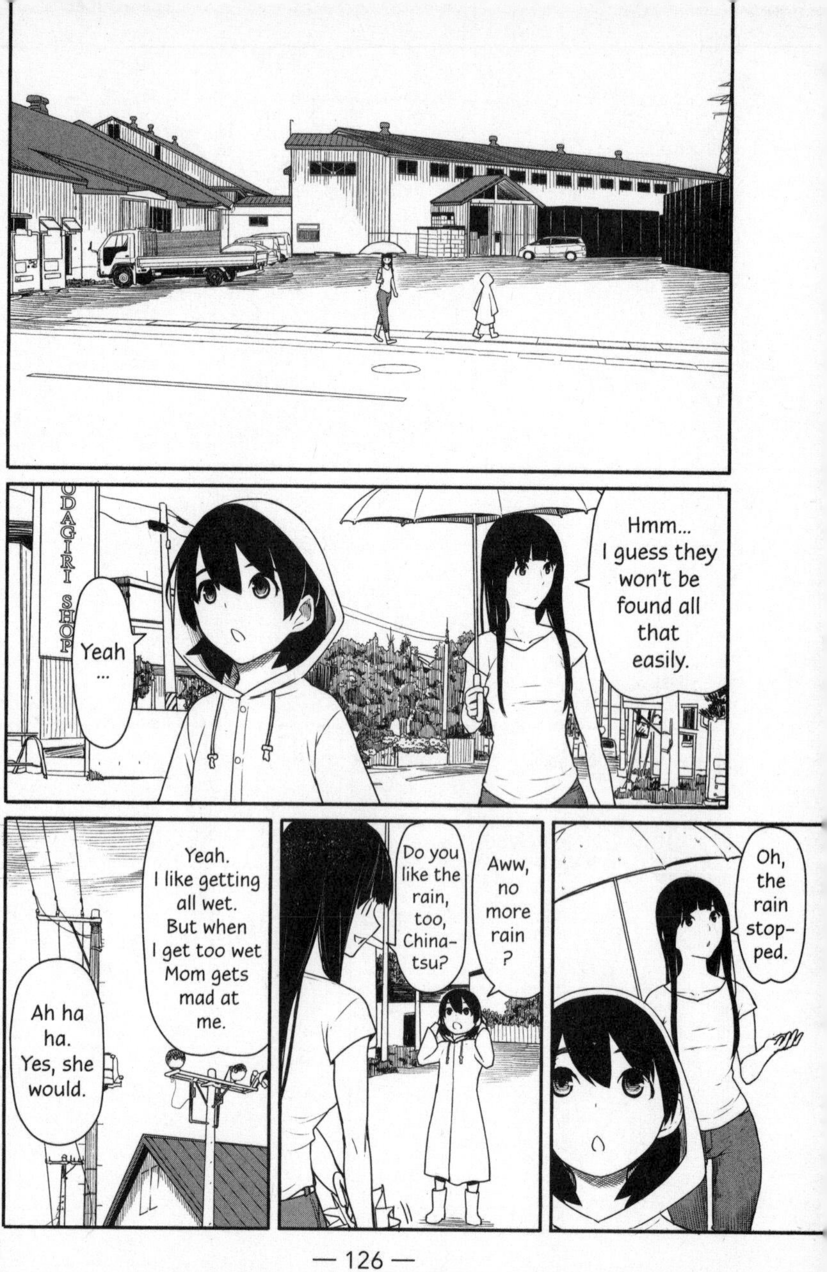
Hmm... I guess they won't be found all that easily.
Yeah ...
ODAGIRI SHOP
Oh, the rain stop-ped.
Aww, no more rain?
Do you like the rain, too, China-tsu?
Yeah. I like getting all wet. But when I get too wet Mom gets mad at me.
Ah ha ha. Yes, she would.

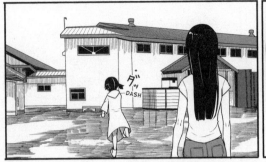

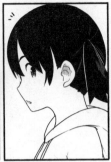

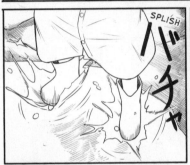

ダッ
DASH
SPLISH
バチャ
Ha ha ha! I'm king of this pond!
パチャ
SPLASH
パチャ
SPLASH
What are you doing?
There're always really big puddles around here to jump in.
It's a good spot.
Oh, they are big!

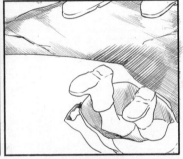

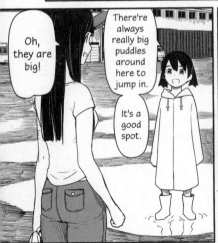

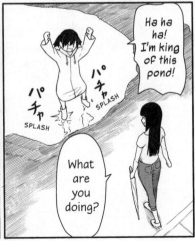

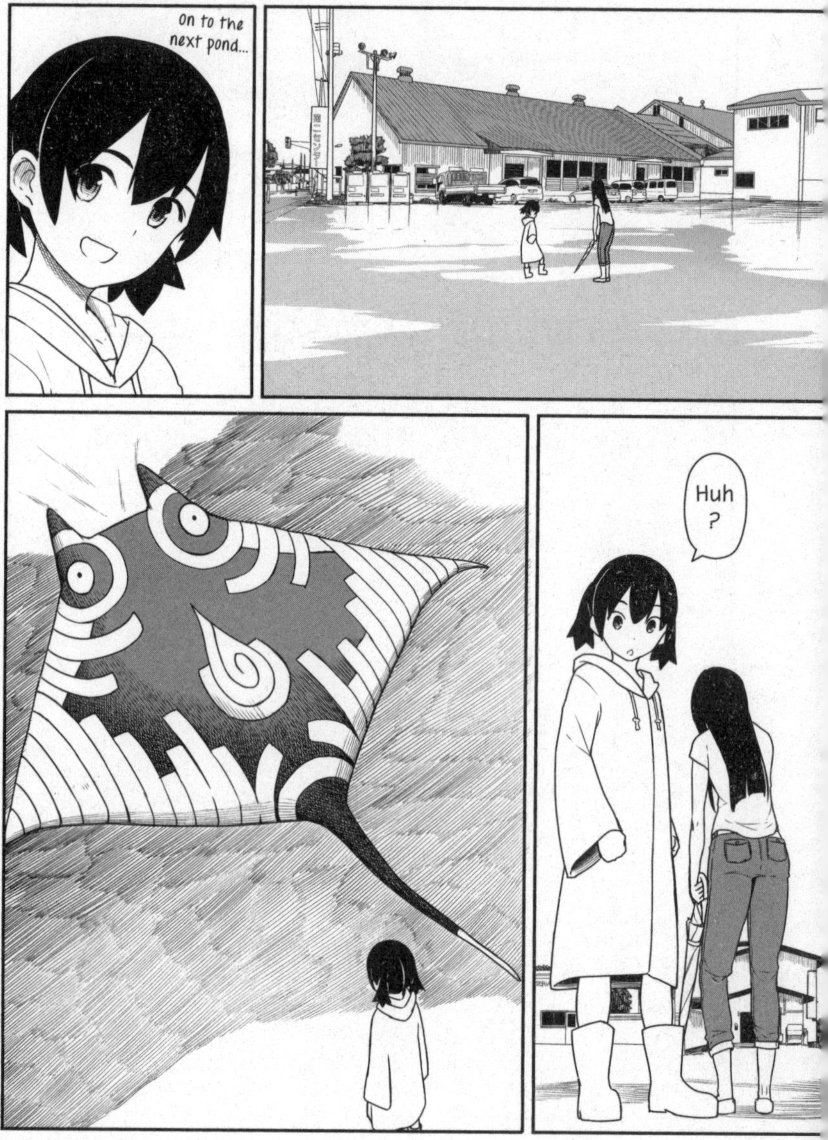
on to the next pond...
Huh ?

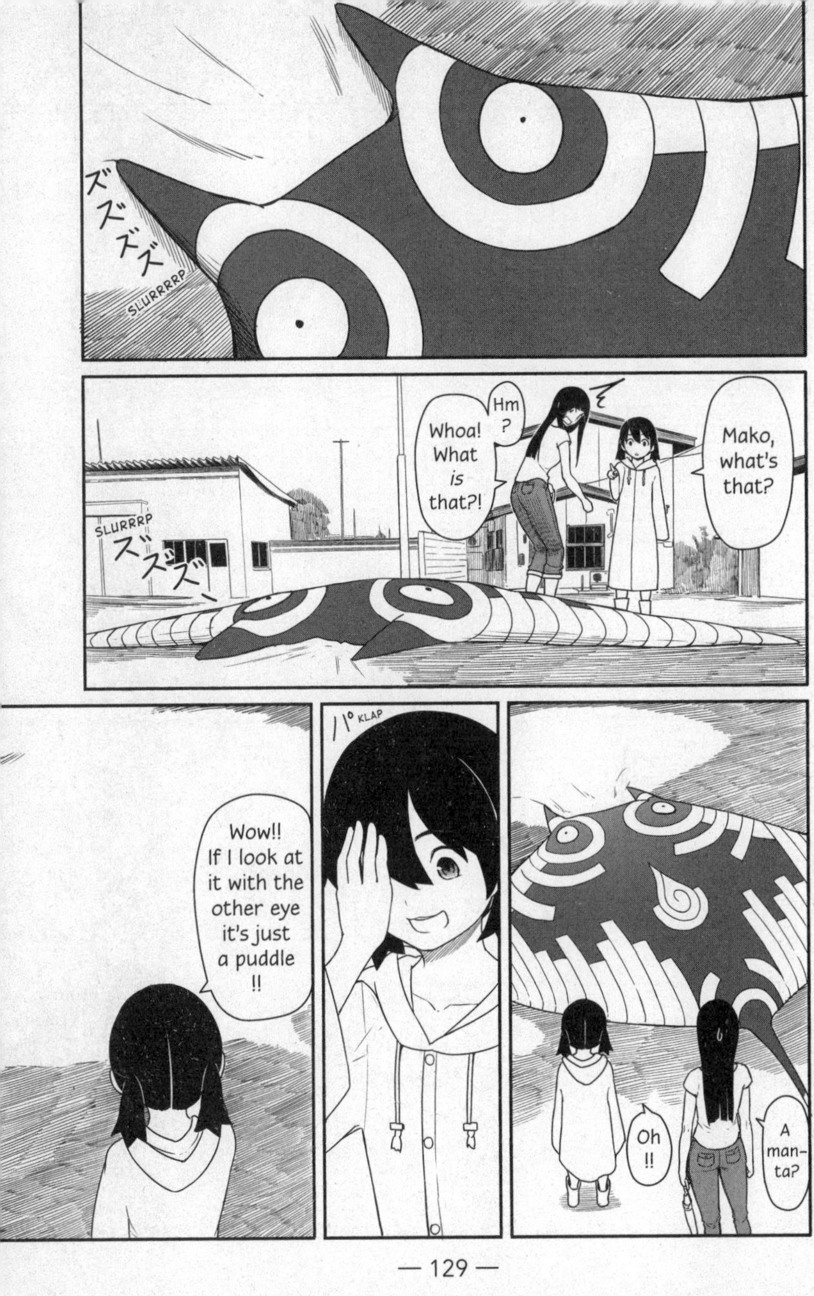
ズズズズ
SLURRRRP
Mako, what's that?
Hm ?
Whoa! What is that?!
SLURRRP
ズズズ
A man-ta?
Oh !!
パ
KLAP
Wow!! If I look at it with the other eye it's just a puddle !!

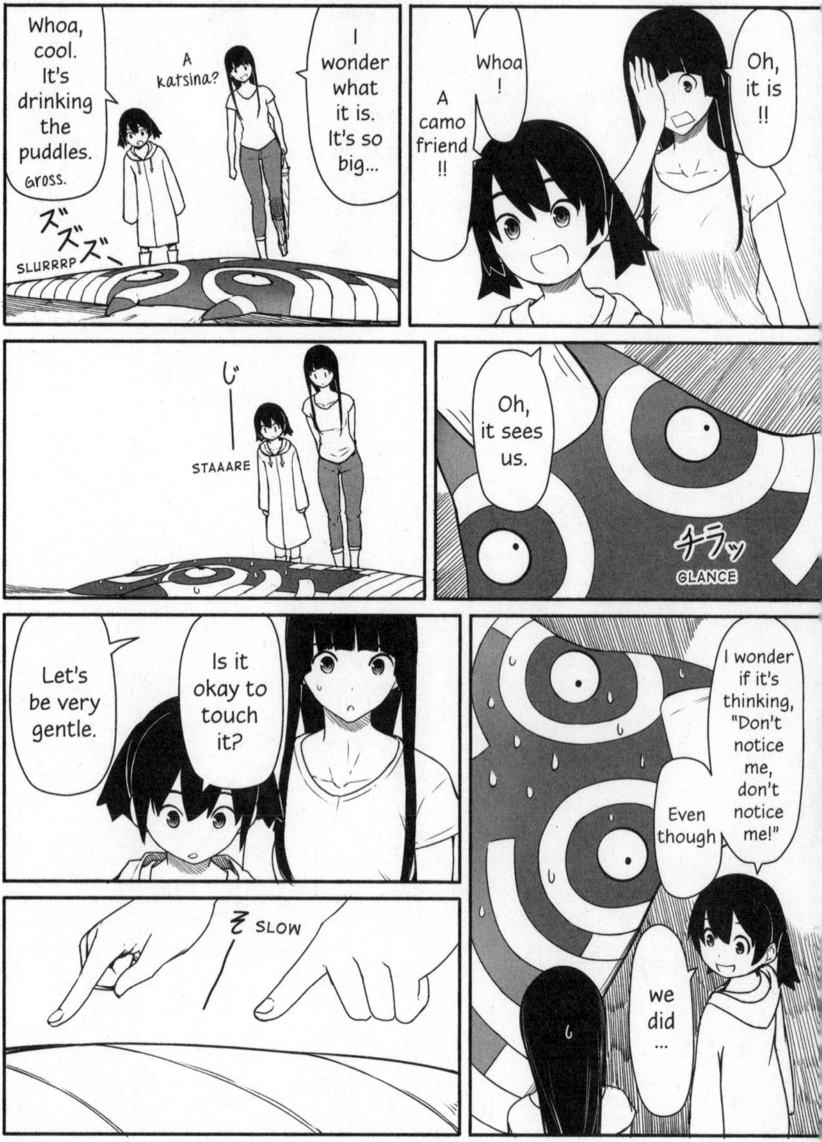
Oh, it is !!
Whoa !
A camo friend !!
I wonder what it is. It's so big...
A katsina?
Whoa, cool. It's drinking the puddles.
Gross.
ズズズ
SLURRRP
Oh, it sees us.
チラッ
GLANCE
じー
STAAARE
I wonder if it's thinking, "Don't notice me, don't notice me!"
Even though
we did ...
Is it okay to touch it?
Let's be very gentle.
ぞ
SLOW

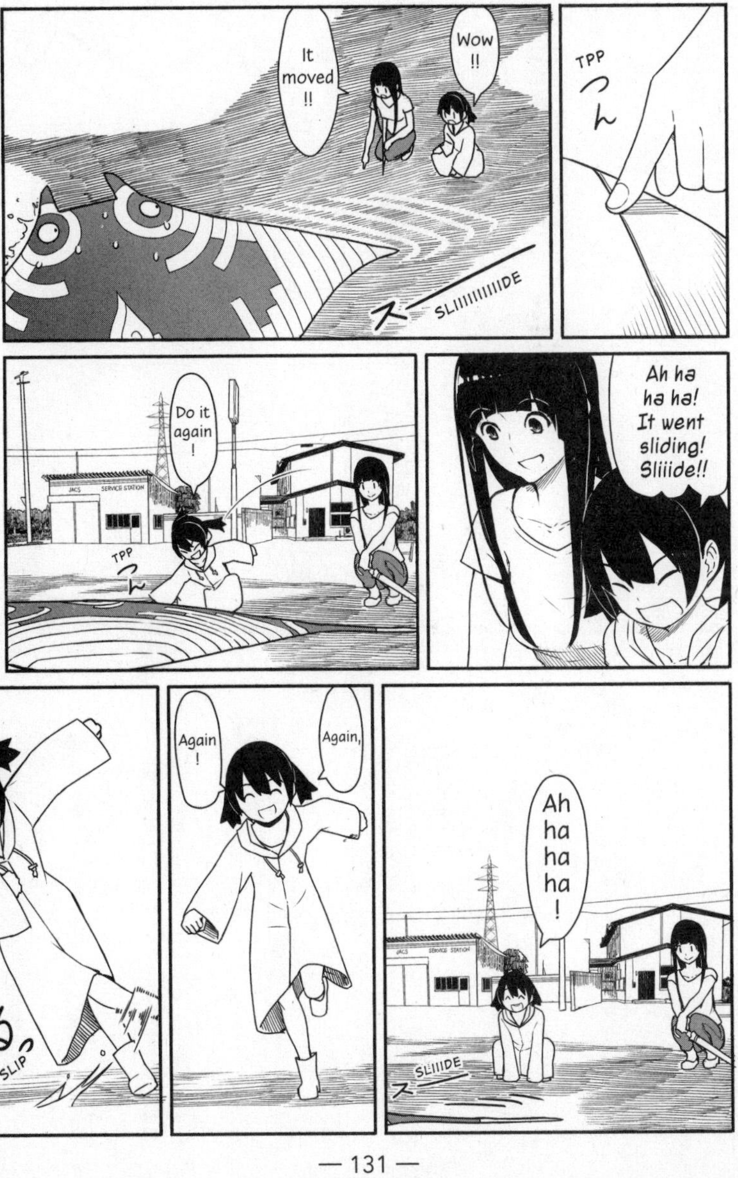

TPP
つん
Wow!!
It moved!!
ス
SLIIIIIIIIIDE
Ah ha ha ha! It went sliding! Sliiide!!
Do it again!
JACS SERVICE STATION
TPP
つん
Ah ha ha ha!
JACS SERVICE STATION
ス
SLIIIDE
Again,
Again!
ずるっ
SLIP

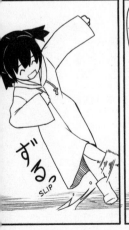

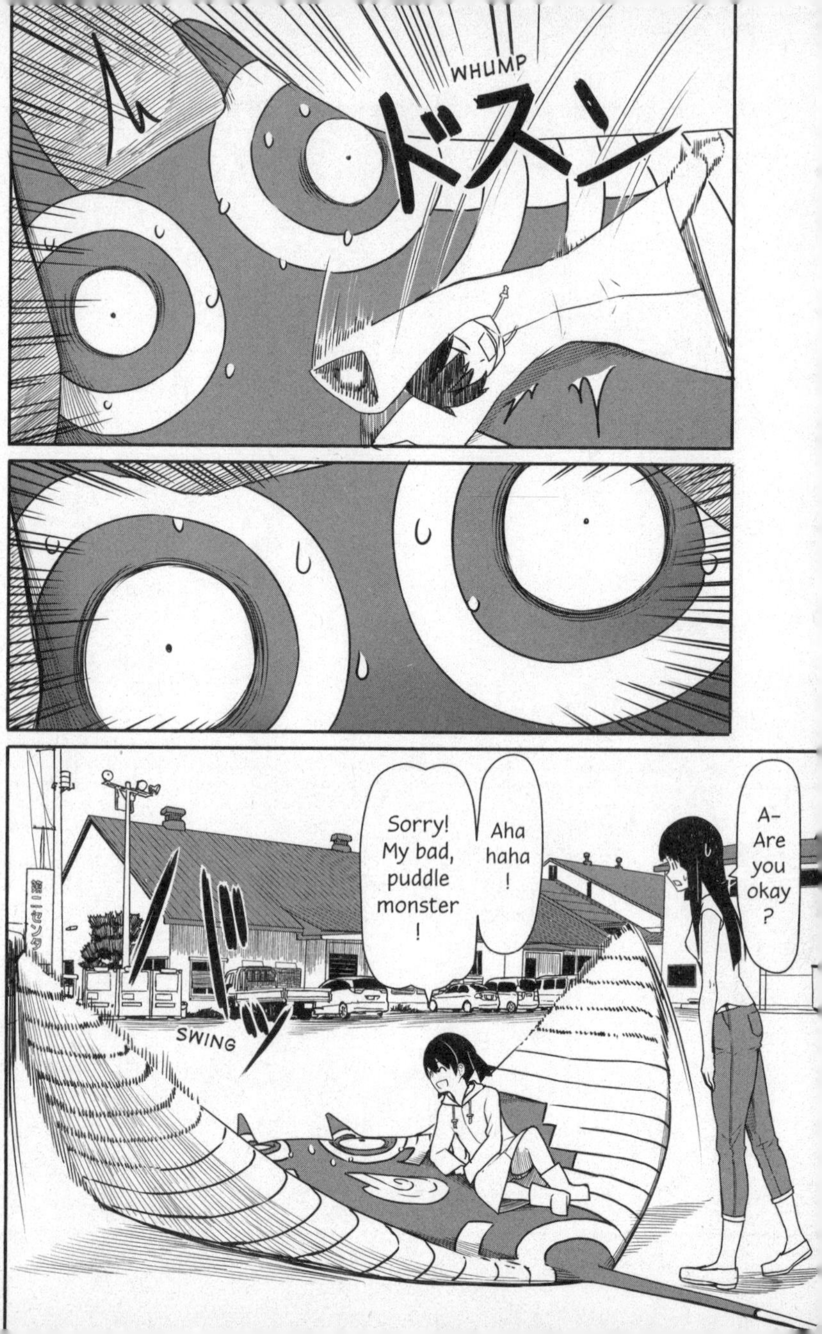
WHUMP
ドスン
A– Are you okay?
Aha haha!
Sorry! My bad, puddle monster!
SWING

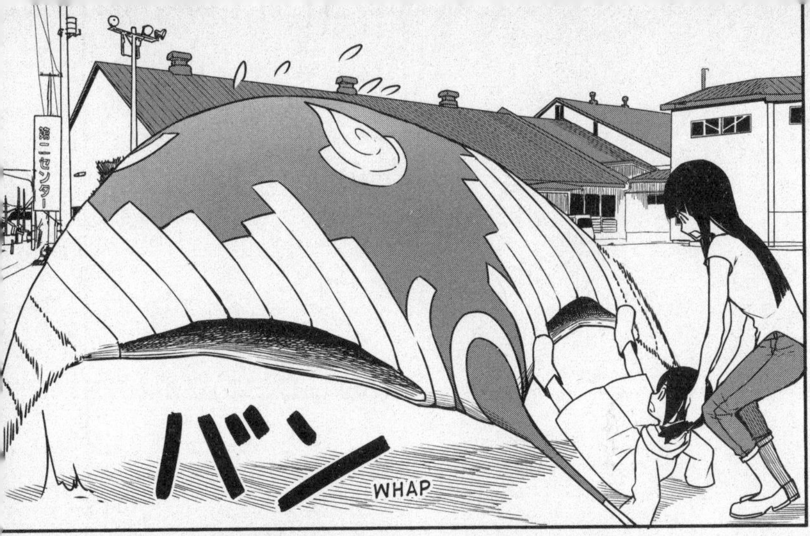
第二センター
バンッ
WHAP
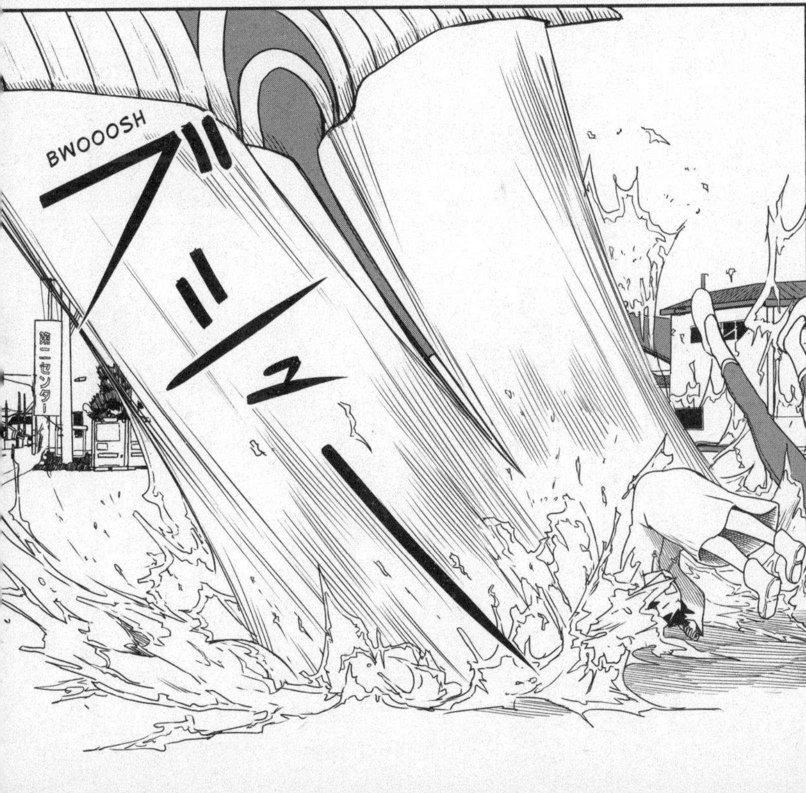
BWOOOSH
ブシュー
第二センター

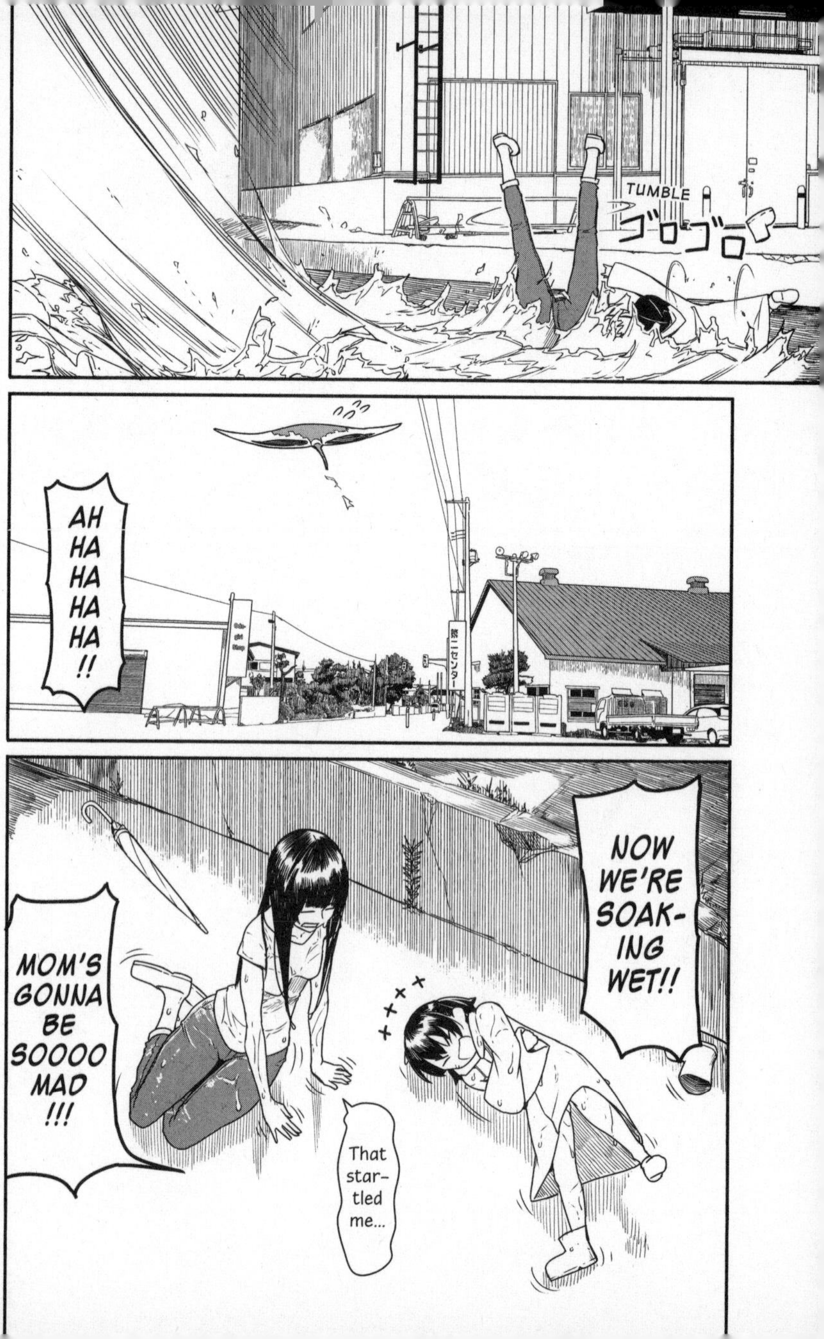
TUMBLE
ゴロゴロ
AH HA HA HA HA!!
NOW WE'RE SOAK-ING WET!!
MOM'S GONNA BE SOOOO MAD!!!
That star-tled me...

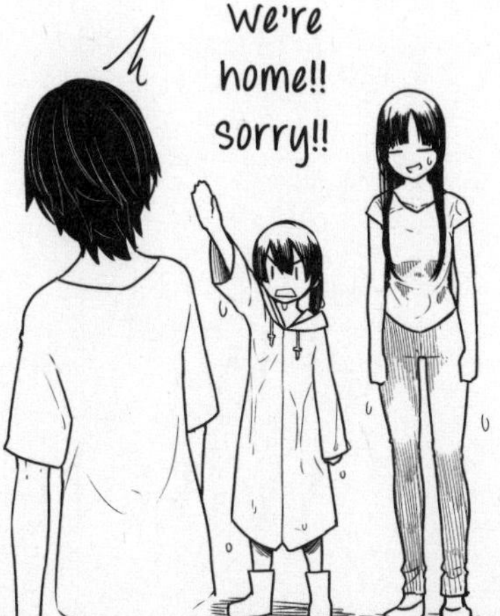
We're home!! sorry!!

Flying Witch

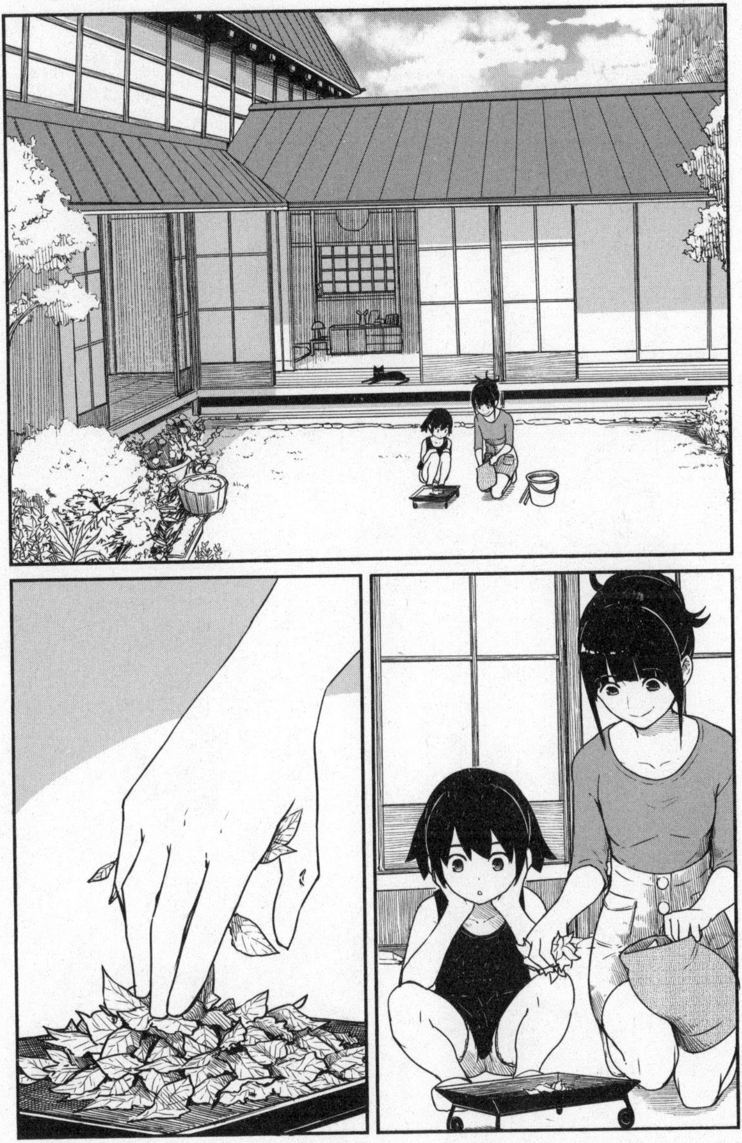

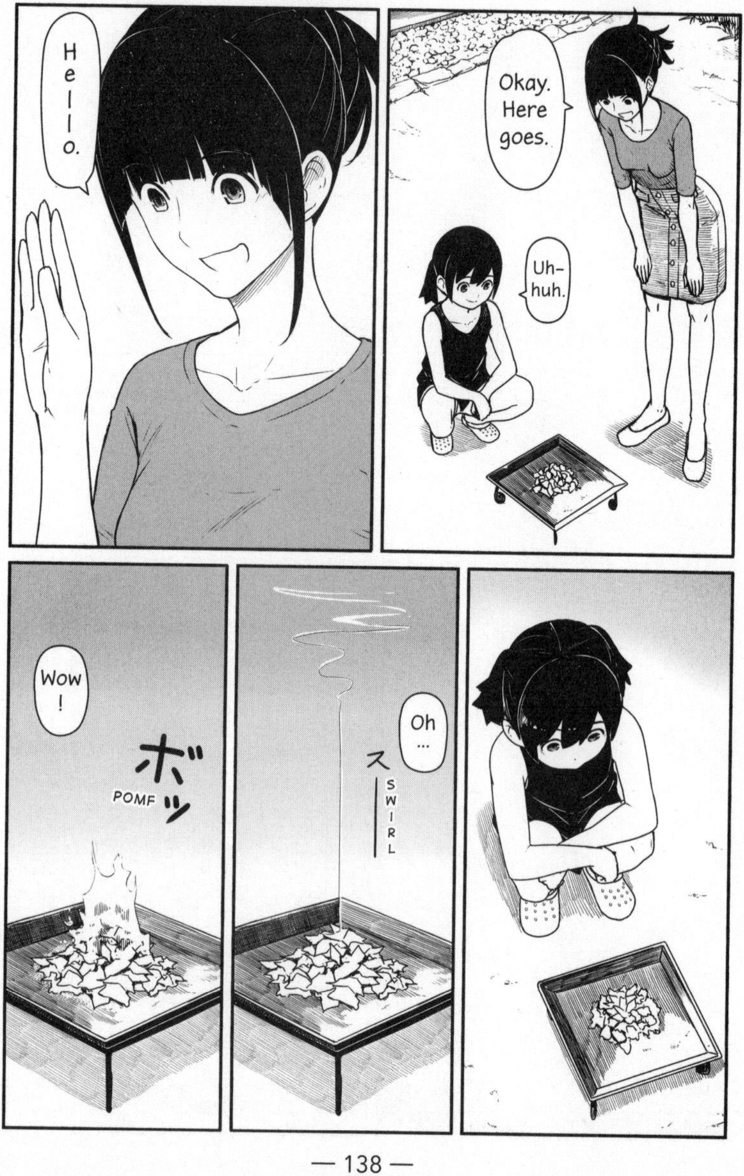

Okay. Here goes.
Uh-huh.
Hello.
Oh ...
ス
SWIRL
Wow!
ボッ
POMF

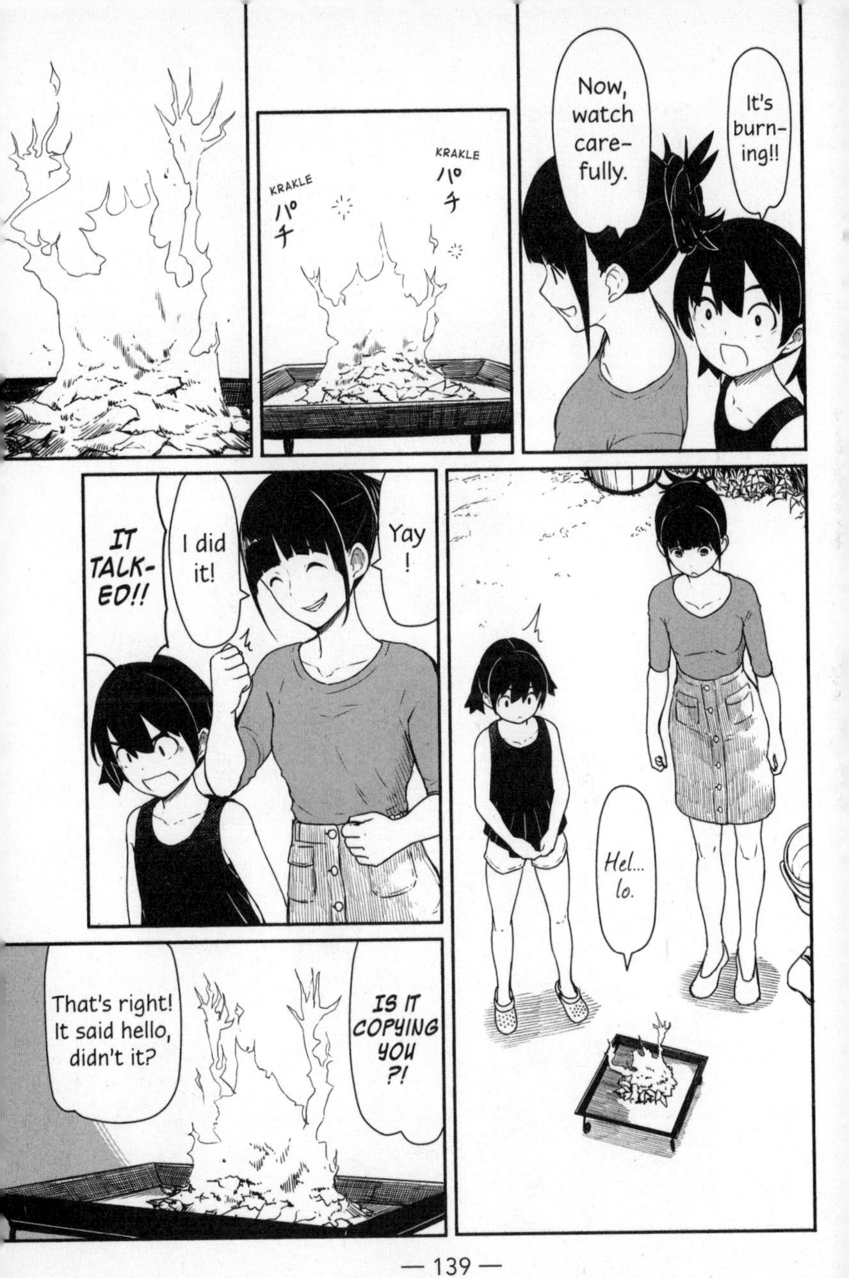
It's burn-ing!!
Now, watch care-fully.
KRAKLE パチ
KRAKLE パチ
Hel... lo.
Yay!
I did it!
IT TALK-ED!!
IS IT COPYING YOU?!
That's right! It said hello, didn't it?

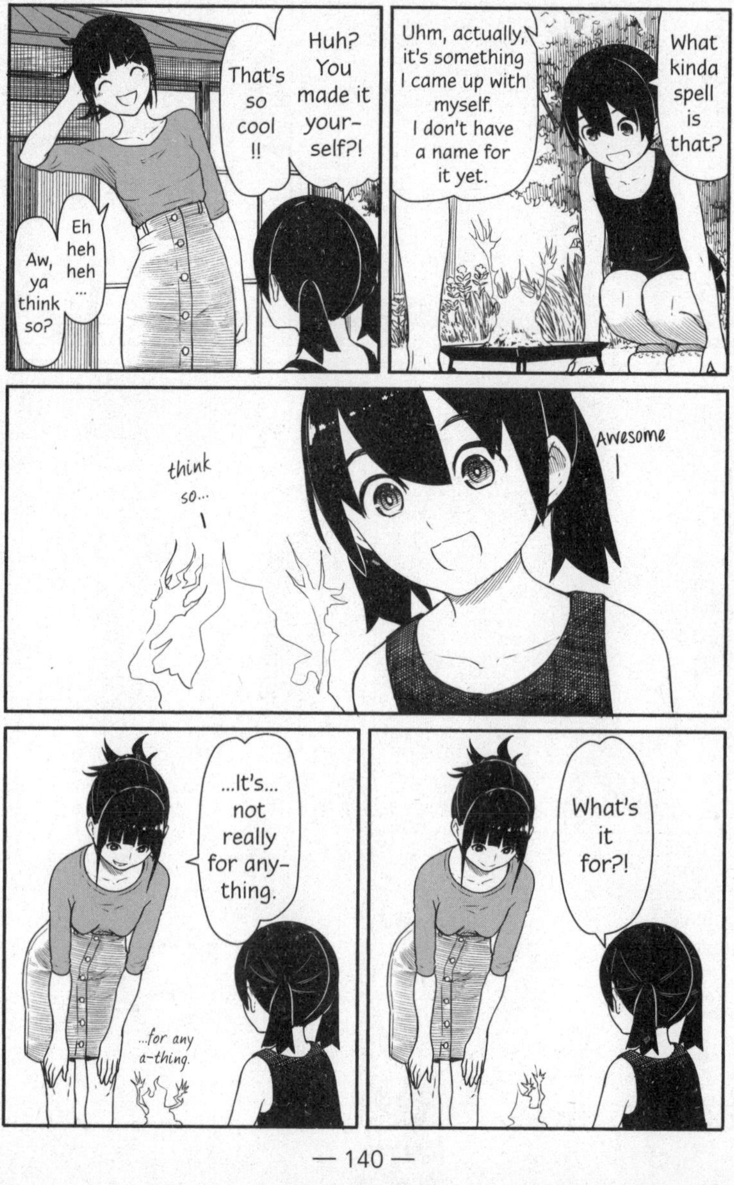
What kinda spell is that?
Uhm, actually, it's something I came up with myself. I don't have a name for it yet.
Huh? You made it your-self?!
That's so cool !!
Eh heh heh ...
Aw, ya think so?
Awesome
think so...
What's it for?!
...It's... not really for any-thing.
...for any a-thing.

Chapter 30
The Witch in the Backyard

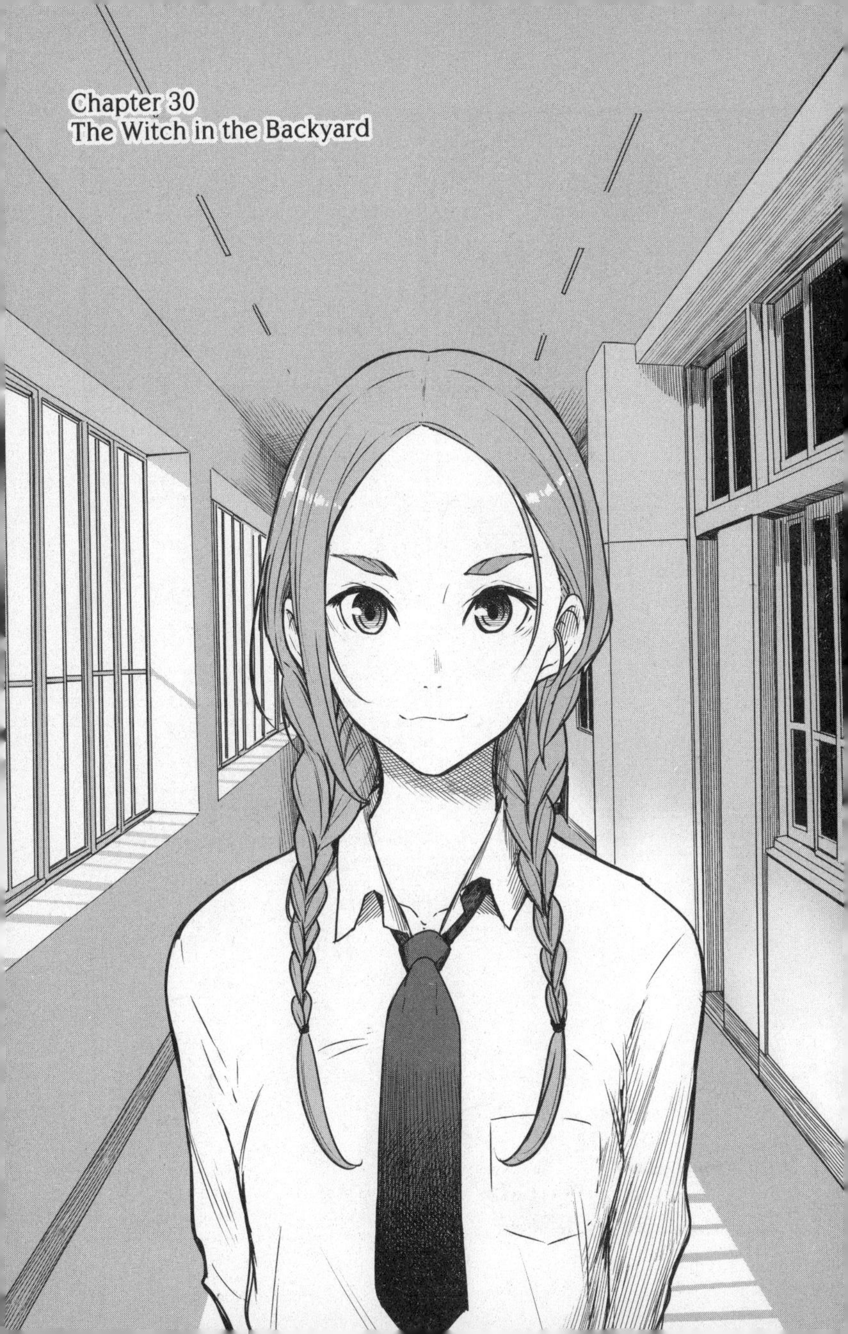

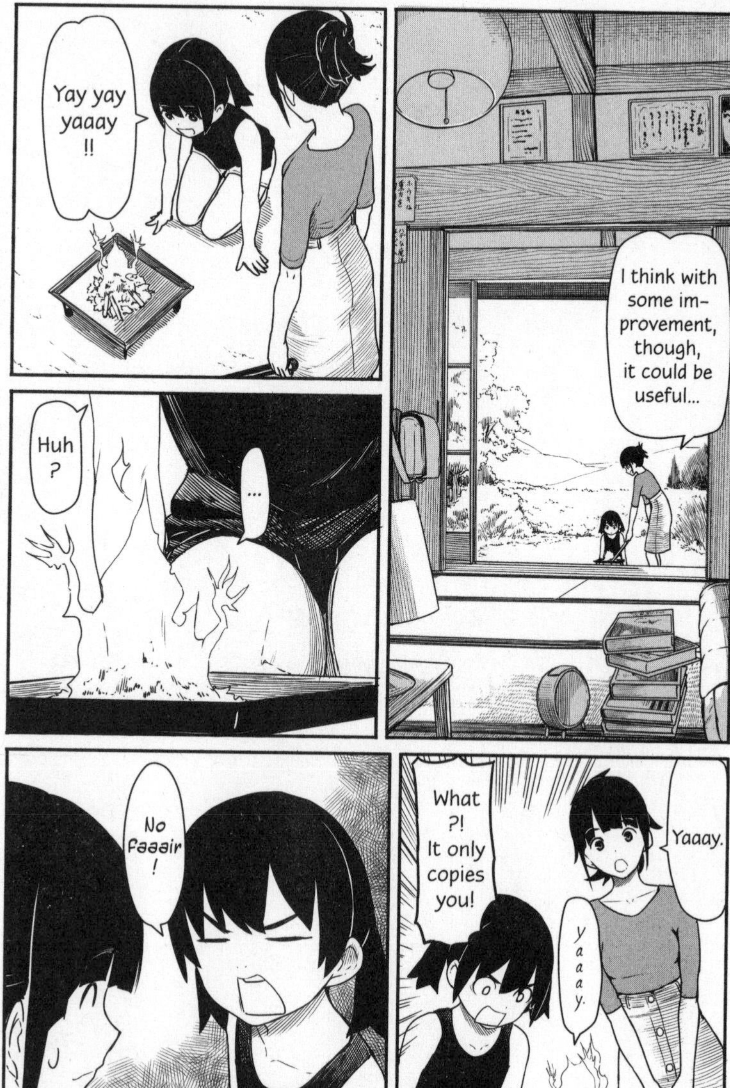
I think with some improvement, though, it could be useful...
Yay yay yaaay!!
...
Huh?
Yaaay.
Yaaay.
What?! It only copies you!
No faaair!

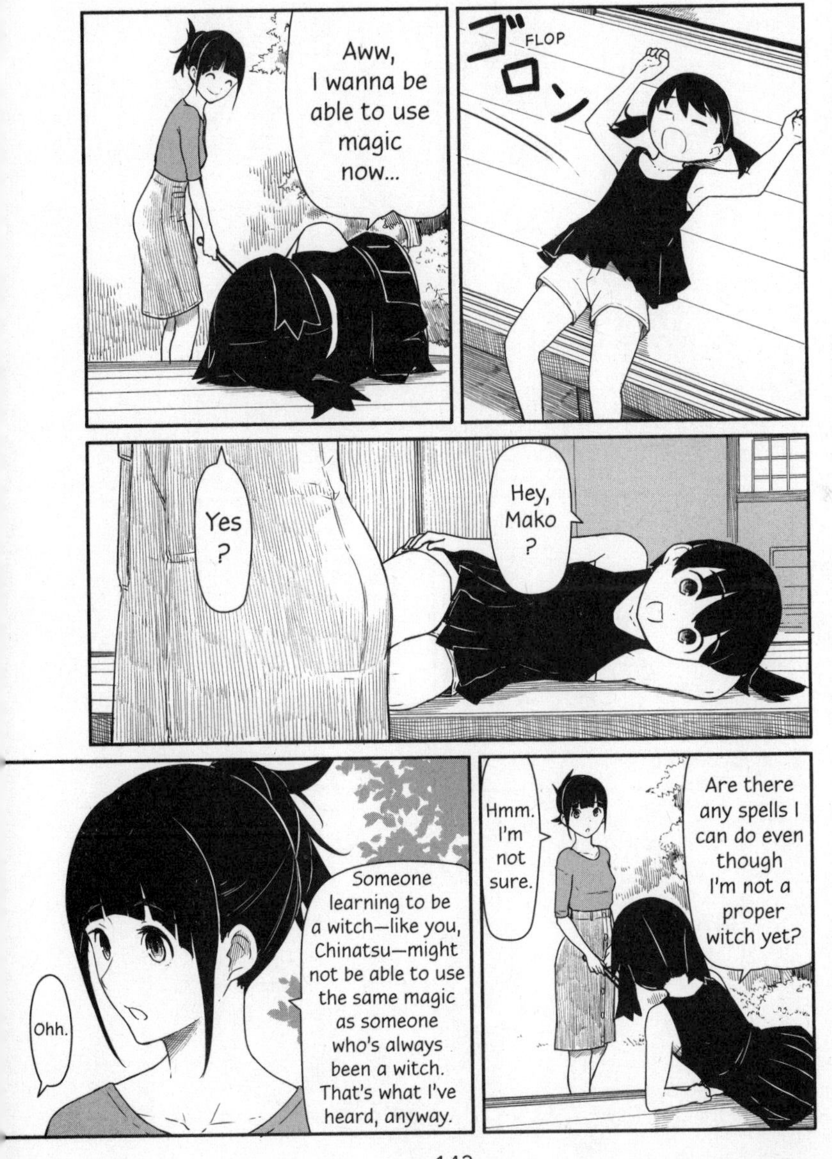
ゴロン
FLOP
Aww, I wanna be able to use magic now...
Hey, Mako?
Yes?
Are there any spells I can do even though I'm not a proper witch yet?
Hmm. I'm not sure.
Someone learning to be a witch—like you, Chinatsu—might not be able to use the same magic as someone who's always been a witch. That's what I've heard, anyway.
Ohh.

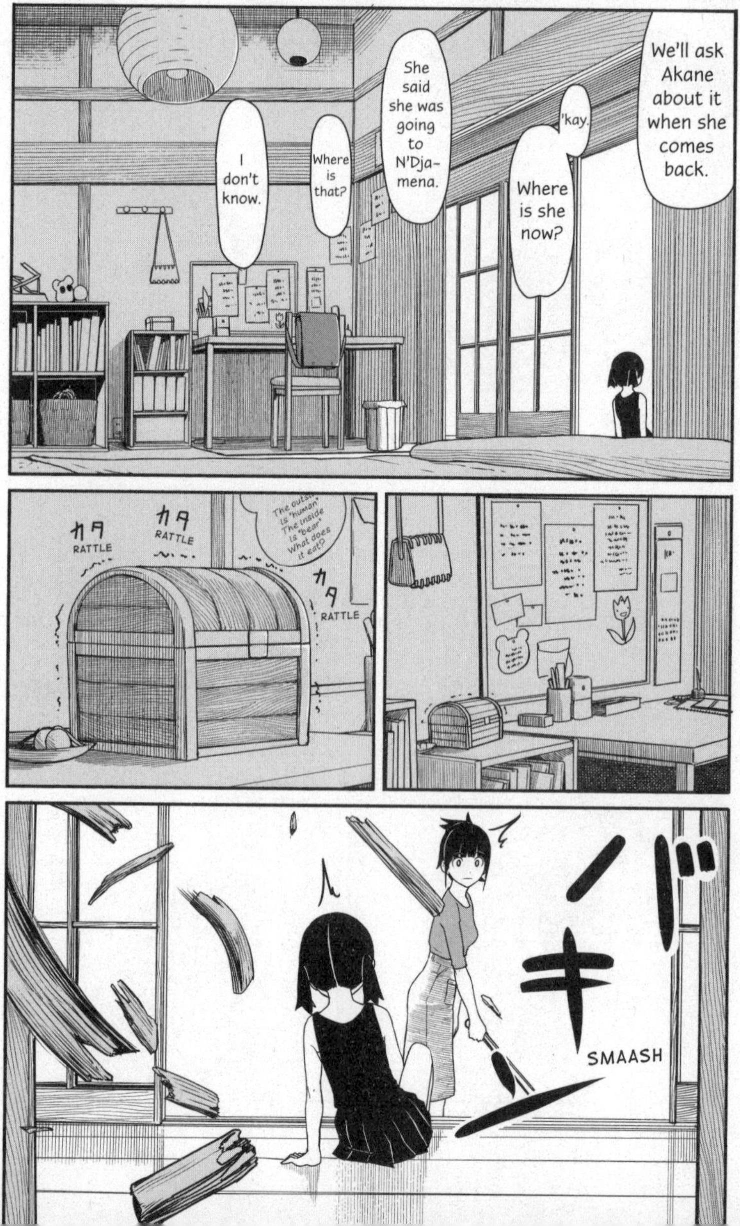

We'll ask Akane about it when she comes back.
'kay.
Where is she now?
She said she was going to N'Dja-mena.
Where is that?
I don't know.
カタ
RATTLE
カタ
RATTLE
The outsi is "human" The inside is "bear" What does it eat?
カタ
RATTLE
バキ
SMAASH

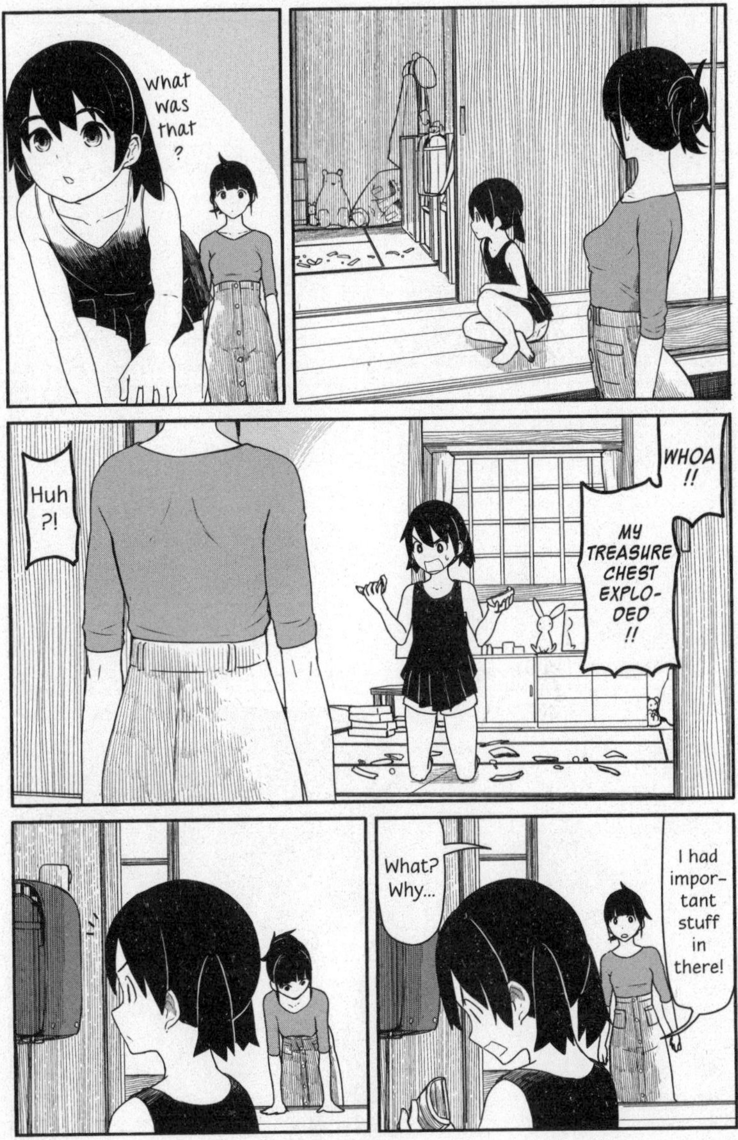
what was that ?
WHOA !!
MY TREASURE CHEST EXPLODED !!
Huh ?!
I had important stuff in there!
What? Why...

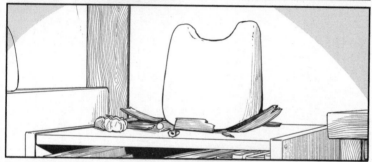

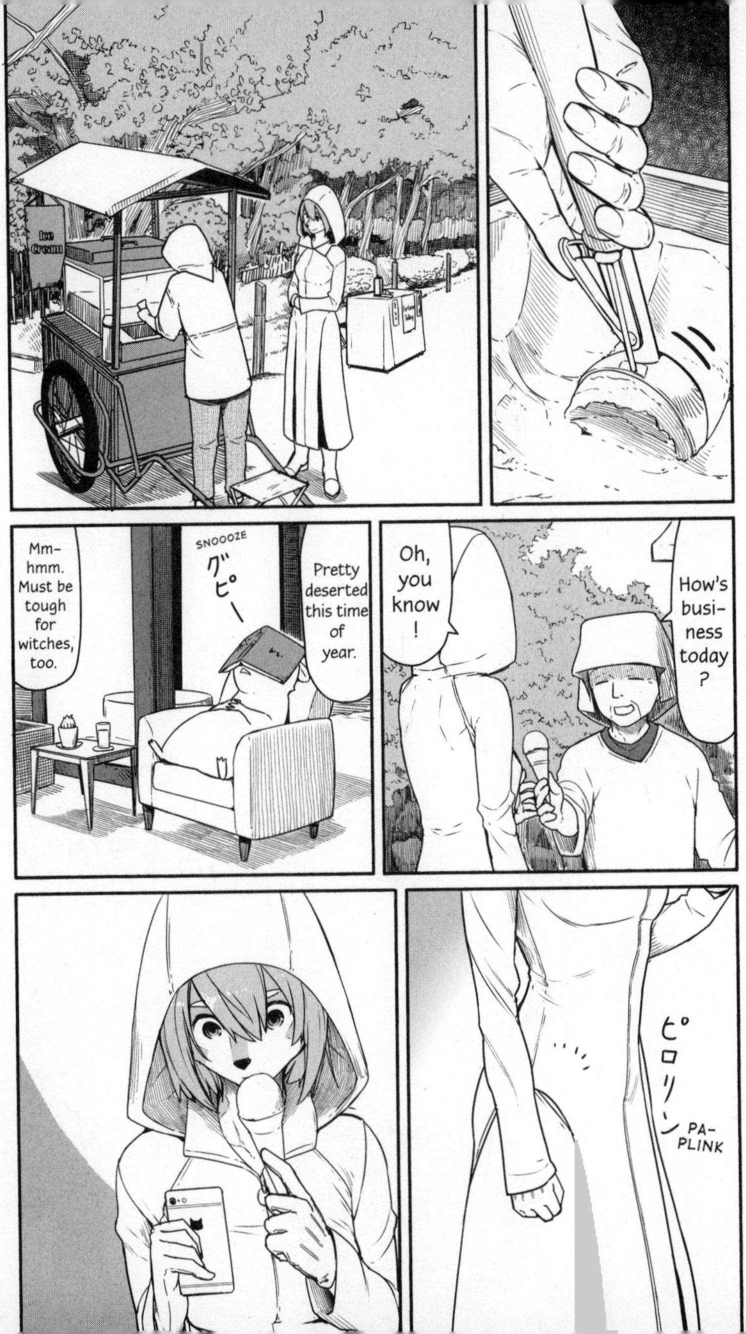
Ice Cream
How's busi-ness today?
Oh, you know!
Pretty deserted this time of year.
SNOOOZE
グピー
Mm-hmm. Must be tough for witches, too.
...
ピロリン
PA-PLINK

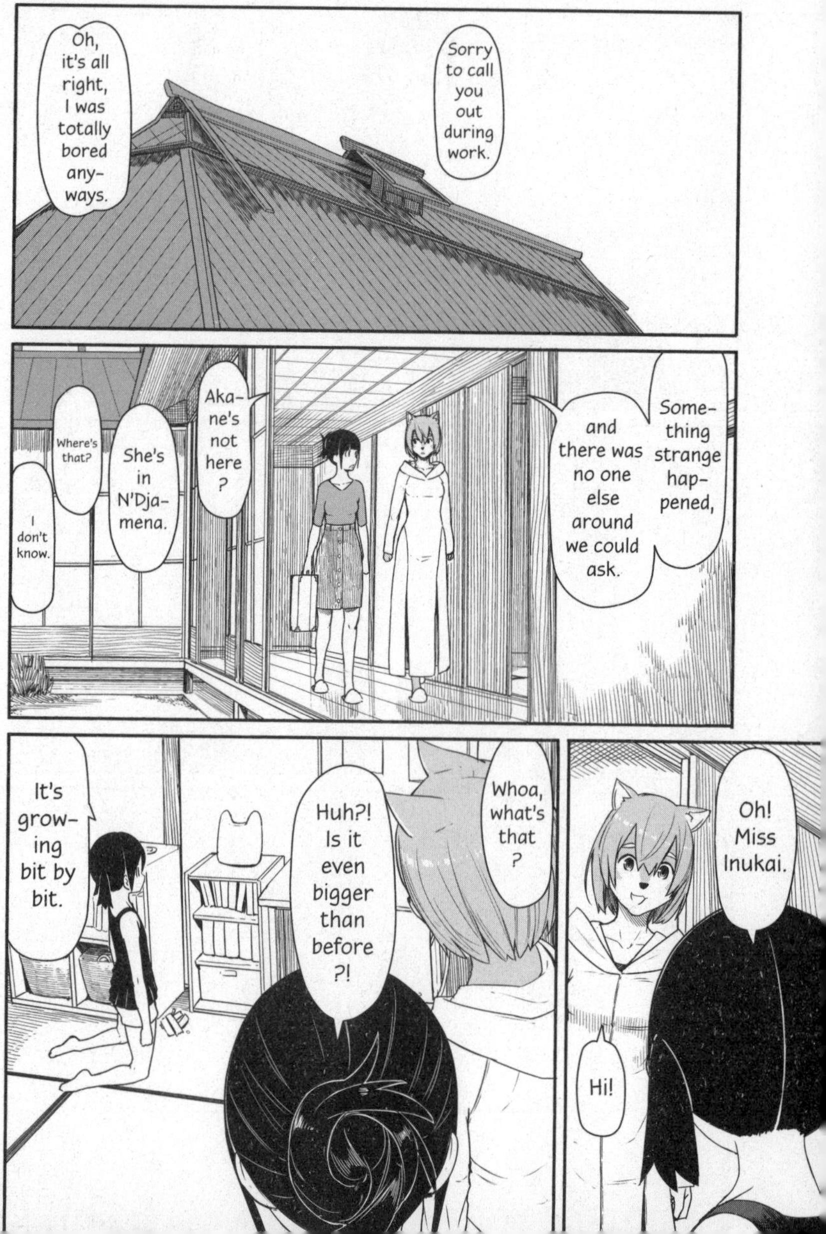
Sorry to call you out during work.
Oh, it's all right, I was totally bored anyways.
Something strange happened,
and there was no one else around we could ask.
Akane's not here?
She's in N'Djamena.
Where's that?
I don't know.
Oh! Miss Inukai.
Hi!
Whoa, what's that?
Huh?! Is it even bigger than before?!
It's growing bit by bit.

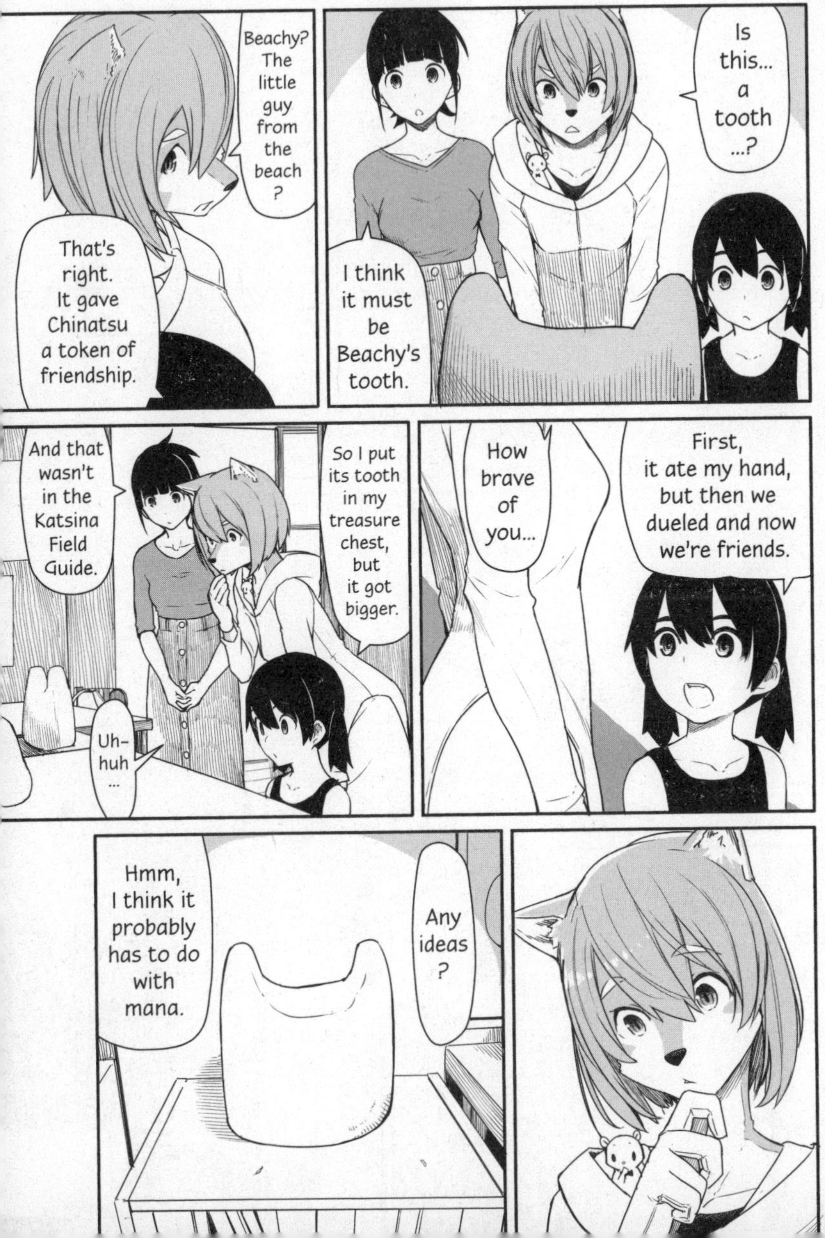

Is this... a tooth ...?
I think it must be Beachy's tooth.
Beachy? The little guy from the beach ?
That's right. It gave Chinatsu a token of friendship.
First, it ate my hand, but then we dueled and now we're friends.
How brave of you...
So I put its tooth in my treasure chest, but it got bigger.
And that wasn't in the Katsina Field Guide.
Uh-huh ...
Any ideas ?
Hmm, I think it probably has to do with mana.

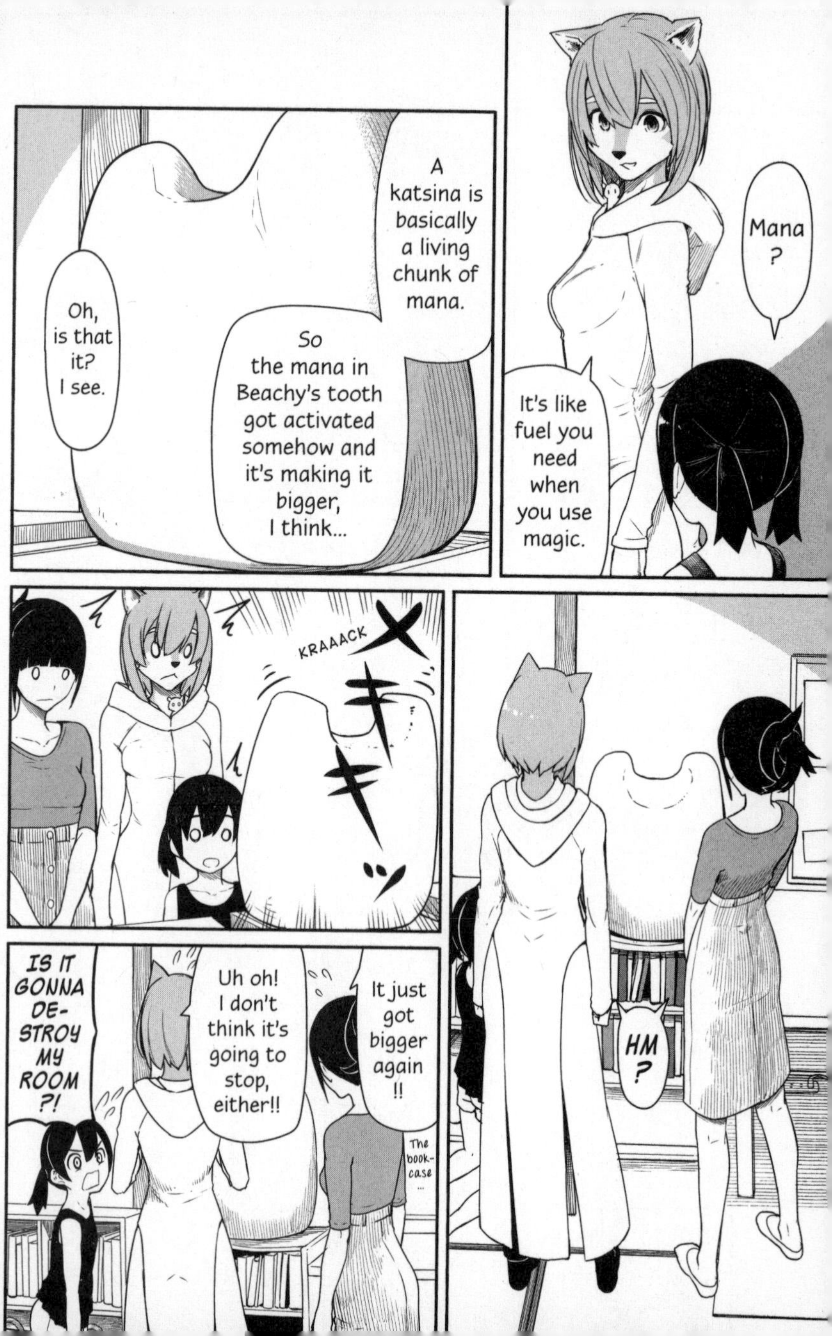

Mana?
It's like fuel you need when you use magic.
A katsina is basically a living chunk of mana.
Oh, is that it? I see.
So the mana in Beachy's tooth got activated somehow and it's making it bigger, I think...
HM?
KRAAACK
It just got bigger again!!
Uh oh! I don't think it's going to stop, either!!
IS IT GONNA DE-STROY MY ROOM?!
The book-case...

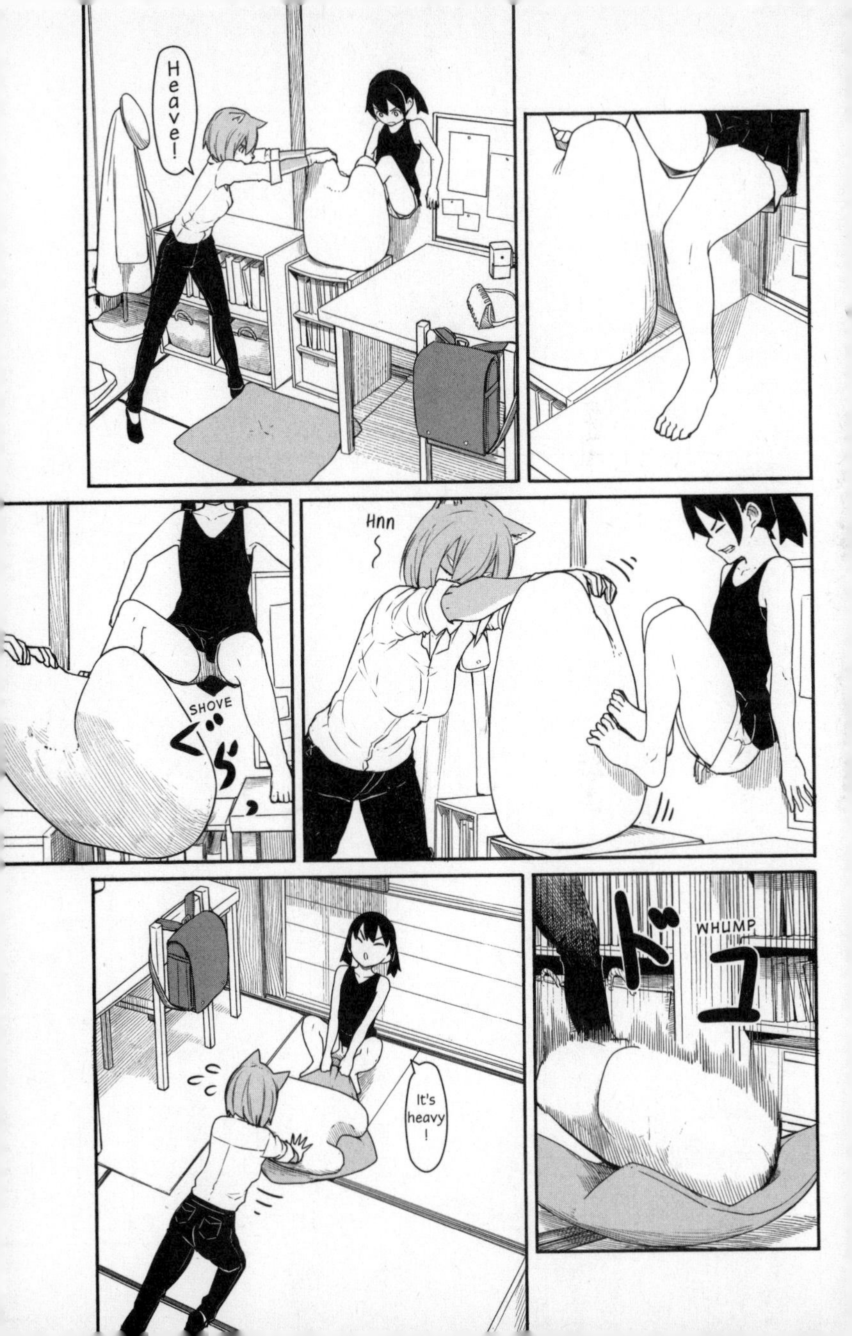
Heave!
SHOVE
ぐぐっ
Hnn
WHUMP
ドコ
It's heavy!

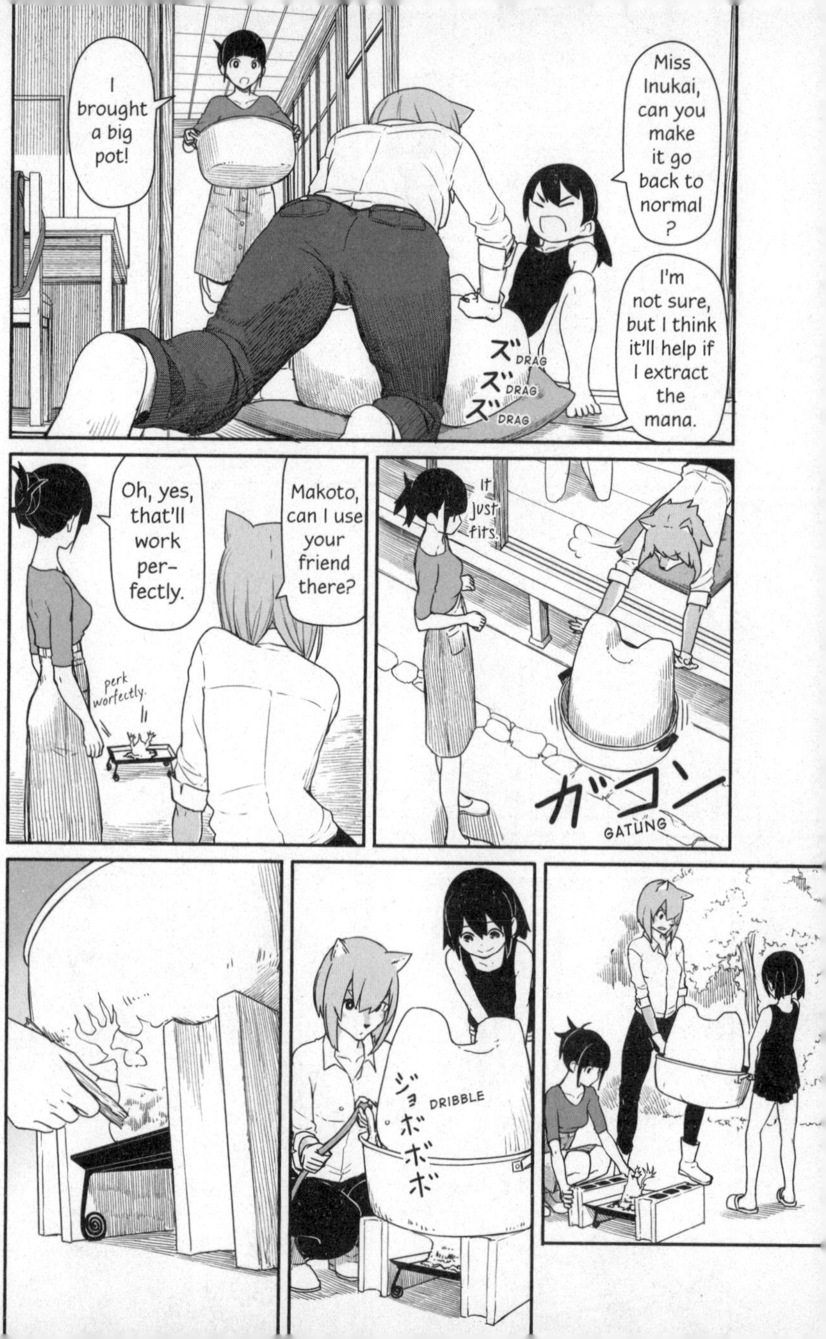
Miss Inukai, can you make it go back to normal?
I'm not sure, but I think it'll help if I extract the mana.
I brought a big pot!
ズズズ
DRAG DRAG DRAG
It just fits.
ガコン
GATUNG
Makoto, can I use your friend there?
Oh, yes, that'll work per-fectly.
perk
worfectly.
ジョボボボ
DRIBBLE

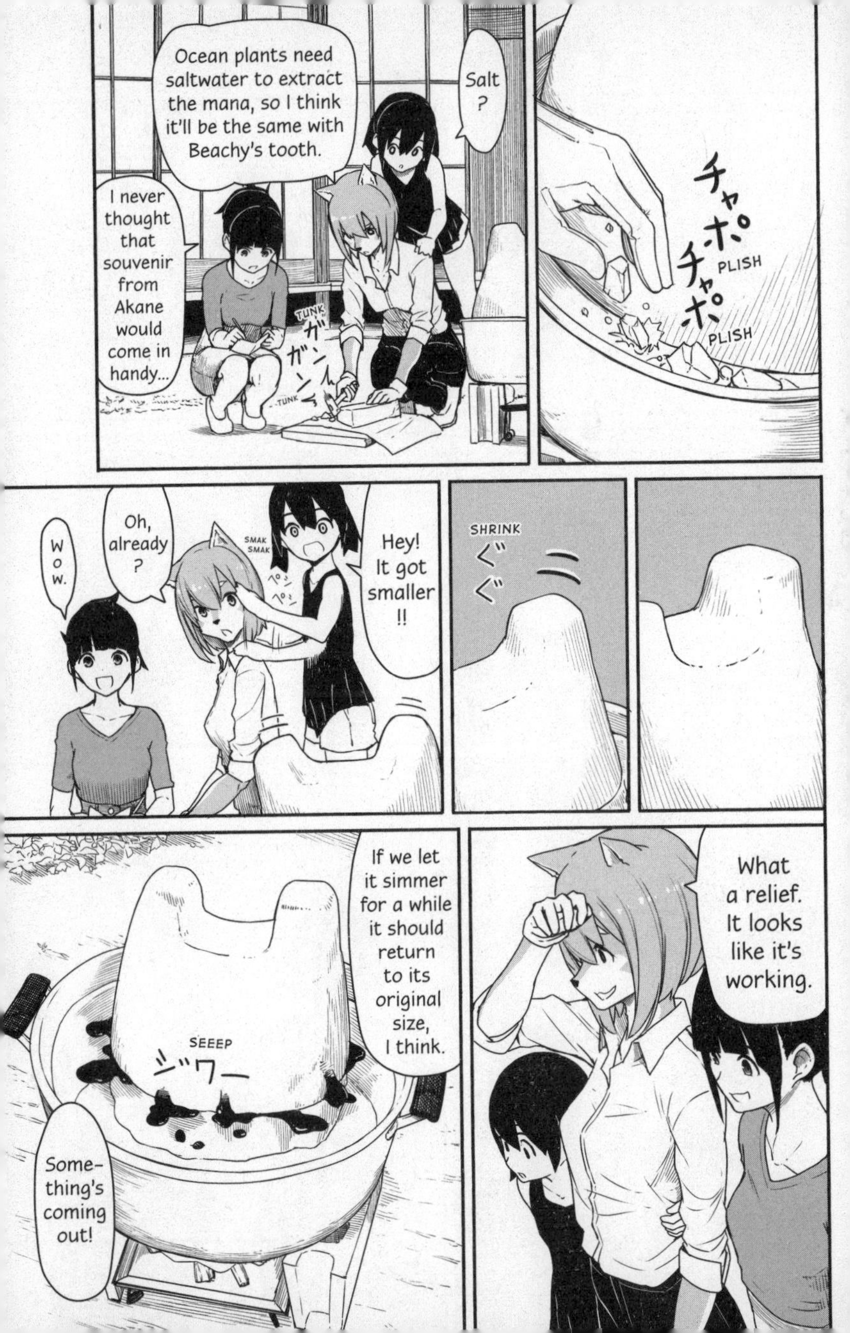
チャポ
PLISH
チャポ
PLISH
Salt ?
Ocean plants need saltwater to extract the mana, so I think it'll be the same with Beachy's tooth.
I never thought that souvenir from Akane would come in handy...
TUNK
ガン
TUNK
SHRINK
ぐぐ
Hey! It got smaller !!
SMAK SMAK
ぺしぺし
Oh, already ?
Wow.
What a relief. It looks like it's working.
If we let it simmer for a while it should return to its original size, I think.
SEEEP
ジワー
Some-thing's coming out!

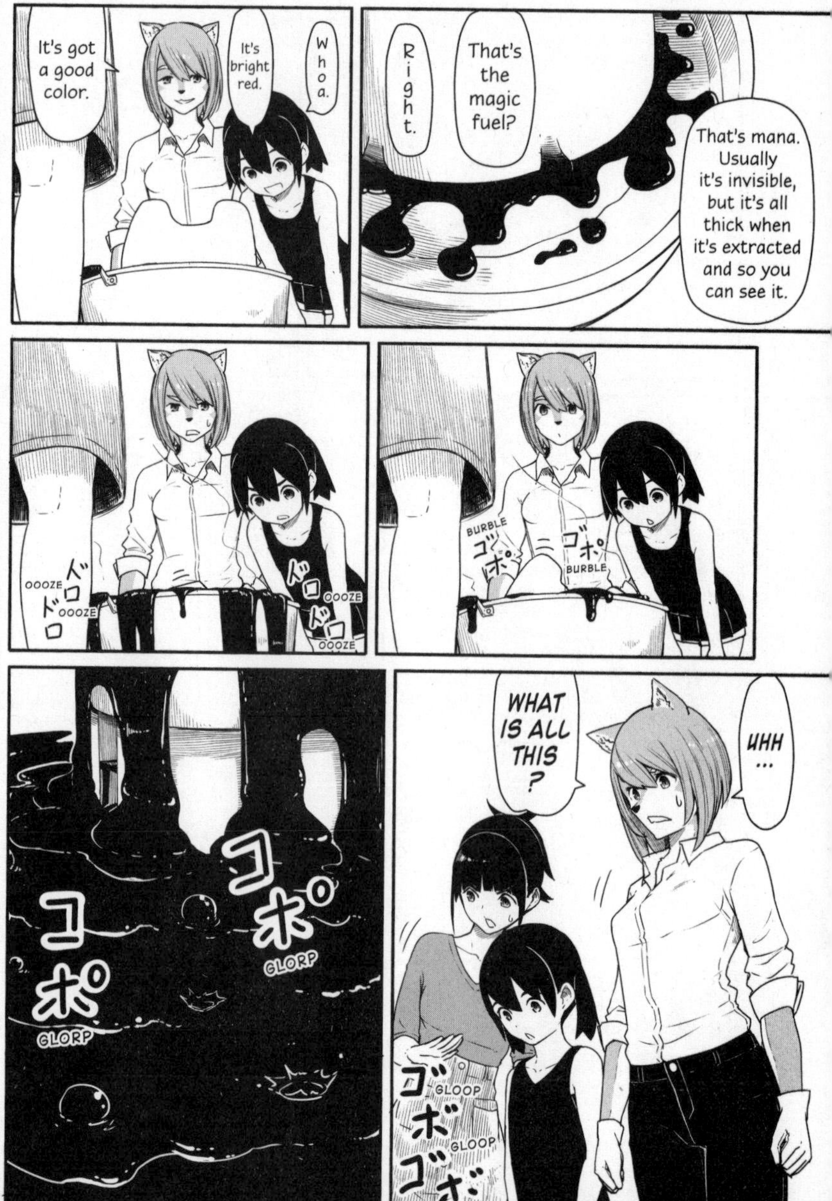
That's the magic fuel?
Right.
That's mana. Usually it's invisible, but it's all thick when it's extracted and so you can see it.
Whoa.
It's bright red.
It's got a good color.
ゴポ
BURBLE
ゴポ
BURBLE
ドロドロ
OOOZE
OOOZE
ドロドロ
OOOZE
OOOZE
UHH ...
WHAT IS ALL THIS ?
ゴボゴボ
GLOOP
GLOOP
コポ
GLORP
コポ
GLORP

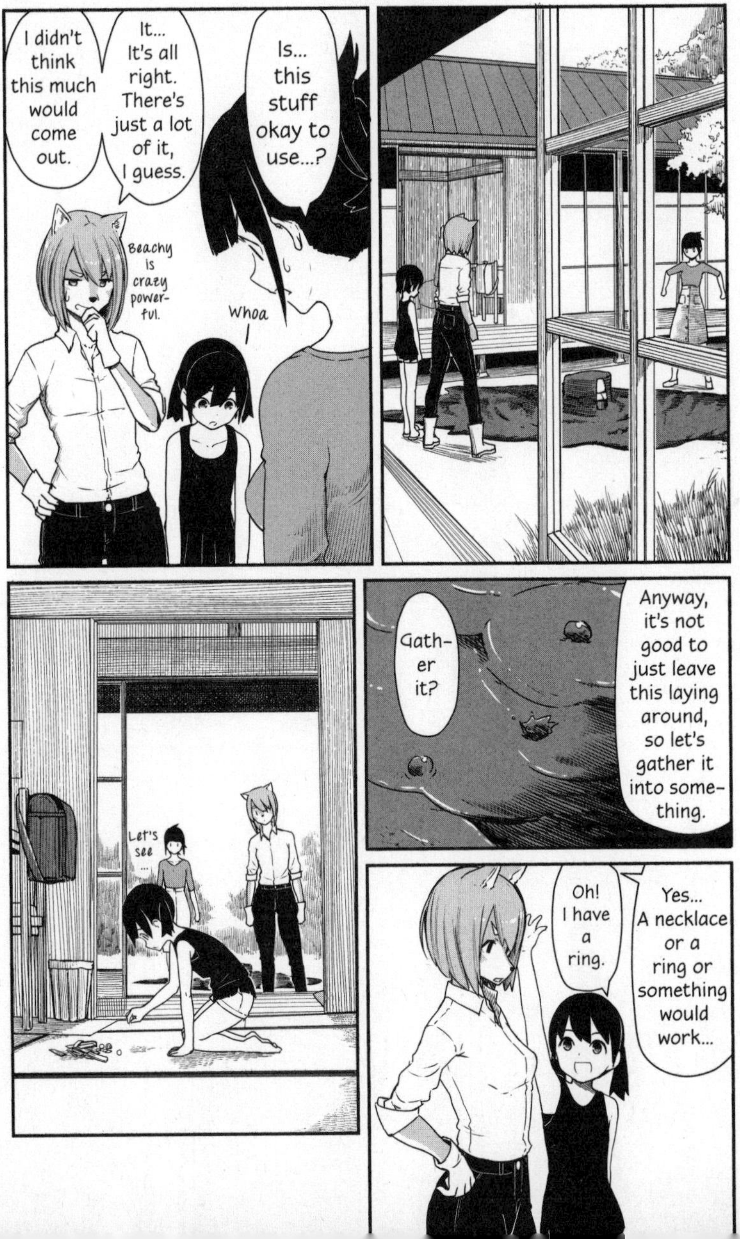

Is... this stuff okay to use...?
It... It's all right. There's just a lot of it, I guess.
I didn't think this much would come out.
Beachy is crazy powerful.
Whoa
Anyway, it's not good to just leave this laying around, so let's gather it into something.
Gather it?
Yes... A necklace or a ring or something would work...
Oh! I have a ring.
Let's see...

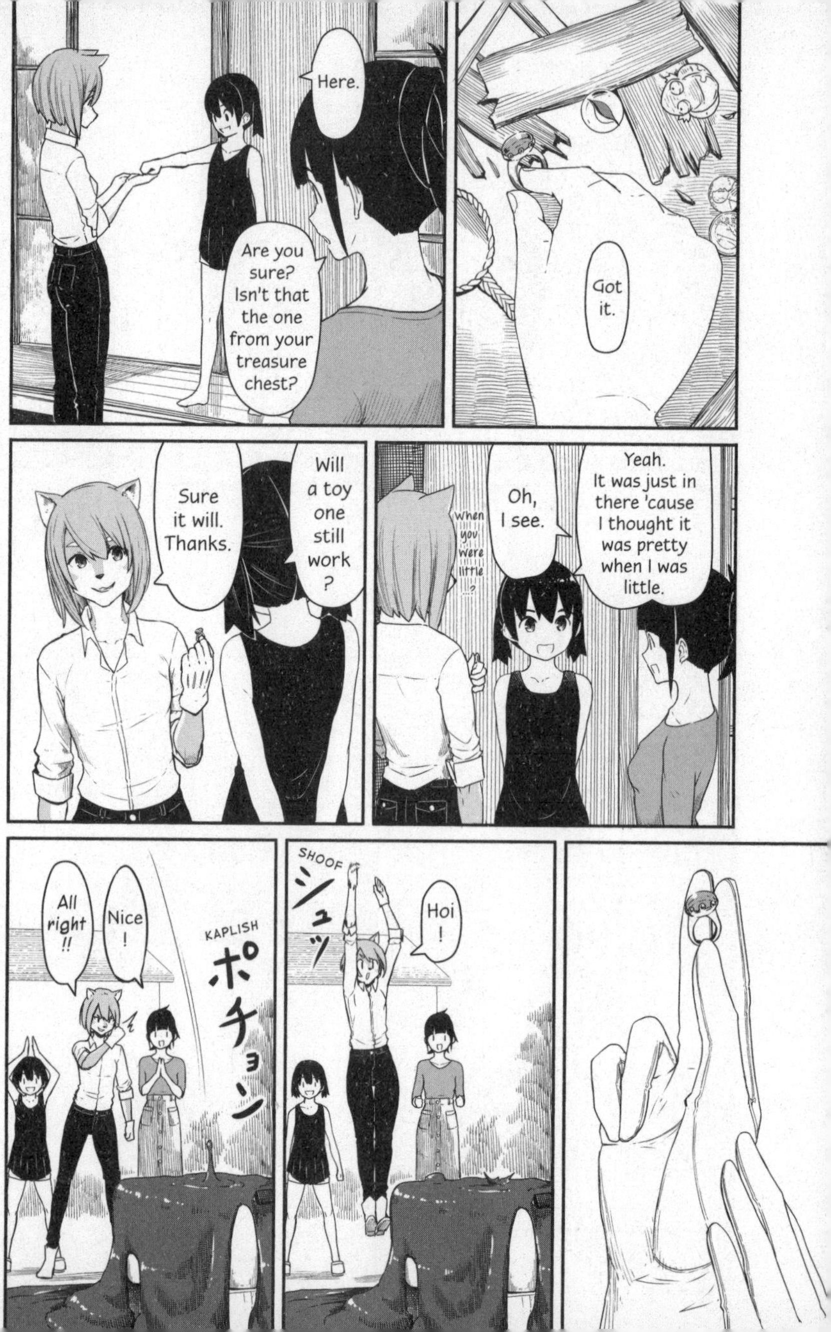
Got it.
Here.
Are you sure? Isn't that the one from your treasure chest?
Yeah. It was just in there 'cause I thought it was pretty when I was little.
Oh, I see.
When you were little ...?
Will a toy one still work?
Sure it will. Thanks.
SHOOF
シュッ
Hoi!
KAPLISH
ポチョン
Nice!
All right!!

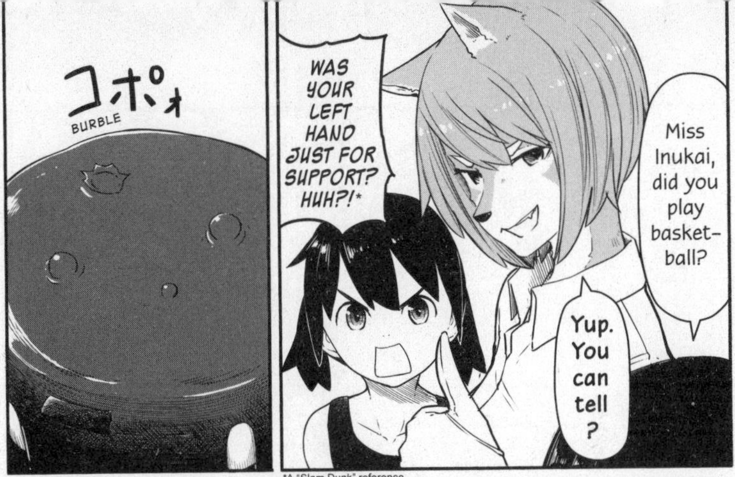
Miss Inukai, did you play basket-ball?
WAS YOUR LEFT HAND JUST FOR SUPPORT? HUH?!*
Yup. You can tell?
コポォ
BURBLE

*A "Slam Dunk" reference.

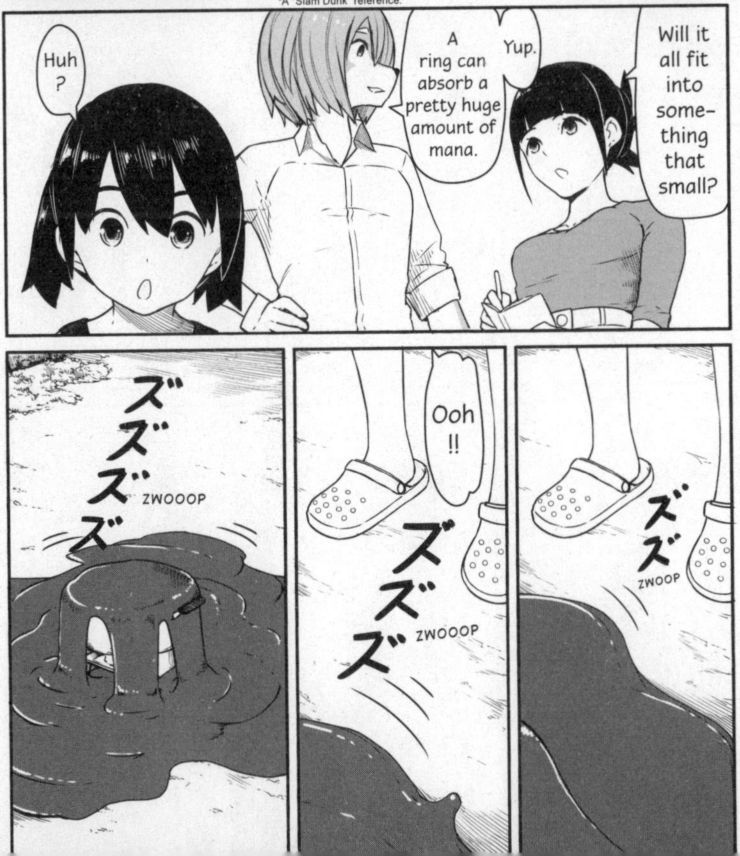
Will it all fit into some-thing that small?
Yup.
A ring can absorb a pretty huge amount of mana.
Huh?
ズズ
ZWOOP
Ooh!!
ズズズ
ZWOOOP
ズズズズ
ZWOOOP

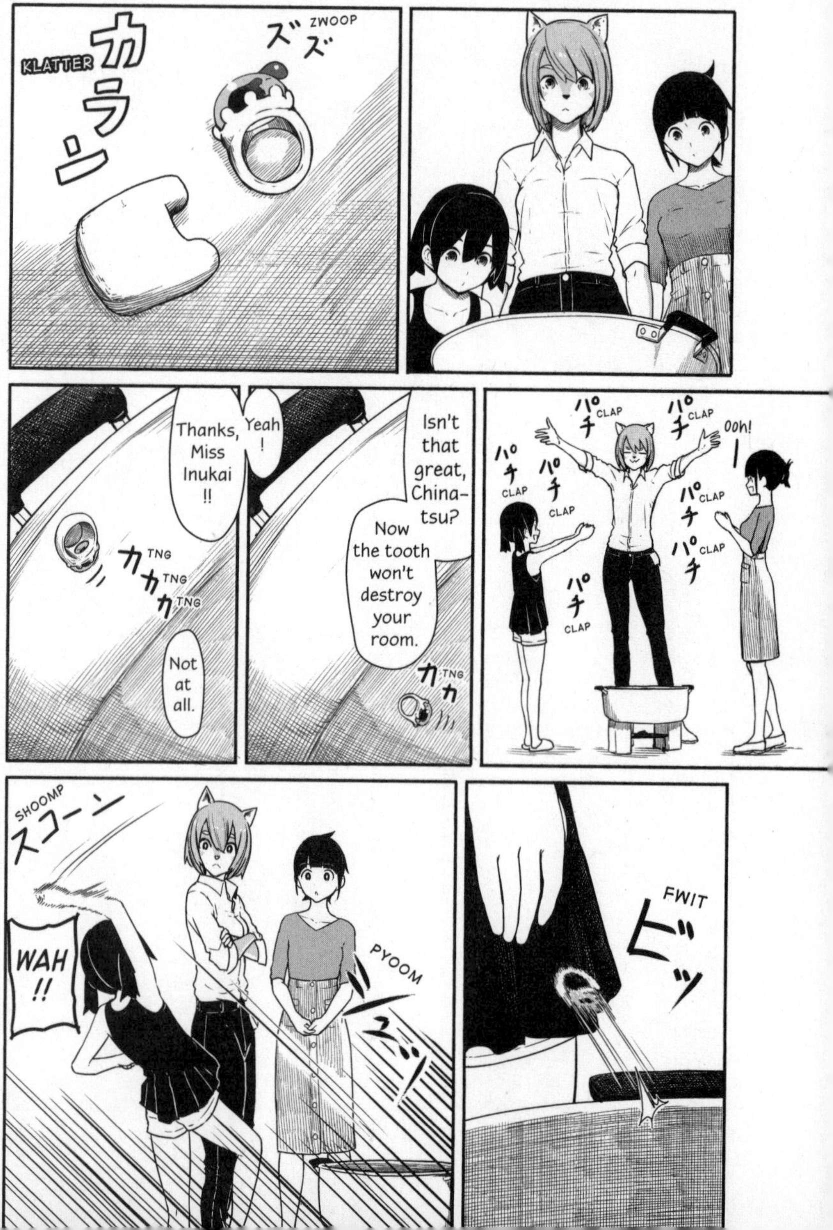

ZWOOP
ズズ
KLATTER
カラン
パチ CLAP
パチ CLAP
Ooh!
パチ CLAP
パチ CLAP
パチ CLAP
パチ CLAP
パチ CLAP
パチ CLAP
Isn't that great, China-tsu?
Now the tooth won't destroy your room.
カカ TNG
Yeah!
Thanks, Miss Inukai!!
カカカ TNG TNG TNG
Not at all.
FWIT
ビッ
SHOOMP
スコーン
PYOOM
ズッ
WAH!!

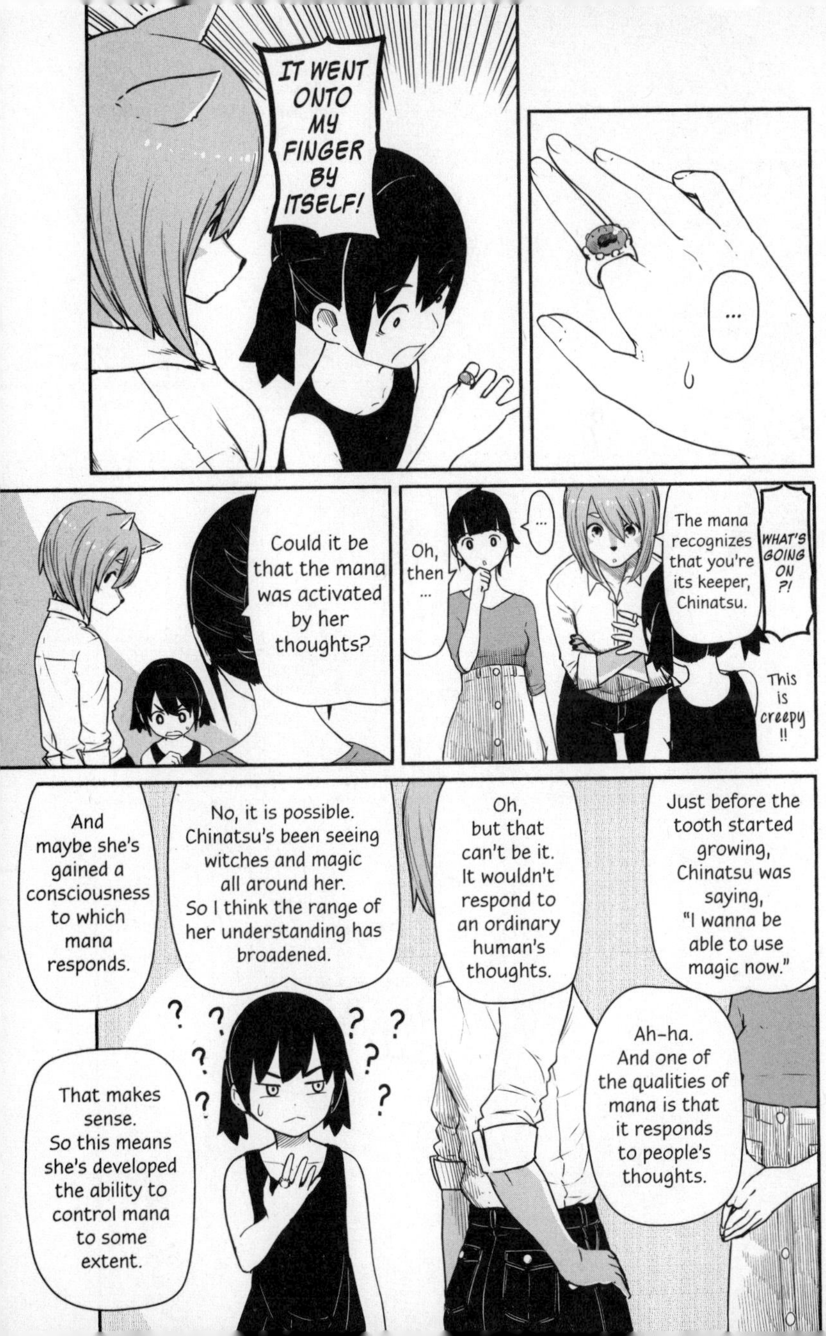
...
IT WENT ONTO MY FINGER BY ITSELF!
The mana recognizes that you're its keeper, Chinatsu.
WHAT'S GOING ON ?!
This is creepy !!
...
Oh, then ...
Could it be that the mana was activated by her thoughts?
Just before the tooth started growing, Chinatsu was saying, "I wanna be able to use magic now."
Ah-ha. And one of the qualities of mana is that it responds to people's thoughts.
Oh, but that can't be it. It wouldn't respond to an ordinary human's thoughts.
No, it is possible. Chinatsu's been seeing witches and magic all around her. So I think the range of her understanding has broadened.
And maybe she's gained a consciousness to which mana responds.
That makes sense. So this means she's developed the ability to control mana to some extent.
? ? ? ? ? ? ? ?

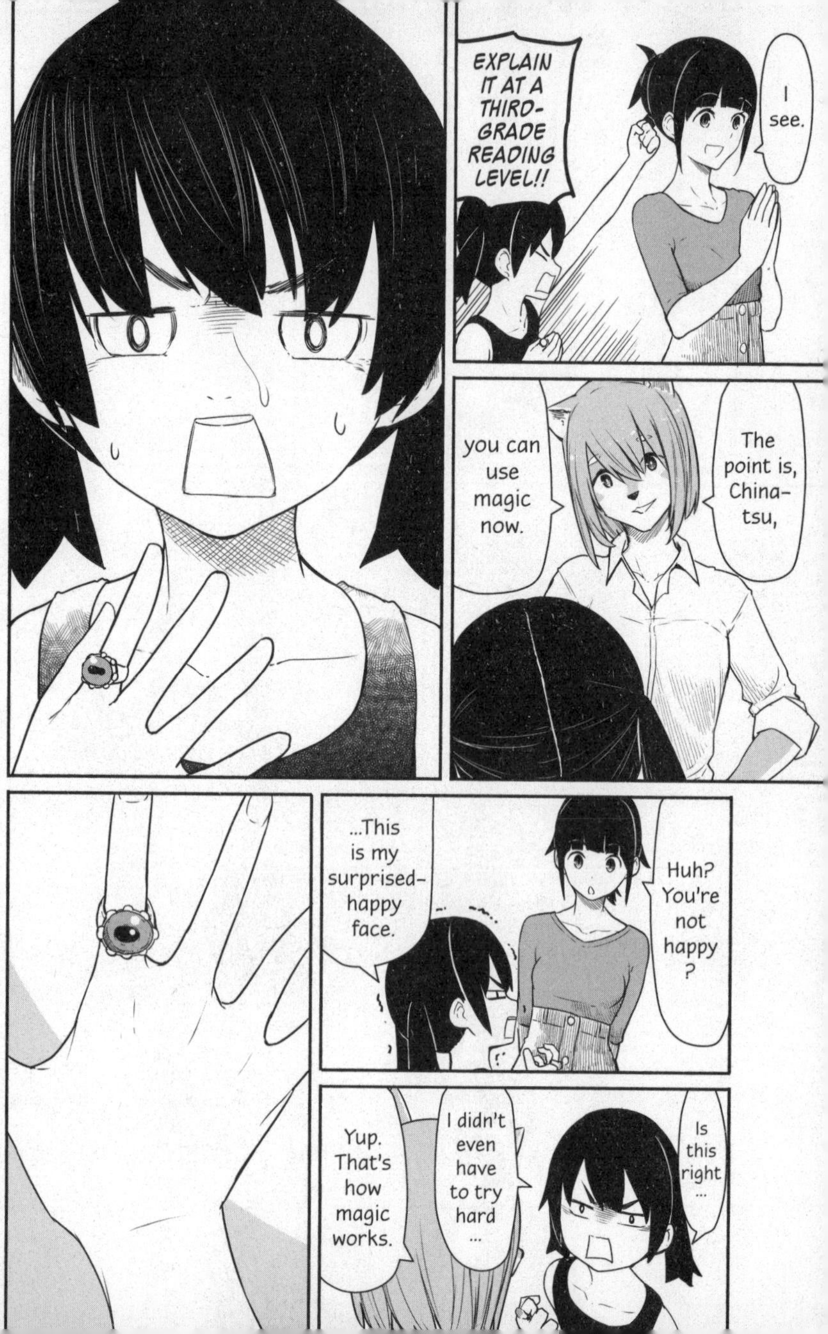
I see.
EXPLAIN IT AT A THIRD-GRADE READING LEVEL!!
The point is, China-tsu,
you can use magic now.
Huh? You're not happy?
...This is my surprised-happy face.
Is this right...
I didn't even have to try hard...
Yup. That's how magic works.

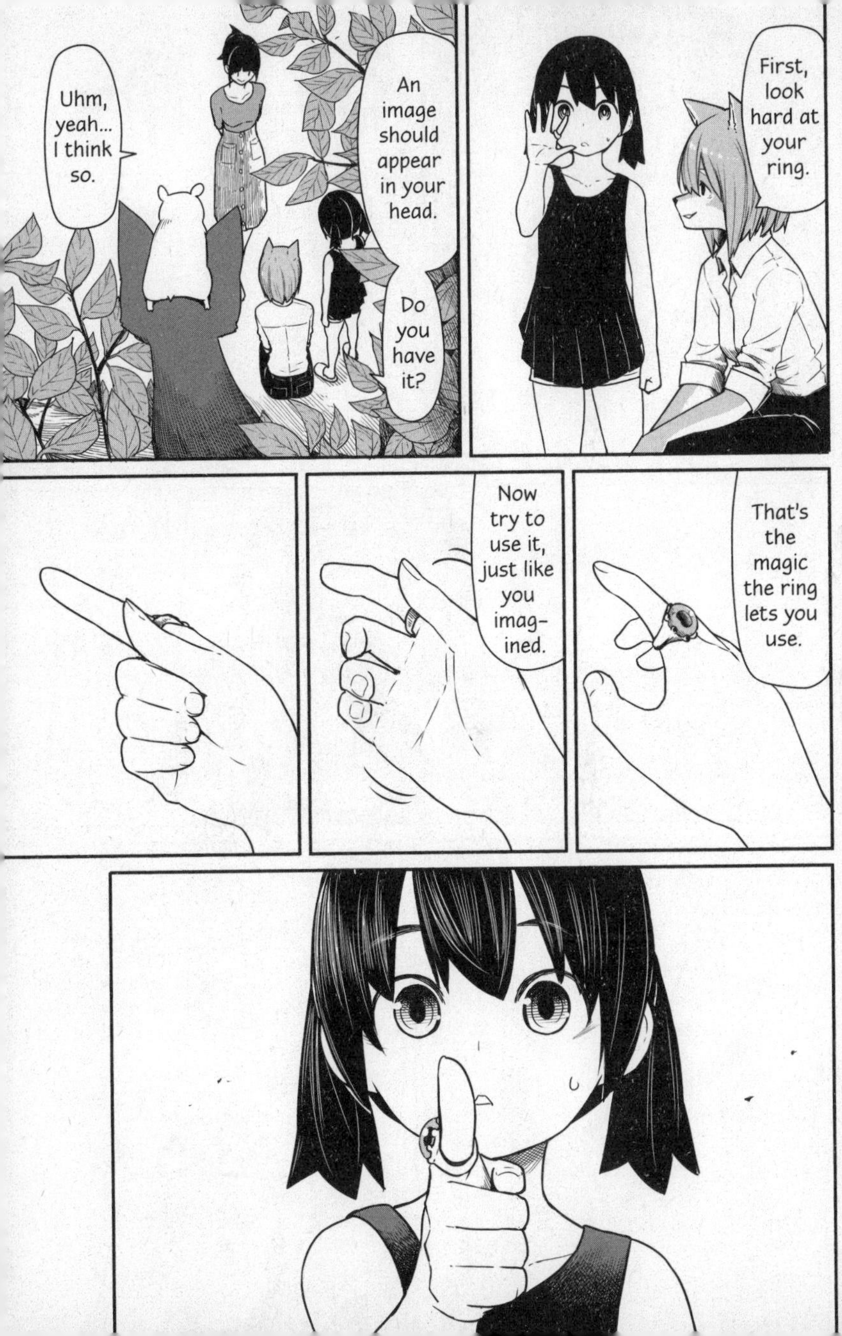
First, look hard at your ring.
An image should appear in your head.
Do you have it?
Uhm, yeah... I think so.
That's the magic the ring lets you use.
Now try to use it, just like you imagined.

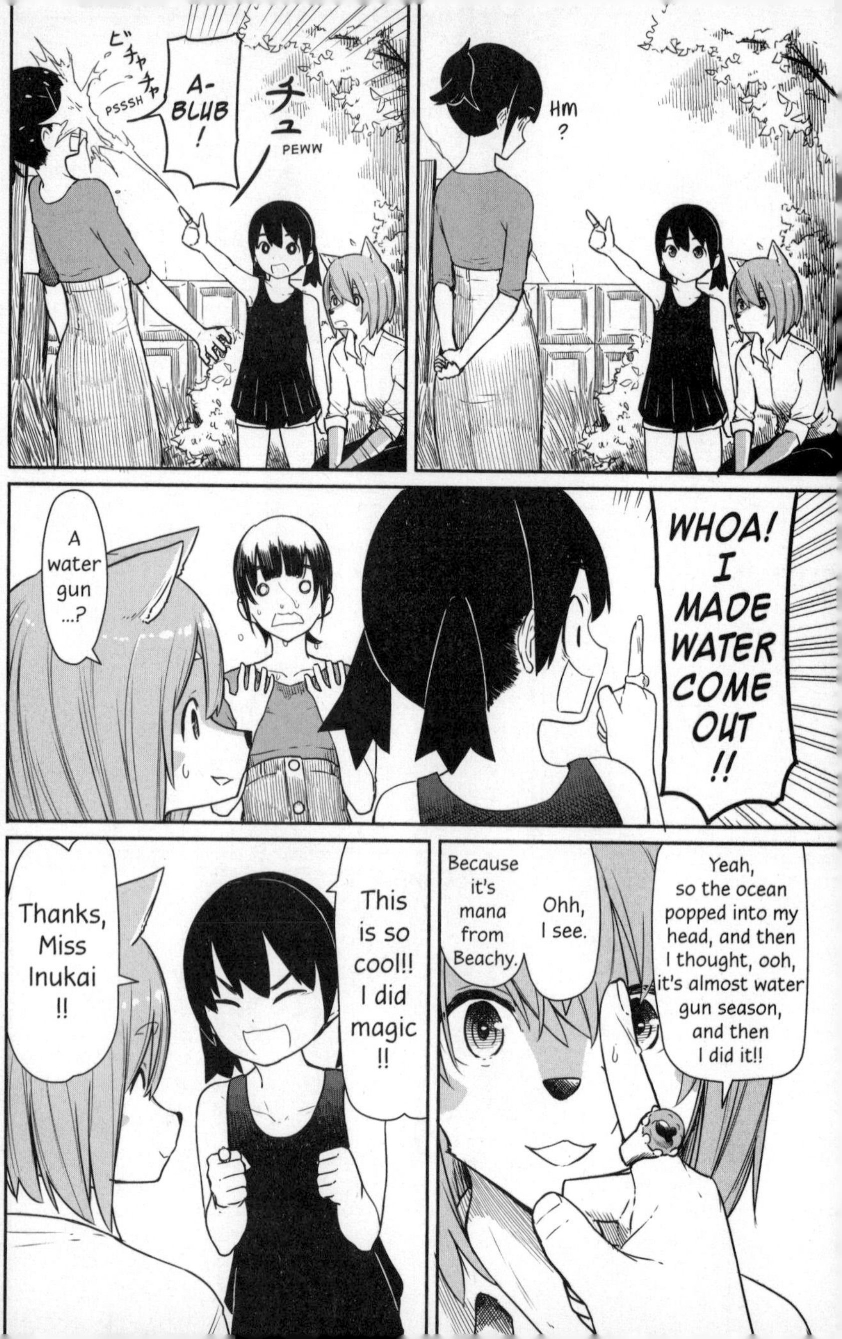
Hm ?
チュ
PEWW
A-BLUB !
ビチャチャ
PSSSH
WHOA! I MADE WATER COME OUT !!
A water gun ...?
Yeah, so the ocean popped into my head, and then I thought, ooh, it's almost water gun season, and then I did it!!
Ohh, I see.
Because it's mana from Beachy.
This is so cool!! I did magic !!
Thanks, Miss Inukai !!

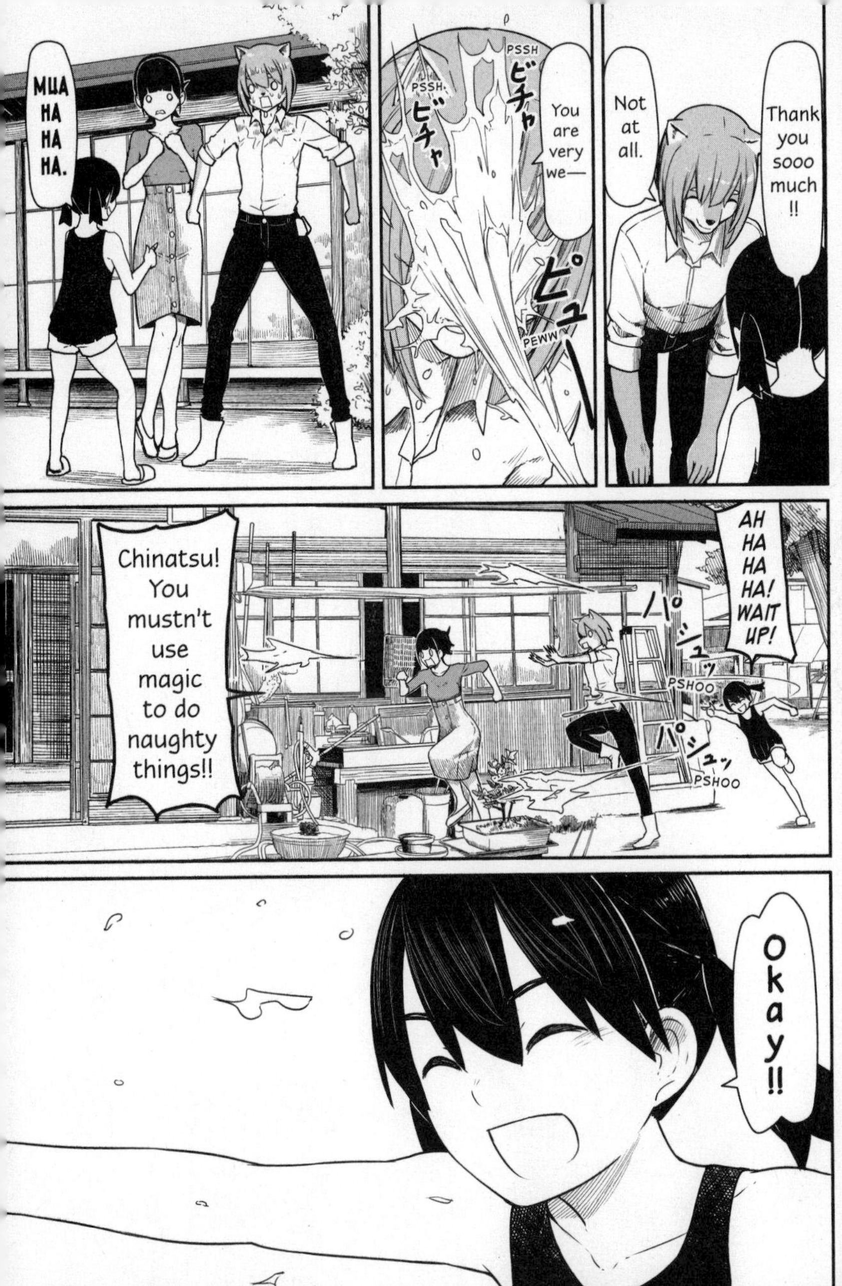
Thank you sooo much!!
Not at all.
PSSH ビチャ
PSSH ビチャ
You are very we—
ピュ
PEWW
MUA HA HA HA.
AH HA HA HA! WAIT UP!
Chinatsu! You mustn't use magic to do naughty things!!
パシュッ
PSHOO
パシュッ
PSHOO
Okay!!

Fly again in Volume 6

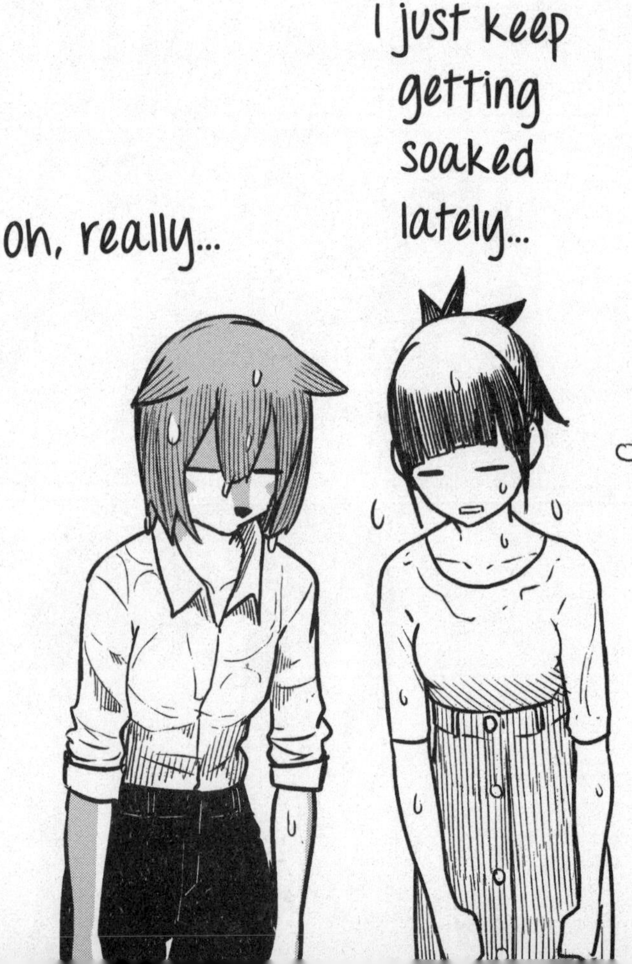
I just keep getting soaked lately...
Oh, really...

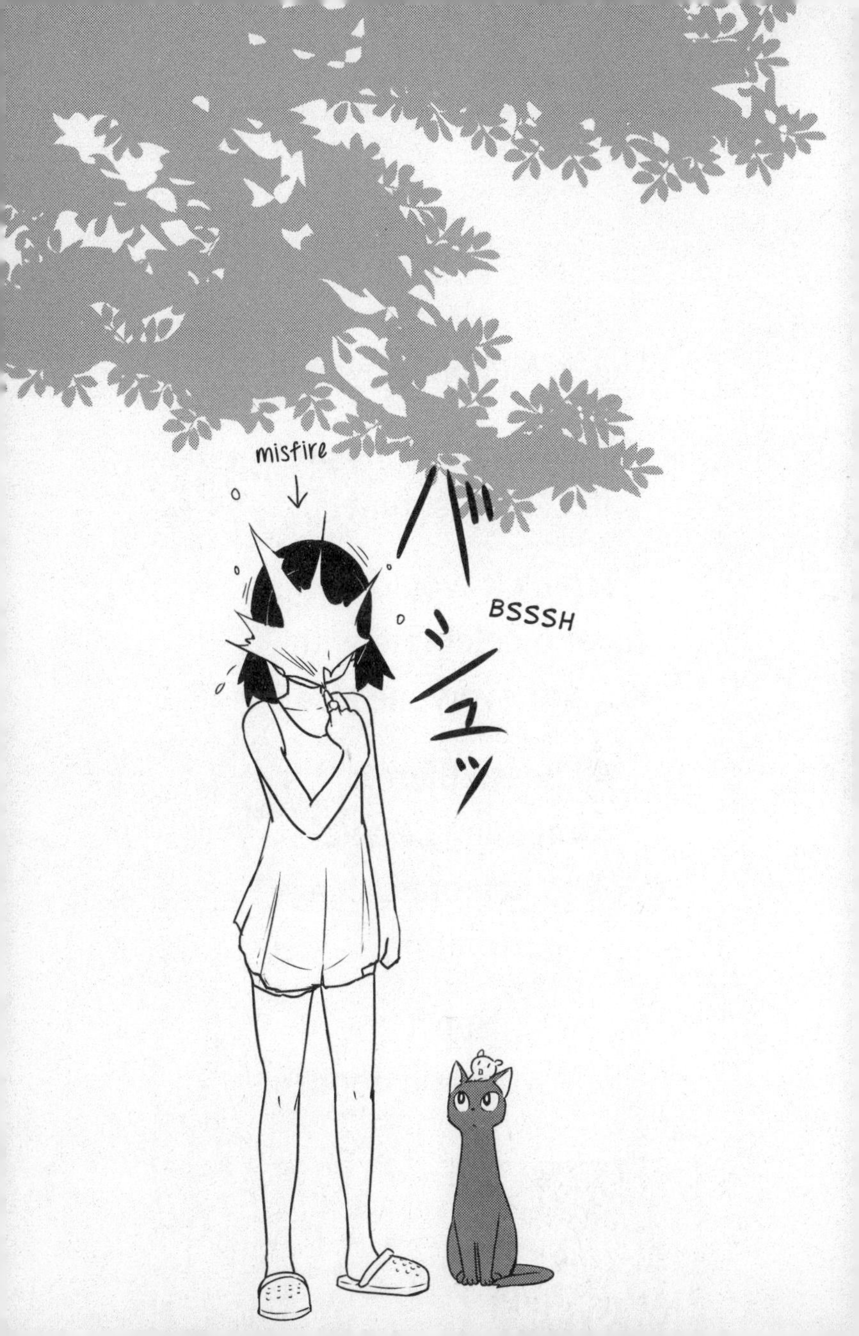
misfire
BSSSH
バシュッ

Volume 6
preview

flying witch ✳ kon flying witch preview for next volume ✳ flying witch ✳ kon

This is Makoto Kowata!

Chinatsu used magic for the first time!

I think it would be nice to celebrate with Kei and everyone else.

I heard there's something people cook to celebrate things in Aomori...

...Huh?!
That's what you cook?!

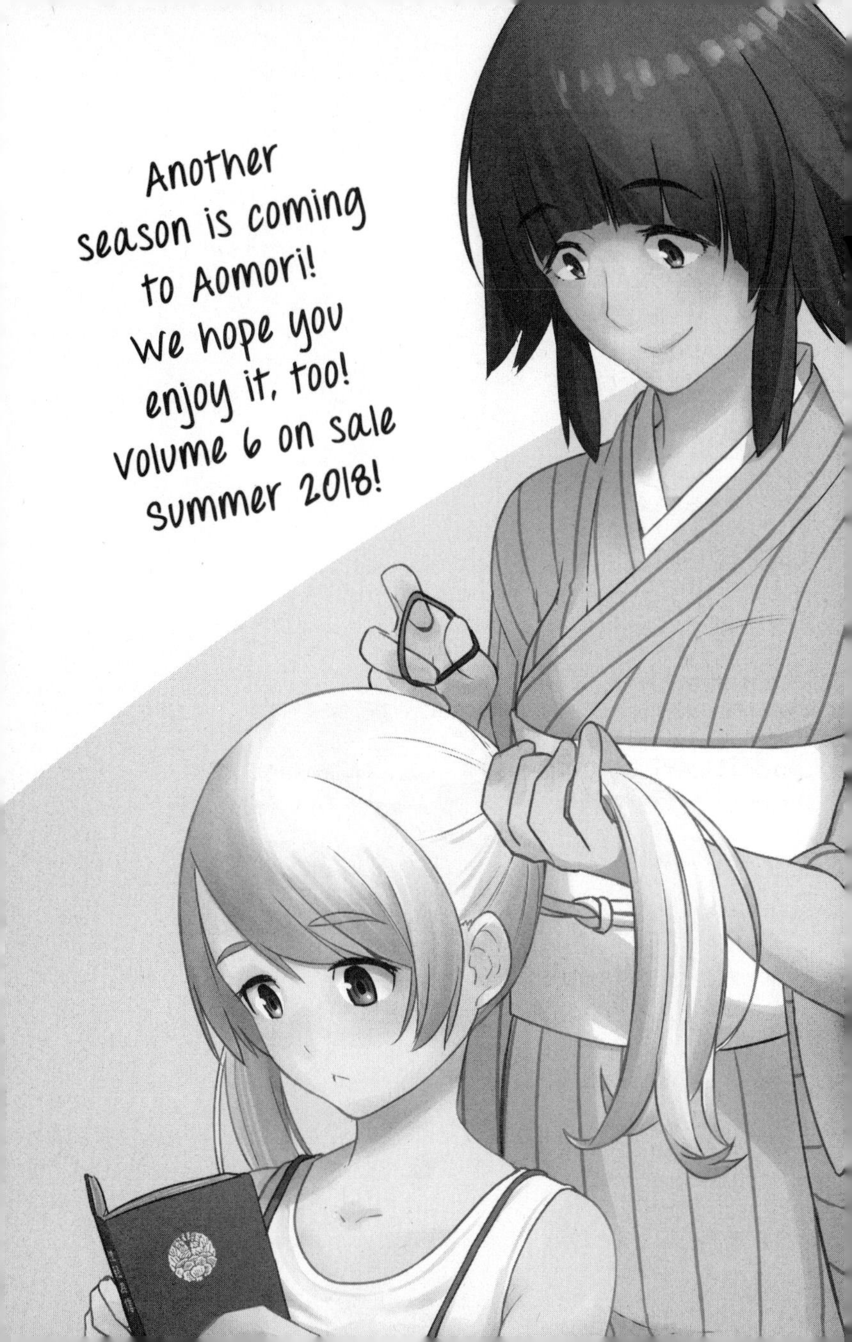
Another season is coming to Aomori! We hope you enjoy it, too! Volume 6 on sale Summer 2018!

Flying Witch 5

Translation - Melissa Tanaka
Production - Grace Lu
Tomoe Tsutsumi

First published in Japan in 2016 by Kodansha, Ltd., Tokyo
Publication for this English edition arranged through Kodansha, Ltd., Tokyo

Translation provided by Vertical Comics, 2018
Published by Vertical Comics, an imprint of Vertical, Inc., New York

Originally published in Japanese as *Flying Witch 5* by Kodansha, Ltd., 2016
Flying Witch first serialized in *Bessatsu Shonen Magazine*, Kodansha, Ltd., 2013-

ISBN: 978-1-945054-67-9

Manufactured in the United States of America

First Edition

Vertical, Inc.
451 Park Avenue South, 7th Floor
New York, NY 10016
www.vertical-comics.com

Vertical books are distributed through Penguin-Random House Publisher Services.